MONTGOMERY COLLEGE
ROCKVILLE CAMPUS

WITHDRAWN FROM LIBRARY

W9-DFW-555

THE CRAZY FABRIC

Essays in Irony

THE
CRAZY FABRIC

Essays in Irony

By
A. E. DYSON

Essay Index Reprint Series

BOOKS FOR LIBRARIES PRESS
PLAINVIEW, NEW YORK

Copyright © A. E. Dyson 1965
Reprinted 1973 by special arrangement
with St. Martin's Press, Inc.

Library of Congress Cataloging in Publication Data

Dyson, A   E
  The crazy fabric.

  (Essay index reprint series)
  CONTENTS: Swift: the metamorphosis of irony.--
Fielding: satiric and comic irony.--Sterne: the
novelist as jester. [etc.]
  1. English literature--Addresses, essays, lectures.
2. Irony in literature. I. Title.
[PR931.D9 1973]   820'.9'1   72-10871
ISBN 0-8369-7214-7

PRINTED IN THE UNITED STATES OF AMERICA

To my Mother
and Father

ACKNOWLEDGEMENTS

THE debts I am conscious of are recorded in the select bibliography, but there must have been many others, now forgotten about, in the course of reading over the years.

I should like especially to put on record the stimulation and encouragement received in conversation, particularly from Professor John F. Danby and Mr C. B. Cox. There have, again, been innumerable discussions with students, in the University College of North Wales where most of this was written, and more recently in the University of East Anglia. Above all, perhaps, I should thank the Extra-Mural Class in Wrexham, which I came during the course of five years to know so well. A number of these papers were first tried out in Wrexham, and discussed when they were still in a formative stage.

The author and publishers wish to acknowledge their indebtedness to the following, who have kindly given permission for the use of copyright material: Chatto and Windus and Harper & Row, for extracts from *Point Counter Point* and the 1946 Introduction to *Brave New World* by Aldous Huxley; Martin Secker & Warburg and Brandt & Brandt, for extracts from *1984* by George Orwell; Lord Russell, for an extract from an article in *The Observer*; Chatto and Windus and Harcourt, Brace & World, for extracts from *Eminent Victorians* by Lytton Strachey; and Mr Evelyn Waugh, for extracts from *Decline and Fall* and *Brideshead Revisited*.

CONTENTS

'In the meantime, he drank Madeira, and laid deep schemes for a thorough repair of the crazy fabric of human nature.'

Thomas Love Peacock

PREFACE

'Poetry comes dearer,' as Silas Wegg pointed out, on being hired to read it to Mr Boffin; 'for when a person comes to grind off poetry night after night, it is but right he should expect to be paid for its weakening effect on his mind.' Mr Wegg recognised other mental dangers by which a sensitive man might be assailed; he warned his friend Mr Venus, for instance, against the consequences of 'floating his powerful mind in tea'. Irony, on the other hand, he took much more readily in his stride: when Mr Boffin's attention turned from poetry to Gibbon's *Decline and Fall*, Mr Wegg experienced some slight difficulties with the names of his Roman heroes, but none at all with his author's tone.

Most students of literature will differ from Mr Wegg at least in this, and find irony very challenging, if not exactly weakening, to the mind. M. H. Abrams has even gone so far as to assert, in his *Glossary of Literary Terms*, that 'following the intricate manœuvres of a great ironist like Swift or Henry James is an ultimate test of a student's skill in reading'. Certainly, the accounts we have had of the 'meaning' of the great ironists show how much scope there is for radical divergences of interpretation; how entangled the naïvely unravelling critic can become. Some present-day reviewers, perhaps aware of these dangers, seem to be simplifying irony into their own images; making of it, indeed, a peg upon which any reader's personal feelings of iconoclasm, cynicism, anger and moral outrage can be conveniently hung.

The studies comprising this present volume were written over a number of years and make no claim to offer either a theory of irony or any criteria that can be universally applied. My main contention is that no embracing theories or criteria are possible and that the attempts to seek for them are invariably misplaced. Nearly all of the classic definitions of 'satire' and 'comedy' overlook the deviousness of the writings on which they purport to be based. The great ironists are so much more ambivalent than the theorists normally think them, so much

ix

more genuinely flexible in their style. We have been told, for
instance, that satirists can be divided into two main groups, the
Juvenalian, who are moralistic and astringent, and the Horatian, who are genial and urbane. But do not most great satirists
share both of these possibilities? — and many more such possibilities, since to love what is hated, to be attracted by what
repels, is not unusual among men to whom irony comes naturally as a mode. We have been told, again, that satirists can be
divided into those who are motivated solely by moral outrage
and those who are motivated chiefly by iconoclasm, which
moral outrage is merely co-opted to serve. But do not most
satirists have both iconoclasm and moral outrage in their make-
up? To draw up proportions or rules that they 'should' adhere
to is like defining the tiger's proper habitat as a zoo.

For irony relates not only to events, but to the temperament
and personality of the man who records events. Its colourings
may come from passing moods, or from a deep-seated habit of
mind; its directions may obey the logic of a particular chain of
events, or may originate in a vision of the universe which particular events are chosen to typify or represent. Even its subject
matter ranges freely over matters political and religious, sexual
and personal; there are very few beliefs or achievements of
men, and still fewer actions, that remain invulnerable to its
shafts. And always, whatever the configuration of ingredients,
irony is complex and oblique. To understand it we must be
able to look beyond the literal meanings of words to meanings
only to be sensed beyond the page. Sometimes there is a simple
reversal of meaning, as in a schoolmaster's sarcasm, or in the
routine 'pleasantries' of everyday: '*You're* a pretty sight!';
'Why, the boy's a genius!' But often, the real meaning is not
an exact reversal of what is actually said. It may exist somewhere between the literal meaning and its logical opposite, in
a no-man's-land where we feel our way delicately and sensi-
tively, among many puzzling nuances of mood and tone.
When Swift writes:

> I have been assured by a very knowing American of my
> acquaintance in London, that a young healthy child well
> nursed is at a year old a most delicious, nourishing and
> wholesome food, whether stewed, roasted, baked or boiled . . .

the opposite of this, whether true or false, has little to do with
what he means. The irony, rather, is bound up with Swift's
bland assumption of brutality and inhumanity in his readers;
he is saying something profoundly shocking, but in the tone of
voice appropriate to ordinary gentlemanly good sense. We
notice the implied equation between capitalism and canni-
balism (very normal with Swift, when England's dealings with
Ireland are his concern); and we notice the balance between
relish and revulsion in the finely judged nuances of tone.

An even more complex irony is offered, with deceptive simplicity, by Oscar Wilde, when he writes: 'The brotherhood of
man is no mere poet's dream, it is a most depressing and
humiliating reality.'

The 'meaning' of this certainly cannot be found by reversing
the sense in some simple way; and analysis merely throws the
sparkling compression of the original into sharper relief. The
diehards (Wilde is really saying) call the brotherhood of man a
mere poet's dream, because this is what they want it to be.
But in fact it is already a reality; an infinitely depressing one,
created by the diehards themselves from the misery and squalor
of the human heart, instead of from its exuberance and joy.
The irony, in fact, is that Wilde does mean what he says, but not
in the way in which his words would normally be understood.
He looks as though he is being light-heartedly cynical about
the ideal of human brotherhood; his irony is really at the expense
of those who would normally be cynical in exactly this way.

In the studies that follow, my approach has been through the
individual flexibilities of the various writers and through close
attention to their personal mood and tone. I have restricted
myself to prose writers for reasons of space, since to have introduced poets among them would have been to double the length
of the book. I have omitted writers like Jane Austen, Dickens
and Henry James who would have taken up too much room;
their irony is intricately related to their whole techniques and
purposes as novelists, and they would need far more extended
attention than there is space for here. And I have omitted writers
who are primarily ironists in another sense; those like the
Greek tragic dramatists, or Hardy, whose irony is more essentially a feeling about the universe than a stylistic technique.
My own concern, as will already have become clear, is with

irony in its primary definition as a figure of speech, and not with
the secondary meaning defined in the *Shorter Oxford English
Dictionary* as 'a contradictory outcome of events as if in mockery
of the promise and fitness of things'. Naturally many ironists
included here are ironists in this secondary sense as well, and
some of them, like Swift and Orwell, come very close to the tragic
sense of life. But this, for my present purpose, is by the way; a
study of tragic irony would certainly centre on the drama, and
would produce a wholly different type of book.

I am not suggesting, then, that the ironists discussed here are
the only major ironists of their kind in the English tongue
(clearly they are not); nor that they in any meaningful sense
form a 'school'. There are many similarities between them, as
one would expect: they are all in one way or another oblique
and devious, since irony prescribes this; and Swift has been to
some degree tutor to all the rest. But their views on life are
widely different, and so are their strategies. Only an exact
attention to their differences brings us to the place where
detailed criticism can begin.

There can be no question, moreover, of a 'definitive' interpretation, and indeed the life of these, as of all other considerable writers, would be extinguished if there could. Criticism is
always a dialogue between the writer and his readers at one
point in time: the writer living 'then', the reader living
'now'; the writer having one background, temperament,
philosophy of life, the reader having another which, however
similar, is certainly never the same. The purpose of criticism
must be to illuminate the possibilities and the rewards of this
dialogue; to keep it alive by the very recognition, if need be,
that the critic is more ephemeral than the authors whom he
chooses to serve; that he is one link in a long and unfolding
chain which their living influence becomes. A critic may hope,
of course, that a reader will find much in what he says to agree
with; but to stimulate a personal response measured against
his own, to stimulate excited disagreement if need be, is the one
legitimate function he can claim.

I have, therefore, tried not to generalise; and when I have
generalised, I have tried to do so as a local convenience, as in
the chapter on Fielding where definitions of 'satire' and
'comedy' are meant to be useful for a particular discussion and

no more. A few brief generalised comments may however be in place here, of the type that cannot be wholly ignored. Some readers are worried, I think, by the fact that ironists are not ironic all the time: 'is this meant seriously or not?' they ask, uneasily aware that the ironist may be dancing them on a string. Sometimes, of course, the passage *is* meant seriously; straightforward narrative or moralising intervenes, and the ironic tone is suspended for a while. But the rule for readers is to remain always and unremittingly on guard. An ironist's whole context is attuned to the hints and nuances he needs. In *Gulliver*, in *Erewhon*, in *Brave New World*, in *1984* a fantasy world is constructed, to carry ironic implications beyond purely verbal manipulation, into the plot and structure of the whole; even in the more realistic worlds of Fielding and Thackeray, Twain and Waugh, everything is still assimilated to ironic needs. The mocking tone can always break in at a moment's notice; and can be suspected, indeed, for the greater part of the time. A reader will test his suspicions whenever they occur to him; he will try to sense an intention in the structure and organisation of the work, even when verbal irony cannot be found.

Perhaps a deeper worry for some readers is this: that though an ironist's main intention is often moralistic, his mood is attuned to ridicule, rejection, mockery, even despair. The very attitudes he employs for moralistic purposes are intrinsically suspect. We may agree that some people and actions are hateful, but is hatred the best response to them that can be made? We may agree that some people and actions are disgusting, but is the man who cultivates disgust the best moral guide we can find? Charity and forgiveness might be more constructive, even though (perhaps significantly?) they are the last responses an ironist can employ. For hatred and disgust can be vices in themselves, and not least so when prudence and respectability are on their side. They can even mirror a disease in the man who succumbs to them, which he merely imagines to be a form of astringent moral health. When Bosola shrinks from the Duchess of Malfi's pregnancy, it is not she whom his disgust condemns. When the Ancient Mariner sees a horror at the heart of the universe, his own damnation has conjured and projected it there.

All of this may seem obvious, yet it warns us to scrutinise the ironist's moral credentials with particular care. At best, he is a moralist to whom cruelty and rejection come more naturally than forgiveness and charity. At worst, he may be a sick man, shuddering at evils which have their true origin in himself. Any reader approaching this field will have to bear such possibilities in mind. But he will have to bear in mind also, perhaps more importantly, that he *is* concerned now with life-through-art and not with life direct. The fact that certain negative emotions belong to irony as a literary mode does not prove that the ironist is incapable of more tender responses as a man; he may or may not be, and this is one of the many things we must try to detect. This paradox is not peculiar to irony, moreover, even though the ironist presents it in a particularly challenging form. Nor is this other paradox, somewhat related to it, peculiar to irony: that the ironist often seems to be denying the possibility of form and order in our human affairs, in a work which actually exemplifies the qualities it denies. To some degree, such a paradox is common to all literature with a propensity to total gloom, and perhaps to all art. However tragic the content might be, or pessimistic the conclusion, in all great writing there is harmony, and even exuberance, of form. The most negative thinker becomes a creator as he writes; if his works live on after him, this is because there is beauty and meaning in what they are, no matter how great the discord in what they say. Nor is this to deny that great art always is a union of form and content; for the very fusion of these two aspects of literary creation underlines this other simple truth, that literature always is a creative achievement as well as a record; that it belongs to the history of what man can make as well as to the history of what he can say. T. S. Eliot reminded us of the distinction between the man who suffers and the artist who creates; we can well imagine that a work which is agonising in its content might have been in some degree pleasurable to create. The work of art which is created is, in any event, more self-contained and permanent than its maker. In ironic writing it need not surprise us if a writer's achievement is more orderly and creative than the account of human nature embodied in it would seem to permit.

A.E.D. 1964

CHAPTER I

SWIFT: THE METAMORPHOSIS OF IRONY

I

In an age of few or shifting values irony becomes, very often, a tone of urbane amusement; assuming the right to be amused, but offering no very precise positives behind the right. It can degenerate into a mere gesture of superiority, superficially polished and civilised, but too morally irresponsible to be really so. *Eminent Victorians* is an example of such irony which springs to mind. Lytton Strachey uses the tone of Gibbon in order to deflate the Victorians, but divorces the tone from any firm moral viewpoint, and so makes of it a negative and somewhat vicious instrument.

Irony can, also, become a mode of escape, as we have good cause to know in the twentieth century. To laugh at the terrors of life is in some sense to evade them. To laugh at oneself is to become less vulnerable to the scorn or indifference of others. An ironic attitude is, as we should all now agree, complex and unpredictable: fluctuating with mood and situation, too subtle in its possibilities for any simple definition in terms of moral purpose or a 'test of truth' to be generally applied.

This is not, however, a state of affairs as new, or unusual, as we might be tempted to think. Even in that great age of moral irony, the eighteenth century, the technique is far from being simple. Irony is, in its very nature, the most ambivalent of modes, constantly changing colour and texture, occasionally suffering a sea-change into something rich and strange. In the work of Swift, who will concern us here, we find, at characteristic moments, that the irony takes a leap. It escapes from its supposed or apparent purpose and does something not only entirely different from what it set out to do, but even diametrically opposite. Nor is this just a matter of lost artistic control or structural weakness. At the moments I have in mind the irony is at its most complex and memorable. It seems, in undergoing its metamorphosis, to bring us nearer to Swift's inner vision of man and the universe. It ceases to be a functional technique serving a moral purpose, and becomes the embodiment of an attitude to life. And just as Alice was forced, on consideration, to accept the metamorphosis of the Duchess's baby into a pig as an improvement ('it would have made a dreadfully ugly child; but it makes rather a handsome pig, I think'), so the readers of Swift will have to agree that the final impact of his irony, however disturbing, is more real, and therefore more worth-while, than its continuation as simple moral satire would have been.

II

But this is to anticipate. We must begin by reminding ourselves that Swift *is* a satirist: and that satire, fiercer than comedy in its moral intentions, measures human conduct not against a norm but against an ideal. The intention is reformative. The satirist holds up for his readers to see a distorted image, and the reader is to be shocked into a realisation that the image is his own. Exaggeration of the most extreme kind is central to the shock tactics. The reader must see himself as a monster, in order to learn how far he is from being a saint.

The Augustan age, as Professor Willey has most interestingly shown, was especially adapted to satiric writing. An age which does not really believe in sin, and which imagines that its most rational and enlightened ideals have been actualised as a norm, is bound to be aware also, at times, of a radical gulf between theory and practice. '. . . if you worship "Nature and Reason", you will be the more afflicted by human unreason; and perhaps only the effort to see man as the world's glory will reveal how far he is really its jest and riddle.'[1]

Economic and acquisitive motives were coming more and more into the open as mainsprings of individual and social action; Hobbes's sombre account of human nature in terms of competition and conflict was altogether too plausible on the practical level for the comfort of gentlemen philosophers who rejected it, as a theory, out of hand. The turning of Science,

[1] Basil Willey, *Eighteenth Century Background*, Chapter VI.

Britannia and The Moderns into idols was bound, in any case, to produce sooner or later some iconoclasm of the Swiftian kind. Satire thrives on moral extremes: and at this period, with Hobbes at hand to provide a view of man which was at once alarmingly possible and entirely opposite to the prevailing one, satire was bound to be very much at home.

It should follow from this, and to some extent really does, that Swift was a moralist, concerned, as he himself puts it, to 'wonderfully mend the world', in accordance with the world's most ideal picture of itself. *Gulliver's Travels* is far more complex and elusive, however, than this intention would suggest. It is, indeed, a baffling work: you have only to dip into the many excellent and stimulating commentaries on Book IV to find disagreements upon the most fundamental points of interpretation. Clearly, we cannot arrive at Swift's 'true' meaning merely by reversing what he actually says. The illusion that he is establishing important positives with fine, intellectual precision breaks down when we try to state what these positives are.

On the surface, at least, the irony does work in ways that can be precisely defined. Swift has a number of techniques which he is skilled in using either singly, or in powerful combination. At one moment he will make outrageously inhuman proposals with a show of great reasonableness and an affected certainty that we shall find them acceptable; at another he will make soundly moral or Christian proposals which are confidently held up for scorn. Again, we find him offering, with apparent sympathy and pride, an account of our actual doings, but in the presence of a virtuous outsider whose horrified reactions are sufficient index of their true worth. Swift can, notoriously, shift from one technique to another with huge dexterity; setting his readers a problem in mental and moral gymnastics if they are to evade all of his traps. In Book III, for example, the Professors at Balnibarbi are presented as progressive scientists, of a kind whom the Augustan reader would instinctively be prepared to admire. We quickly find that they are devoid of all common sense; and that unless we are to approve of such extravagant projects as 'softening marble for pincushions' we have to dissociate ourselves from them entirely. But when we do this, Swift is still ready for us. 'In the school of political projectors', says Gulliver, 'I was but ill entertained; the Professors appearing in my judgement wholly out of their senses' (a pleasant reassurance this, that we have done well to come to a similar conclusion some time before). The crowning absurdity is that these 'unhappy people were proposing schemes for persuading monarchs to choose favourites upon the score of their wisdom, capacity and virtue . . . of rewarding merit, great abilities and eminent services . . .'. Dissociated from the Professors, we find ourselves once more in Swift's snare.

The technique is, of course, one of betrayal. A state of tension, not to say war, exists between Swift and his readers. The very tone in which he writes is turned into a weapon. It is the tone of polite conversation, friendly, and apparently dealing in commonplaces. Naturally our assent is captured, since the polite style, the guarantee of gentlemanly equality, is the last one in which we expect to be attacked or betrayed. But the propositions to which we find ourselves agreeing are in varying degrees monstrous, warped or absurd. The result is the distinctively satiric challenge: why, we have to ask, are we so easily trapped into thinking so? And is this, perhaps, the way we really do think, despite our normal professions to the contrary?

The technique of betrayal is made all the more insidious by Swift's masterly use of misdirection. No conjuror is more adept at making us look the wrong way. His use of the polite style for betrayal is matched by his use of the traveller's tale. The apparently factual and straightforward narrative with which *Gulliver's Travels* opens (the style of *Robinson Crusoe*) precludes suspicion. We readily accept Gulliver as a representative Englishman fallen into the hands of an absurd crew of midgets, and realise only gradually that the midgets, in fact, are ourselves, and Gulliver in this instance the outside observer. The same technique is used, I shall argue, in Book IV: though there the misdirection is even more subtle, and the way to extricate ourselves from a disastrous committal to Gulliver's point of view far harder to find.

III

So much, then, for the purpose of the irony and its normal methods. It is, we notice, accomplished, full of surprises and admirably adapted to the task of shocking the reader for his

moral good. For a great part of the time, moreover, it func-
tions as it is intended to. When Swift is satirising bad lawyers,
bad doctors, bad politicians and *id genus omne*, he is driven by
the conviction that people ought not to act in this way, and
need not act so. His tone of savage indignation is justified by
the content, and relates directly to normal ideals of justice,
honesty and kindness in human affairs.

On looking closer, however, we find that his irony is by no
means directed only against things which can be morally
changed. Sometimes it is deflected, and turned upon states of
mind which might or might not be alterable. Consider, for
example, the Laputians. These people never, we are told, enjoy
a moment's peace of mind, 'and their disturbances proceed
from causes which very little affect the rest of mortals'. They
are preoccupied with fears of cosmic disasters, and apprehensions that the world will come to an end. The ironic treatment
presupposes that Swift is analysing a moral flaw, but it seems
doubtful whether such fears can be regarded wholly as culpable
weakness, and even more doubtful whether ridicule could hope
to effect a cure. The problem exists in a hinterland between the
moral and the psychological, between sin and sickness. The
Laputians are temperamentally prone to worry: and worry is
not usually regarded, except by the most austerely stoical, as
simply a moral weakness in all its forms.

This dubious usage points the way to the real metamorphosis,
which occurs when the irony is deflected again, and turned
against states of mind, or existence, which cannot be changed
at all. The irony intended to 'wonderfully mend the world'
transmutes itself into a savage exploration of the world's essential unmendability. It is turned against certain limitations, or
defects (as Swift sees them), in the human predicament that
are, by the nature of things, inevitable. When this happens,
Swift seems to generate his fiercest intensity. The restless energy
behind the style becomes a masochistic probing of wounds. The
experience of reading him is peculiarly disturbing at such
moments; and it is then that his tone of savage indignation
deepens into that *disgust* which Mr T. S. Eliot has called his
distinctive characteristic.

In the first two books of *Gulliver* alterations of perspective
usually precipitate this type of irony. The Lilliputians are

ridiculous not only because they are immoral, but because they are small. The life of their court is as meaningless as it is unpleasant: their intrigues and battles a game, which Gulliver can manipulate like a child playing with toys, and as easily grow tired of. Gulliver himself becomes ridiculous when he is placed beside the Brobdingnagians; whose contempt for him, once again, is not wholly, or even primarily, a moral matter. The King, after hearing Gulliver prattling about his 'beloved England', comments 'how contemptible a thing was human grandeur, which could be mimicked by such diminutive insects', and continues:

> Yet I dare engage, these creatures have their titles and distinctions of honour; they contrive little nests and burrows, that they call houses and cities; they make a figure in dress and equipage; they love, they fight, they dispute, they cheat, they betray.

The force, here, is in 'mimicked', 'diminutive insects', 'creatures', 'little'. The smallness of Gulliver and his kind makes anything they do equally contemptible, their loves as much as their battles, their construction of houses and cities as much as their destructiveness. The survey is Olympian; and the human setting, seen from this height, becomes, irrespective of moral evaluation, a tale of little meaning though the words are strong.

Likewise, the hugeness of the Brobdingnagians makes them potentially horrible. The sight of a huge cancer fills Gulliver with revulsion, as, too, does the sight of giant flies who 'would sometimes alight on my victuals, and leave their loathsome excrement or spawn behind'.

What do these alterations in perspective suggest? We are made to feel that perhaps all beauty or value is relative, and in the last resort of little worth. To be proud of human achievement is as absurd as to be proud of our sins. The insignificance of men in space suggests an inevitable parallel in time. Perhaps men really *are* no more.than ants, playing out their fleeting tragi-comedy to an uninterested or scornful void. The irony, now, is an awareness of possible cosmic insignificance. It is exploring a wound which no amount of moral reformation would be able to heal.

IV

In Book IV of *Gulliver* the irony completes its transformation, and is turned upon human nature itself. Swift's intensity and disgust are nowhere more striking than here. This is the classic interpretative crux: and Aldous Huxley's remark, that Swift 'could never forgive man for being a vertebrate mammal as well as an immortal soul' still seems to me to be the most seminal critical insight that has been offered.

The crux centres, of course, upon what we make of Swift's relationship to Gulliver. How far is Gulliver a satiric device, and how far (if at all) does he come to be a spokesman for Swift himself? The answer seems to me to be by no means clear. If we accept Gulliver as Swift's spokesman, we end in a state of despair. On this showing, it would seem that Swift has openly abandoned his positives, and that when he avows that he has 'now done with all such visionary schemes' as trying to reform the Yahoos 'for ever', he has passed from ironic exaggeration to sober truth. Few readers will be willing to take this view, especially when they reflect upon the dangers in store for those who identify themselves with Gulliver too readily. And yet, if we reject this, what is the alternative view to be? Swift leads us very skilfully to follow Gulliver step by step. If at some point we depart from his view of himself we have to depart also from the Houyhnhnms: who seem, however, to be an incarnation of Swift's actual positives, and the very standard against which the Yahoos are tried and found wanting. What happens in Book IV is that Gulliver is converted gradually to an admiration of the Houyhnhnms, and then to an acceptance of their judgements upon himself and his kind. The result of this enlightenment is that he comes to realise also the unattainability of such an ideal for himself. He sinks into bitterness and misanthropy and ends, as a result of his contact with the ideal, far more unpleasant and unconstructive than he was before. At some stage, it seems, he has taken the wrong turning: but where has the mistake occurred?

The construction of the Book is of great interest. Gulliver first of all comes across the Yahoos, and is instantly repelled by them. 'Upon the whole, I never beheld in all my travels so disagreeable an animal, or one against which I naturally conceived so strong an antipathy.' Soon after this he encounters the noble horses, and is equally strongly impressed, this time in their favour. Almost at once he starts to discover between himself and the Yahoos an appalling resemblance: 'my horror and astonishment are not to be described, when I observed, in this abominable animal, a perfect human figure'. At this stage it is the physical resemblance which disturbs him. But later, as he falls under the influence of the Houyhnhnms, he comes also to accept a moral resemblance. And this is at the core of the satire.

The cleverness of Swift's technique is that at first the horses are only sketched in. They are clean, kindly, rational, but apart from seeing them through Gulliver's eyes we learn little in detail about them. Gulliver is first 'amazed to see . . . in brute beasts . . . behaviour . . . so orderly and rational, so acute and judicious'. But almost at once he finds that they regard *him* as the 'brute beast', and with somewhat more justice, 'for they looked upon it as a prodigy, that a brute animal should discover such marks of a rational creature'. From this moment, the Houyhnhnms start to insinuate into Gulliver's mind a vision of himself that becomes increasingly repellent. They begin by rejecting his claim to be truly rational, speaking of 'those appearances of reason' in him, and deciding that he has been taught to 'imitate' a 'rational creature'. When they compare him with the Yahoos, Gulliver at first objects, acknowledging, 'some resemblance', but insisting that he cannot account for 'their degenerate and brutal nature'. The Houyhnhnms will have none of this, however, deciding that if Gulliver does differ, he differs for the worse. 'He said, I differed indeed from other Yahoos, being much more cleanly, and not altogether so deformed; but in point of real advantage, he thought I differed for the worse.' The reason for this judgement — a reason which Gulliver himself comes to accept — is that his 'appearance of reason' is a fraud; and that what seems reason in him is no more than a faculty which makes him *lower* than the Yahoos.

. . . when a creature pretending to reason, could be capable of such enormities, he dreaded, lest the corruption of that faculty might be worse than brutality itself. He seemed therefore confident, that instead of reason, we were only possessed of some quality fitted to increase our natural vices.

SWIFT 9

Up to this point the reader might feel fairly confident that he sees what is happening. The Houyhnhnms really are ideal, and Gulliver's conversion to their point of view is the lesson we should be learning. The contemptuous view of mankind formed by the Houyhnhnms is the main satiric charge. The view that man *is* a Yahoo and cannot become a Houyhnhnm is satiric exaggeration: near enough to the truth to alarm us, but not intended to be taken literally. We shall be 'betrayed' if we identify ourselves with Gulliver at the points where the horses scorn him, but safe enough if we accept his conversion at their hands.

This, I fancy, is what many readers are led to feel: and to my mind, in so leading them, Swift sets his most subtle trap of all. The real shock comes in the middle of Chapter VIII, when Gulliver turns, at long last, to give us a more detailed description of the horses. We have already been aware, perhaps, of certain limitations in them: they have a limited vocabulary, limited interests, and an attitude to life that seems wholly functional. But Gulliver has explained all these limitations as virtues, and persuaded us to see them as a sign of grace. No doubt, we feel, these horses are noble savages of some kind, and their simplicity a condition and a reward of natural harmony. It remains for the fuller account to show us two further truths about the horses: the first, that they are not human at all, so that their way of life is wholly irrelevant as a human ideal; and the second, that their supposedly rational way of life is so dull and impoverished that we should not wish to emulate them even if we could.

Their society, for instance, is stoic in appearance. They accept such inevitable calamities as death calmly; they eat, sleep and exercise wisely: they believe in universal benevolence as an ideal, and accordingly have no personal ties or attachments. The family is effectually abolished: marriage is arranged by friends as 'one of the necessary actions in a reasonable being'; husband and wife love one another, and their children, just as much and as little as they love everyone else. Sex is accepted as normal, but only for the purpose of procreation. Like all other instincts, it is regarded as entirely functional, and has no relevance beyond the begetting of a standard number of offspring. The Houyhnhnms have no curiosity; their language, their arts and their sciences are purely functional, and restricted to the bare necessities of harmonious social existence. Life is lived 'without jealousy, fondness, quarrelling or discontent'; and it is lived in tribal isolation, since they are 'cut off from all commerce with other nations'.

This impoverished and devitalised society is the one which Gulliver uncritically accepts as an ideal, and on the strength of which he sinks into a most negative and unedifying misanthropy. And yet, so plausibly does Swift offer this as the ideal of Reason and Nature which his own age believed in, so cunningly does he lead us to think that this is the positive against which a satiric account of the Yahoos is functioning, that the trick is hard to detect. Even the fact that Gulliver is in an escapist frame of mind is not immediately apparent, unless we are on the alert. We see at once, it is true, that the Houyhnhnms are not *like* men: that physically Gulliver might be a monkey but is nothing like a horse, and that this physical placing is linked with a moral one. Yet we assume that this placing is only one more satiric technique: and it is with a distinct shock that we realise that it exists at a more fundamental level than any *moral* amendment on the part of a man could resolve. The Houyhnhnms are literally not human: they are inaccessible to Gulliver not because they are morally superior, but because they are physically non-existent. They are mental abstractions disguised as animals: but they are no more animals, really, than the medieval angels were, and nothing like any human possibility, bad or good.

The horses have, in fact, no passions at all. Their 'virtue' is not a triumph over impulse and temptation, but a total immunity from these things — and an immunity which is also, by its very nature, an absence of life and vitality. They have no compulsive sexual impulses, no sensuous pleasures, no capacity for any degree of human love. They have no wishes and fears, and scarcely any ideas. If they are incapable of human bestiality they are even less capable of human glory or sublimity; and it is only because Swift prevents us from thinking of humanity as anything other than a real or potential Yahoo that this is not at once immediately apparent.

What is the true force of Book IV, then? Swift seems to my mind to have posed, in new form, and with appalling consequences, the old riddle of man's place as the microcosm. Instead of relating him to the angels and the beasts, he relates him to the Houyhnhnms and the Yahoos. The Houyhnhnm is as non-bodily and abstract, in its essential nature, as an angel, the Yahoo a beast seen in its most disgusting lights. As for man, represented by Gulliver, he is left in a disastrous microcosmic vacuum. Instead of having his own distinctive place, he has to *be* one or other of the extremes. Swift drives a wedge between the intellectual and the emotional, makes one good, the other evil, and pushes them further apart, as moral opposites, than any except the most extreme Puritans have usually done. The result is the kind of tormenting and bitter dilemma which always lies in wait for those who do this and, to quote Huxley again (a writer temperamentally very similar to Swift himself), who cannot 'forgive man for being a vertebrate mammal as well as an immortal soul'. The ideal is unattainable, the vicious alternative inescapable, and both so unattractive, that one is at a loss to decide which one dislikes the more.

Once again, then, the irony intended for moral satire has undergone a metamorphosis: and starting as an attempt to improve man, ends by writing him off as incurable.

V

But how far did Swift intend this to be so? This is the question which now becomes relevant, and the answer cannot, I think, be a straightforward one. My own feeling is that we are faced with a split between conscious intention and emotional conviction, of a kind which modern criticism has familiarised us with in Milton. Perhaps Swift really did intend a simple moral purpose, and was not consciously betraying his reader into despair. And yet the unpleasantness of the Yahoos is realised so powerfully, and any supposed alternative is so palpably non-existent, that he must have been to some degree aware of his dilemma. He must have known that men do, for better or worse, have bodily desires, and that the Houyhnhnms were therefore an impossible ideal. He must have known, too, as a man himself, that the Houyhnhnms were both very limited and very unattractive. And in identifying Reason and Nature with them, he must have been aware that he was betraying his own positives and those of his age: leaving the Yahoos in triumphant possession of all the reality and the life, and removing the possibility of any human escape by way of Reason or Nature from their predicament.

As a satire, *Gulliver* can work normally only if we can accept the Houyhnhnms as a desirable human possibility: and this, I do not for a moment believe Swift thought we could. The very energy of the style is masochistic — a tormenting awareness of its own impotence to do, or change, anything. Swift is publicly torturing both himself and the species to which he belongs. The irony, then, intended for moral reformation, has undergone a more or less conscious metamorphosis; and the total effect of Book IV, as Dr Leavis has insisted, is largely negative.

There are, nevertheless, before this is finally asserted, one or two compensating factors to notice. The first, often surprisingly overlooked, is that Swift cannot really have supposed his readers to be Yahoos, if only because Yahoos could not have responded at all to *Gulliver's Travels*. The deliberate obtuseness with which Gulliver prattles of his 'beloved England' will register only with a reader much less obtuse. The reader must not only be betrayed but see that he has been betrayed: and in order for this to happen he must have more intelligence and more moral sense than a Yahoo. Swift knew, in any case, that his readers were Augustan gentlemen with ideals of human decency that he had in common with them, and that however much a case against them could be both thought and felt, the ultimate fact of Augustan civilisation — a fact embodied in his own style as much as anywhere — was not to be denied. *Gulliver's Travels* might leave us, then, with a wholly negative attitude, but the very fact of its being written at all is positive proof that Swift's own total attitude was not negative.

This may seem commonplace: but it leads on to another consideration, equally important, which most commentators upon *Gulliver* seem oddly afraid of: namely that Swift, writing for gentlemen, intended to give pleasure by what he wrote. When Gulliver says of the Yahoos (his readers), 'I wrote for their amendment, and not their approbation', there is a general readiness to accept this at its face value, and to credit Swift with a similar sternness. Sooner or later most writers about *Gulliver* hit upon the word 'exuberance', and then pause doubtfully, wondering whether, if Swift is so moral and so misanthropic as we think, such a word can have any place in describing him. Yet 'exuberant' he certainly is, even in Book IV of *Gulliver*. The *vive la bagatelle*, the flamboyant virtuosity of *A Tale of a Tub* is less central, but it is still to be detected, in the zest with which Gulliver describes bad lawyers, for example, and in the fantastic turns and contortions of the irony. Clearly, Swift enjoyed his control of irony: enjoyed its flexibility, its complex destructiveness, his own easy mastery of it. Clearly, too, he expects his readers to enjoy it. The irony is not *only* a battle, but a game: a civilised game at that, since irony is by its very nature civilised, presupposing both intelligence, and at least some type of moral awareness. The 'war' is a battle of wits: and if one confesses (as the present writer does) to finding *Gulliver* immensely enjoyable, need one think that Swift would really, irony apart, have been surprised or annoyed by such a reaction?

On a final balance, I fancy that we have to compromise: agreeing that *Gulliver* ends by destroying all its supposed positives, but deducing, from the exuberance of the style and the fact that it was written at all, that Swift did not really end in Gulliver's position. He was, at heart, humane, and his savage indignation against cruelty and hypocrisy in the straightforwardly satiric parts reflects a real moral concern. He was, also, iconoclastic and disillusioned about the ultimate dignity of man at a deep level: and when his irony undergoes the type of metamorphosis that has been discussed here, it is as disturbing and uprooted as any we can find. But he always, at the same time, enjoyed the technique of irony itself, both as an intellectual game and as a guarantee of at least some civilised reality. Very often, even at the most intense moments, we may feel that pleasure in the intellectual destructiveness of the wit is of more importance to him than the moral purpose, or the misanthropy, that is its supposed *raison d'être*. Irony, by its very nature, instructs by *pleasing*. To ignore the pleasure, and its civilised implications, is inevitably to oversimplify and falsify the total effect.

CHAPTER 2

FIELDING: SATIRIC AND COMIC IRONY

I

WHEN Fielding came on the literary scene, influences of senti-
mentalism were already at work. He was not a gentleman
philosopher writing for the cultured *élite*, as so many of his
predecessors had been. The audience he had in mind was the
new middle-class one, which was destined to adopt the form in
which he chose to pioneer and make it pre-eminent on the
literary landscape for two hundred years.

The history of the novel is far too vast to retell here, but we
all know how this child of the printing press was born with
Shandeyan belatedness in the eighteenth century. No doubt the
true pioneer was Defoe, but *Robinson Crusoe* and *Moll Flanders*
were somewhat ahead of their time. Richardson and Fielding
were the first novelists to find an audience ready and eager for
what they had to give. Horace Walpole might sneer, Lord
Chesterfield might sigh for the golden days of Addison and
Pope, but the future reading public was on the novelists' side.

And what did these new readers want? They were far less
interested in logic than the readers of *The Spectator* would have
been; their interest in philosophical empiricism existed scarcely
at all. What they chiefly wanted was to be entertained, and
perhaps a little moved as well, by tales of people not too unlike
themselves. They were interested in love, and in marriage; in
thrift, in prosperity and in success. They wanted plots and
characters that would be colourful, and possibly a little
heightened towards the dramatic: but not so heightened that
the sense of realism would be destroyed. And like Lewis
Carroll's Duchess, they wanted a moral; that final luxury without which no middle-class entertainment is complete. It was
not exactly that they confused literature with religion, or with
moral philosophy, or with life itself, as moralistic critics since

Matthew Arnold have been inclined to do. But they did sense that this new form could depict life with a seriousness and fulness inseparable from moral concern; and surely they were right?

Fielding cannot be judged then by the same canons of taste as his immediate predecessors, though he is clearly indebted to them in a great variety of ways. His satire was profoundly influenced by Swift, to whom in style he is often closely akin. The pessimistic view of man on which he sometimes falls back derives from Hobbes, though this also may have come to him by way of Swift. His more usual and characteristic optimism, and the particular moral vision it rests upon, owes a very great deal to Shaftesbury. In all these ways his roots are in the past, but the whole bent of his genius is original and forward-looking to a remarkable degree.

Satiric and comic elements mingle in all his works, but his primary instinct is for the comic. He uses ridicule in the service not of idealism, as a satirist would, but of ordinary benevolent good sense. In *Tom Jones* the readers are reminded that because a character is not good it does not follow that he is wholly bad. Does this seem obvious to us? — perhaps it does; yet a thorough-going satirist seldom thinks in this way. It gives us a clear indication, at any rate, of the manner in which Fielding's ridicule is to work. There is to be no great gulf fixed between the sheep and the goats. Instead, there is to be a series of graded distinctions between the bad, the not so bad, the good, the better and the best. The discrimination between these categories is keen, and the moral observation tough, for all Fielding's geniality of tone. For if the refusal to see men as either black or white is a commonplace of ordinary good sense, it is a commonplace of the kind that literature exists to give subtlety and depth to, in place of the everyday familiarity that breeds contempt.

In the Preface to *Joseph Andrews* Fielding goes so far as to suggest that ridicule is appropriate only to 'affectation' and not to true vice, which can arouse in us nothing but disgust. But here we should be on our guard, since 'affectation' is defined to include hypocrisy and vanity, both of which are extremely vicious in the presentation that Fielding normally chooses to give. Nor does this attempt to limit the scope of ridicule take *Jonathan Wild* into account, for there a savage irony plays around vice of the vilest kind. As critics, we shall have to distinguish more clearly than Fielding himself did between the satiric and comic elements in his work. When we have done this, we shall have gone far towards discovering where his true success as a writer is to be found.

For there is a paradox in Fielding's development as a novelist, as these preliminary remarks have already made clear. As a stylist he was indebted to Swift, but as a man he was about as dissimilar to Swift as he could have been. It is not only that he lacks the genuine fervour of the idealist — though this in itself is damaging to satire, unless there is some corresponding obsession to take its place. It is, rather, that he is too good-humoured for satire. He lacks the misanthropy to carry off the disgust which he must frequently profess to feel. He is, indeed, prejudiced in favour of the human race as it normally is — accepting *homo sapiens* at exactly the point of robust animality where Swift rejects him, and exhibiting a corresponding exuberance and geniality of style. The quality of exuberance in the two writers is as good a pointer as any to their differences. For whereas Swift's exuberance is in defiance of his content — an *animus* deriving partly from intellectual virtuosity, partly from the sheer strength of his disgust — Fielding's is much closer to the simple enjoyment and acceptance of life. In personality he is nearer to Rabelais than to Swift. His place is on the other side of that great watershed which separates those who view the human body with laughter or with reverence — or with both — from those who view it solely with dismay. It is no accident that he can be mistaken for Swift only in passages that are emotionally neutral. Both writers are remarkably similar in their prefaces and digressions, in the game with mock-logic and pseudo-scholarship which in company with many later ironists they loved to play. But turn to any passage where human experience is in question, and the differences between them leap at once to the eye. The spirit of good humour and tolerance keeps breaking into Fielding's work, in a manner that satire is ill-fitted to survive.

II

Let us turn, then, to the novels themselves. *Shamela Andrews* (which is almost certainly by Fielding and an early work) sets out as a parody of Richardson's *Pamela*. Fielding's unpuritanical

good humour could not swallow the cult of the pure but per-
secuted servant girl, so he reinterpreted Pamela for his own
amusement. *Shamela Andrews* makes two main ironic points; the
first that servant girls may not always be as pure as middle-
class moralists like to think, the second that Richardson's book
offers a larger measure of vicarious sexuality than its author
could possibly have known. For the most part the fun at
Richardson's expense is pure frivolity. There is Parson Tickle-
text's moral rapture, for instance, ('Oh! . . . methinks I see
Shamela at this instant, with all the pride of ornament cast
off'); and the solicitude of Henrietta as she advises her daughter
on the ways of the world: 'Remember the first lesson I taught
you, that a married woman injures only her husband, but a
single woman herself.' There are Shamela's well-spent hours
between the bedroom scenes, discussing her 'vartue' and reading *The Whole Duty of Man*. All these things are sheer good
humour, with Richardson as a mere jumping-off ground.

Joseph Andrews is also, in its origin, a parody of *Pamela*, but
Fielding is now ready to widen his scope. Satiric elements
continue to be of importance, but the main conception of the
work is a comic one. The ridicule is no longer reserved for the
hypocrites: Fielding's good characters are to come in for their
share of it as well. Parson Adams is a sympathetic character, a
religious leader whom Fielding very obviously admires. But he
is laughed at for failing to preach what he practices: his sermons
are full of a harshness that is abundantly belied in his life. Even
Joseph and Fanny do not escape without some good-humoured
laughter, again for the very virtues that endear them to us.
Fielding wholly approved of chastity, but he was the last man
to be solemn about it. Betty is allowed to exist in the novel as
well as Fanny, less virtuous to be sure, but with a compensating
liveliness of her own.

There are moments in *Joseph Andrews* when Fielding makes a
nearer approach to satire. Slipslop and Lady Booby are merci-
lessly exposed; the early life of West is an unpleasant picture of
a prodigal's life among the swine. The character of Leonora is
a much more serious exposure of wickedness than anything
Fielding had attempted in the novel before. But more usually
he forgoes the moral intensity of the satirist, and is content to
be amused as a man. The bedroom scenes exemplify his

masculine taste for the bawdy, with ironic situations straight from Boccaccio, but a tone and manner more likely to bring Chaucer to mind. And it is in these that we notice a curious ambiguity of effect, which runs through nearly all of Fielding's work until we get to *Tom Jones*. For whereas the frequent attempts on Fanny's chastity are ostensibly a satiric commentary on human nature, their real inspiration seems to be nearer to farce. And other episodes which in pure satire would have to be taken seriously are presented with all the boisterous gaiety of burlesque. There is, for instance, the famous scene when Joseph is left for dead by two highwaymen who have robbed him, and a coachload of people discover him lying naked by the road.

> The poor wretch, who lay motionless a long time, just began to recover his senses as a stage-coach came by. The postillion, hearing a man's groans, stopt his horses, and told the coachman, he was certain there was a dead man lying in the ditch, for he heard him groan. 'Go on, sirrah,' says the coachman; 'we are confounded late, and have no time to look after dead men.' A lady, who heard what the postillion said, and likewise heard the groan, called eagerly to the coachman to stop and see what was the matter. Upon which he bid the postillion alight, and look into the ditch. He did so, and returned, 'that there was a man sitting upright, as naked as ever he was born'. — 'O J-sus!' cried the lady; 'a naked man! Dear coachman, drive on and leave him'. Upon this the gentlemen got out of the coach; and Joseph begged them to have mercy upon him: for that he had been robbed and almost beaten to death. 'Robbed!' cries an old gentleman: 'let us make all the haste imaginable, or we shall be robbed too'. A young man who belonged to the law answered, 'He wished they had passed by without taking any notice; but that now they might be proved to have been last in his company; if he should die they might be called to some account for his murder. He therefore thought it advisable to save the poor creature's life, for their own sakes, if possible; at least, if he died, to prevent the jury's finding that they fled for it. He was therefore of opinion to take the man into the coach, and carry him to the next inn'. The lady insisted, 'That he should not come into the coach. That if they lifted

him in, she would herself alight: for she had rather stay in
that place to all eternity than ride with a naked man'. The
coachman objected, 'That he could not suffer him to be taken
in unless somebody would pay a shilling for his carriage the
four miles'. Which the two gentlemen refused to do. But the
lawyer, who was afraid of some mischief happening to himself, if the wretch was left behind in that condition, saying
no man could be too cautious in these matters, and that he
remembered very extraordinary cases in the books, threatened
the coachman, and bid him deny taking him up at his peril;
for that, if he died, he should be indicted for his murder; and
if he lived, and brought an action against him, he would
willingly take a brief in it. These words had a sensible effect
on the coachman, who was well acquainted with the person
who spoke them; and the old gentleman above mentioned,
thinking the naked man would afford him frequent opportunities of showing his wit to the lady, offered to join with the
company in giving a mug of beer for his fare; till, partly
alarmed by the threats of the one, and partly by the promises
of the other, and being perhaps a little moved with compassion at the poor creature's condition, who stood bleeding
and shivering with the cold, he at length agreed; and
Joseph was now advancing to the coach, where, seeing the
lady, who held the sticks of her fan before her eyes, he
absolutely refused, miserable as he was, to enter, unless he
was furnished with sufficient covering to prevent giving the
least offence to decency — so perfectly modest was this
young man; such mighty effects had the spotless example of
the amiable Pamela, and the excellent sermons of Mr.
Adams, wrought upon him.

Though there were several greatcoats about the coach, it
was not easy to get over this difficulty which Joseph had
started. The two gentlemen complained they were cold, and
could not spare a rag; the man of wit saying, with a laugh,
that charity began at home; and the coachman, who had
two greatcoats spread under him, refused to lend either, lest
they should be made bloody: the lady's footman desired to
be excused for the same reason, which the lady herself, notwithstanding her abhorrence of a naked man, approved: and
it is more than probable poor Joseph, who obstinately

C

adhered to his modest resolution, must have perished, unless the
postillion (a lad who hath been since transported for robbing
a hen-roost) had voluntarily stript off a greatcoat, his only
garment, at the same time swearing a great oath (for which
he was rebuked by the passengers), 'that he would rather ride
in his shirt all his life than suffer a fellow-creature to lie in so
miserable a condition'.

The open relish for the absurd makes us laugh out loud, as
we are surely intended to do, but the events described are not
without their sombre side. If we respond to this purely as farce,
as we might to the early misadventures of Mr Pickwick, we miss
the whole purpose Fielding had in mind. The toughness of
eighteenth-century life as it is recorded here is matched by
toughness of moral observation and tone. Fielding was far from
being a sentimentalist when it came to understanding his
fellow men; his belief in vitality and good nature rested on no
overestimate of their prevalence in the world. In the passage I
have quoted above there is a clear parallel to the parable of the
Good Samaritan to remind us where the intended moral is to
be found: the implication that a man whom society despises for
his poverty and later deports for robbing a hen-roost should be
the only decent human-being in the coach is one which any
Christian ought to take in his stride. Indeed, Fielding himself is
essentially Christian in his beliefs, and his comic vision is near
to the New Testament in a number of ways. The discrepancy
between social reputation on the one hand and true human
worth on the other is surely fundamental to the whole narrative
on which Christianity is based. What we have to say about a
passage like this, perhaps, is that it is deeply serious at heart,
yet also funny — and even farcical — in a way that serious
satire very seldom is. Fielding is willing to enjoy whatever can
be enjoyed, to 'see the funny side of things' as the popular
phrase has it; and this itself reflects an aspect of his temperament
which differentiates him sharply from Swift — his personal
vitality and resilience, his ability to take evil, and even goodness,
in his stride. He was never obsessed with violence as Swift was,
never tempted to give the Devil too much more than his due.
Hostile critics have seen Fielding's humour as irresponsible,
but no one who attends to his compassion, to his abundant

engagement with life, will make this mistake. Humanly speaking the humour is vastly attractive, but stylistically it can sometimes get out of hand. We are most conscious of this in the dialogue; in the passages when his virtuous characters feel compulsively moved, as most of them too often do, to discourse. For surely Parson Adams's views on virtue should be implied rather than stated? They are the positive standards against which the irony works, and for this very reason ought to be implied obliquely, rather than presented in so many words in the text. By making them explicit in this way — through the mouth of a fallible mortal, and in the same burlesque style that tends to be used throughout — Fielding comes very close to sabotaging his effect. The very standards of virtue sound absurd when men are bombastic: Fielding's presentation even suggests a new and anarchic type of humour, where everything is satirised in turn against differing sets of values. Fanny becomes the standard of chastity who offers a satiric placing of Betty, but Betty the exponent of unchastity who reminds us that the world, after all, does not take kindly to prudes. If this is so it is a superb stroke of gaiety, but gaiety and satire cannot live long together in this way.

Our judgement on this crux will be central to what we make of Fielding as a whole. If the word 'irresponsible' has to be rejected, as I am sure that it does, what are we to put in its place? The answer has to be approached by a number of routes, none of which has been popular in literary criticism of late. One is that the loss of satiric rigour is compensated for by a gain in comic tolerance and poise; and to this I shall return. Another is that the reader, too, has his responsibilities; any reader who sees in Fielding only farce or burlesque is perhaps unfitted to read him at all. And a third is the defence of burlesque which Fielding himself offers in the Preface to *Joseph Andrews*, even while arguing that his own method is of a more serious kind: 'it contributes more to exquisite mirth and laughter than any other (mode); and these are probably more wholesome physic for the mind, and conduce better to purge away spleen, melancholy and ill affections, than is generally imagined.'

However this may be, the mingling of good humour with seriousness is bound to reveal itself as a literary infirmity of purpose in passages where satire rather than comedy is the aim: in *Jonathan Wild* it becomes a source of structural weakness throughout. By the consistency and intensity of its irony, this work clearly announces itself as a satire in the tradition of *Gulliver*. But the Swiftian façade is related only fitfully to a genuine disgust; Fielding has as much insight into evil as Swift, but none of the misanthropy which sustains Swift in a gradually mounting indictment of humanity. As a result, the *jeu d'esprit* works against the total artistic purpose rather than for it. Instead of intensifying the satire, it produces a quite alien note of honest mirth.

I am not suggesting, however, that *Jonathan Wild* fails as a work, or anything so simple. Its very lapses from satire are the occasion for that health and vitality which are the true qualities by which Fielding survives. Nor am I suggesting, as I have already made clear, that Fielding is incapable of depicting evil as it really is. His sense of the depravity of the corrupted soul was a profound one, and none the less so for its refusal to become assimilated to a prevailing misanthropy. The real point that has to be made is that Fielding depicts Wild skilfully, but without ultimate conviction; there is even a hint of glamour in the portrait, of the kind that one associates with street ballads of the time. It is hard for us to believe that Wild is very relevant to the life of ordinary men; far from being alarmed on behalf of the species to which he belongs (as we are alarmed on behalf of the species to which the supposed author of Swift's *Modest Proposal* belongs) we must regard him as an interesting exception. He is little more than a puppet, flawless in performance, but curiously abstract in the quality of his crime. There is even a certain monotony about his techniques. First he will try to gain his ends by a brilliant and persuasive rhetoric, which itself implies a Hobbesian view of human nature; when this fails he resorts to open violence, with immediate and predictable success. But his progress in crime is a mere accumulation of incidents, not a deepening insight into the nature of evil. He has used all his best methods, and Fielding has expended his best irony upon them, before a quarter of the novel is through. So the rest tends to be unsatisfying; well executed in its way, but increasingly tedious by repetition.

And the good characters suffer here, as in *Joseph Andrews*, from the tone of voice in which they speak. Mr Heartfree's moral homilies, like those of Parson Adams before him, sound fantastically bombastic, for all the honest seriousness they convey. The mock-heroic tone touches his words, like Jonathan's, with ridicule, seeming to suggest a further set of man-of-the-world values to ridicule Christian idealism itself. Nor does this tendency stop at what is said, it extends to the action as well. Mrs Heartfree's adventures at sea recall *The Decameron* (Day Two, Novel Seven), on which they were probably based; their effect is considerably more bawdy than satiric, despite the heroine's narrow (and unBoccaccian) escapes. We are forced to conclude that Fielding is not a genuine satirist, measuring *homo sapiens* against his own most exalted ideals and finding him wanting. He is, rather, an essentially unpuritanical commentator, distressed by the sins of men but often amused by them as well. To be unpuritanical is not, however, to be un-Christian, whatever the puritans themselves may say. The puritan's laughter hurts, as the satirist's does, but good humoured laughter can be healing in ways of its own. Fielding's true praise is as a master of this second kind, and it is to this — and to his masterpiece as a writer — that we must now turn.

III

Tom Jones is Fielding's masterpiece, by common consent — and what a splendid masterpiece it is! There is no consistent irony of the kind attempted in *Jonathan Wild*, but at last there is a consistent moral purpose. The inconsistencies due to an insufficiently realised satiric plan are no longer in evidence. We find instead that all of the major characters fit into a pattern, which is large enough to allow them to exist as rounded and convincing people, and delicate enough to ensure that they are understood and judged at every point. W. L. Cross and R. L. Brett have actually called the book 'an attempt to express Shaftesbury's moral theory in fictional form'. I would not myself go this far, since *Tom Jones* seems to me bigger than its moral ideas, important though these undoubtedly are: and the ideas themselves transcend the eighteenth-century framework to which they belong. But the emphasis on moral purpose is at least preferable to the notion that Fielding had no serious values at all. The nature of this purpose is bound up, of course, with plot and characterisation, and the implications are maybe more subtle than they at first appear. At one level we are presented with three moral philosophies to choose from, each current in the early part of the eighteenth century, and each embodied in one important character in the book. The first of these is Butler's prudential morality, which assumes that virtue is at root a very rational affair. The promptings of Conscience have unique authority, but they are reinforced by hedonistic calculations, in which self-love and social duty can be seen to be the same. Butler's ideas are exemplified in Mr Allworthy, who might have stepped straight from the Bishop's sermons into the book. Butler, then, provides the first of the moral philosophies; the next, more warm and genial, is Shaftesbury's, where reason counts for less, and feeling for more. What really matters in life, on this view of things, is warm good nature. Without this quality our highest virtues are mere calculation; with it, our worst vices are touched, at least, with the kind of humanity that saves. This moral view, one need scarcely add, is Fielding's own; the character who embodies it in the purest form is Sophia, though Tom comes very close to it as well. And thirdly, there is the moral primitivism which takes the Noble Savage as its myth; the view which ascribes all our ills to a repressive culture and sees an outsider like Tom — both bastard and rebel — as the true source where virtue is to be found. Tom himself is conceived in accordance with this idea, and naturally he is nearer to Shaftesbury's formula for virtue than he is to Butler's. But in one vital respect there is a difference, on which the moral climax of Fielding's novel is to turn. For whereas the primitivist thinks of civilised society as merely evil, Shaftesbury finds in it our highest good. He sees it, indeed, as the soil in which true virtue must grow — though he agrees with the primitivist that it *can* be a source of evil as well.

It might be said, then, that a choice between Butler, Shaftesbury and the Noble Savage is one of the moral preoccupations that the novel offers. But it might also be said that an even deeper preoccupation, to which these more formal excursions into philosophy are assimilated, is the choice between Reputation and Real Worth: between appearance and reality in virtue, explored in a manner which has to be described as Christian. The initial contrast of this kind is the one between Master Blifil and Tom Jones when they are both very young. From the viewpoint of society Blifil is the good boy, and Tom the bad. And why? Because Blifil keeps the rules or seems to keep them, while Tom breaks them or seems to break them all the time. Blifil is the type of boy who causes little trouble to those set in authority over him. Not only is he exemplary himself, but he is eager that Tom should be exemplary as well; certainly he brings Tom's faults to the notice of authority whenever he can, in a manner that can easily be interpreted as honest concern. In all these good works he is actuated by the virtue of prudence; but by a prudence which senses that you do not really have to keep the rules if your reputation is such that you can appear to keep them instead. Tom, in sharp contrast to Blifil, is a perpetual nuisance to everyone set in authority over him, and has no social reputation at all. He is wholly devoid of prudence, as Mr Allworthy correctly sees; he not only fails to pretend to virtues he lacks, but gains little credit for those he actually has.

In the contrast between the two boys, one central fact emerges with startling clarity: that reputation, which is the yardstick by which society measures its citizens, may have little to do with genuine virtue; little to do with humanity, or compassion, or vitality, or simple goodness of heart. Blifil's very virtues indeed, as society judges them to be, depend upon a lack of these latter qualities; a certain self-righteous callousness is inseparable from the kind of esteem he enjoys. Tom's vices, on the other hand, are the other side of exactly the warmer sentiments and affections that Blifil lacks: the other side of a generous humanity which is acknowledged by Mr Allworthy though not by Square or Thwackum, but which even Mr Allworthy regards as a poor substitute for social reputation and esteem.

From this contrast, a number of further implications arise. Firstly, though Pride is officially supposed to be the deadliest of sins, it is not treated as such by society at large; for whereas sensuality earns instant disapproval, pride is usually rewarded with esteem. Secondly, though Charity is said to be the chief among virtues, in practice it is regarded very little if at all; the Pharisee is nearly always more respectable than the Saint.

Thirdly, the very absence of energy and exuberance is a part of virtue as it is normally defined: indeed these qualities tell against reputation rather than for it, since anyone possessing them is apt to be regarded with envious mistrust. Fourthly, the possession of reputation enables a man to be readily believed even when he is the most accomplished liar like Blifil, whereas the lack of reputation ensures that he will be disbelieved, even when he habitually tells the truth like Tom. Fifthly, the quality of almost open malice and vindictiveness can pass itself off as virtue, even among decent and responsible judges, if it has law and convention on its side. And sixthly, the society which judges in these ways seems radically incapable of looking beyond what people say and do to what they are.

The elaboration of these insights is the moral basis of the novel, which Fielding underlines by his own apparent hostility to Tom. Of course Tom will be hanged on the last page, he assures us, and of course all decent readers will rejoice when he is. The irony of this pose forces upon us, as it is meant to do, the real nature of our moral bearings. As I have already indicated, there is something profoundly Christian in the very presentation of the dilemma. I would be the last to suggest that there is a close parallel of any kind between Tom Jones and any hero from the New Testament: indeed, Tom is obviously flawed, if less seriously than his respectable enemies make out. But the dichotomy between reputation and real worth, posed in exactly the extreme form that Fielding offers, is at the heart of the gospels themselves. Why, a Christian will have to ask, was Christ put to death as a man too wicked to live? How did a respectable and legalistic society come to make such a mistake? The nature of the indictment is well enough known — a liar and blasphemer, a rebel, a Sabbath breaker, a friend of publicans and sinners — yet the Christian reader is committed to finding true worth, in its purest and highest form, in conjunction with a social reputation of this deplorable kind. The challenge of the New Testament is to discover where true virtue is to be found, and why. And this is exactly the challenge upon which Fielding engages us in *Tom Jones*, even though in a fable where natural and not supernatural events are the chosen concern. He nowhere suggests (and surely no one in his right mind would suggest?) that everyone who keeps social rules is bad and everyone who breaks them is good. He nowhere sentimentalises the ruffian, or does less than justice to respectable citizens of a benevolent kind. Nor is there any real antinomianism in his attitude, though one can see how it could be pushed towards the antinomian by writers more intent on paradox than he was himself. What he does suggest, and the whole comic purpose reinforces this, is that true virtue can never be discovered by rule of thumb. To discern it we need a certain added sense, an intuition almost, of the kind which D. H. Lawrence no doubt had in mind when he said he could 'smell people's souls'. The man who possesses such intuition may find more human worth in a man whom society condemns as a scoundrel than in one whom it reveres as a tried and tested moral guide. *This* is the particular iconoclasm behind the irony of *Tom Jones*, just as it is the iconoclasm of the religion in which Fielding firmly believed.

How, then, is the theme followed through? We must turn next to Square and Thwackum, the two teachers who are set over Blifil and Tom in their youth. They are both intelligent men, given to earnest theorising about good and evil, and by no means insincere in their beliefs. Square holds the philosophical rationalism of the deists, maintaining that moral values antedate deity, that the light of Reason is our guide to ethical truth. Thwackum is a Calvinist, holding that men are totally fallen, and wholly dependent for their salvation upon grace. Both men are serious and even honest up to a point, but in neither is there any genuine goodness or warmth of heart. Their judgements habitually justify Blifil at the expense of Tom and this, Fielding makes us feel, is a sufficient pointer to the manner of men they are. In one of the most significant passages in the whole work he goes out of his way to say that he is not really satirising what the men stand for, but what they are:

> Had not Thwackum too much neglected virtue, and Square religion, in the composition of their several systems, and had not both discarded all natural goodness of heart, they had never been represented as objects of derision in this history.

'. . . had not both discarded all natural goodness of heart' . . . here, surely, we have Fielding's central insight in all its simplicity. Lack of natural goodness of heart invalidates any system of ethics, since this alone can make it work in practice, however impressive the theory may be. The possession of such goodness is, however, likely to redeem even the most imprudent of men. It may redeem even Tom himself, whose very vices are tinged with generosity, and therefore somewhat less tainted than the virtues of his foes.

But if this were all that *Tom Jones* had to say, it would be much less impressive than it is. Fielding is concerned not only to shock us out of our habitual discriminations, but to educate us in discriminations of a finer kind. A more subtle problem arises when we turn from Square and Thwackum to Mr Allworthy himself. He, surely, has all the warmth and benevolence we could desire, but he is still very much on their side. It is he, after all, who appoints them, and trusts the moral judgements they have to make. And it is he who finally banishes Tom, on evidence supplied by those whose reputations seem to be of the highest kind.

One of the main contrasts in the novel is between Mr Allworthy and Tom. It is offered with considerable skill and a scrupulous honesty, since for all his irony Fielding is determined not to cheat. Mr Allworthy undoubtedly possesses benevolence, as we have said. He is also a man of wisdom and honour, as his remarks to Tom when he imagines himself to be dying make abundantly clear:

> I am convinced, my child, that you have much goodness, generosity and honour, in your temper: if you will add prudence and religion to these, you must be happy; for the three former qualities, I admit, make you worthy of happiness, but they are the latter only which will put you in possession of it.

To an eighteenth-century reader, Mr Allworthy's courage in the face of death tells its own tale; there can be no doubting the integrity of his words. But how far, we must ask, is Fielding himself identified with such a view? How far might it be the moral of the novel as a whole? The answer to this, to my mind, is abundantly clear. Fielding admires Mr Allworthy and approves of him, but is very far from being convinced by anything he says. For while being morally good is one thing, being morally right is another; and though Mr Allworthy's moral goodness is never in doubt, he is seldom if ever morally right. Prudence comes even before benevolence in his make-up; his judgements, though kindly, are severe. His demands on human nature are high, and he seems unwilling to forgive failure or weakness more than once. This might not in itself be so bad if his judgements were reliable, but again and again they are not. He pursues his moral arithmetic with unfailing zeal for the truth, but his data are wrong, so his answers are wrong as well. He is mistaken about Jenny Jones, about Partridge, about Tom, in a manner which causes them very great hardship before they are through. And he is mistaken about Bridget Allworthy and about Master Blifil, in a manner that delivers him as a dupe into their hands.

But why is Mr Allworthy wrong as often as this? Is it simply because the plot demands that he should be? To take this view would be to reduce the novel unthinkably, and fortunately we can dismiss it at the start. Mr Allworthy's failure of judgement is clearly one of the main strands in the moral texture of the whole, and what it indicates is Fielding's profound mistrust of Reason in ethics. It mirrors indeed his unambiguous conviction that a severely rationalistic ethic like Bishop Butler's cannot be relied upon to sift appearance from reality; for even when the gulf between social reputation and true worth is at its widest, unaided Reason may not even be aware that it exists. The one thing Mr Allworthy lacks is the instinct to smell people's souls. Because he lacks this, all his virtuous striving does not show him where true virtue is to be found.

It is in this, of course, that he contrasts most strikingly with Tom. For Tom has no prudence at all, and his moral judgements are not in the least conventional, or even rational in their approach. Yet always it seems, he is right about people, and at just those points where Mr Allworthy is most disastrously wrong. His very vigour and vitality help him to bypass people's professions, their appearances, their reputations and their social façade. He sees straight through to the reality beneath; and if this is partly because his own lack of reputation frees him from convention, it is also because he has moral perceptions of a positive kind which even Mr Allworthy, for all his goodness, seems to lack. His mercy and compassion are genuine qualities, in the fully Christian sense, whereas Mr Allworthy's are surrounded with some degree of doubt. Mr Allworthy always wants to know whether a person *deserves* mercy; and this is to reject mercy itself in favour of certain notions that are often confused with it — such as the perception of extenuating circumstances, or the generous resolution to give one more chance. Real mercy, like real compassion, is surely undeserved: and both come, in Fielding's presentation of them, from a well of generosity which is very close to the well of vitality and of life itself. In this sense, Tom is actually more virtuous than Mr Allworthy — though Mr Allworthy by the nature of things is unable to understand this for himself. Tom's very faults are tinged with the generosity in which his true worth as a person is to be found. This indeed is why Fielding is on his side, and willing to justify him — and not because he is indulgent to Tom's actual faults, as is sometimes supposed.

In the contrast between Mr Allworthy and Tom, the very style indicates where our sympathies should be. Mr Allworthy's moralising suffers, like that of Parson Adams and Mr Heartfree before him, from the excessively burlesque tone which it adopts. But Tom's mode of speech is refreshingly natural; it moves with the rhythms of feeling, so much more trustworthy in their very spontaneity than the rhythms of thought.

But this, again, is not all that the novel has to say: if it were, we should once more be taking from it a less subtle moral than Fielding has to give. We have established that Tom is better than Mr Allworthy; that he stands outside society, rebuking those inside by the very quality of life which they seem unable to share. But primitivism is only part of the story; Fielding's sense of evil was deeper than this would suggest, nor did he underestimate the darker potentials of the untamed human heart. If Mr Allworthy is good, and Tom is better, there is still in the novel a best: this is Sophia, of course; or even more precisely, the marriage of Tom and Sophia at the end.

That Sophia is nearer to Tom than to Mr Allworthy goes without saying, even though she agrees with Mr Allworthy at certain points where Tom is tempted to dissent. Like Tom, she judges instinctively rather than prudentially; like Tom, she smells out good and evil with an infallible instinct of her own. She knows with absolute certainty that marrying Blifil would be spiritual death for her, just as she knows that marrying Tom is the one true desire of her heart. But she knows also that she cannot marry Tom if he continues his career as a rake. She is as opposed to this as everyone else in the book, but only because she has his happiness wholly at heart. Whereas the other characters profess concern, but often delight in the sufferings that they inflict, Sophia's concern is really selfless; she thinks only of the highest good that Tom deserves.

The contrast is not only between Tom's masculinity and Sophia's femininity; it is also, and perhaps more fundamentally, a contrast between Tom's recklessness and Sophia's thoughtfulness; between Primitivism and Shaftesburyean ethics, if one is to place it in its eighteenth-century context once more. For Sophia senses that social rules are, after all, necessary and good, however perverted they may be in the hands of the Pharisees: however perverted they might be even in Mr Allworthy's hands. She represents the awareness of a true discipline, which is based not on arbitrary rules or restrictions, but upon the law of fruitfulness, and upon the ultimate nature and needs of man himself. Tom, we may allow, embodies the primitivist's insight that a man outside society may be finer and nobler than a man inside. But Sophia embodies the further Shaftesburyean insight that only inside society can a man be fully mature, fully what he has it in himself to be.

So the true moral culmination of *Tom Jones* is its ending. As in all good comedies, the marriage of the hero and heroine is not just a 'happy ending' tacked on as a requirement of the plot. It is also a deeply felt moral resolution, of the issues that have been so finely surveyed. Inside marriage, both Tom and Sophia will fulfil themselves; they will find the happiness which both deserve, but which without marriage neither will finally attain. The delicate femininity and robust masculinity of the two main actors will meet in the way appointed by nature itself, as well as by religion, by society and by the emotional needs of their own humanity. Tom's virility will no longer run to waste as it has been doing; it will be contained inside the larger needs of his own virtue: for loyalty, for tenderness, for returned affection, for the healthy perpetuation of the race.

Tom Jones seems to me one of the greatest novels in the language; and just as certainly as Jane Austen's novels, it exists wholly inside the conventions of comedy. For the purposes of my present thesis, it is an illustration of a major ironic talent achieving its true relation to temperament, after a somewhat uncertain and fluctuating start. In *Tom Jones*, the satiric irony is restricted only to certain local episodes, where it properly belongs; to the struggles of Black George with his conscience, for instance, as he wonders just how much further he dare swindle his friend. But the main irony is wholly assimilated to the comic purpose; to Fielding's grand survey of the nature of true virtue, in which the bad (Blifil, Bridget Allworthy, Square and Thwackum) is held in balance against the not quite so bad (Squire Western), the good (Mr Allworthy), the better (Tom) and the best (Sophia). In this way, a very mature, as well as robust, sense of life is achieved.

Of all the ironists known to me, with the possible exception of Mark Twain, Fielding comes nearest to charity and generosity; to the qualities which irony by its very obliqueness seldom realises in an unambiguous form. Perhaps something of the kind could also be said about our next ironist, Sterne — though *Tristram Shandy* is a very far cry from *Tom Jones*.

CHAPTER 3

STERNE: THE NOVELIST AS JESTER

I

BY the time *Tristram Shandy* came to be written, the eighteenth century had already moved a very long way from the Augustans. It had discovered, for instance, that its own good taste was not as wholly the fruit of discursive reasoning as the most dedicated followers of Locke had been tempted to think. In the opening years of the century Shaftesbury had been somewhat isolated in his emphasis on the part played by feeling and intuition in the building of the moral sense, but as early as the late 1830s these heresies were coming into their own. There was the 'gothic' sensibility, which invaded verse as part of an explicit rejection of 'cold formalism', but was to win its real triumphs a decade or so later in Horace Walpole, Mrs Radcliffe, Monk Lewis and the Novel of Terror. And in 1759 there was the first instalment of *Tristram Shandy*, which erupted on to the literary scene, exalting feeling and flouting rules as if in a spirit of anti-classicism run riot. We have only to glance at Sterne's masterpiece to see that we are dealing with one of the most boldly experimental novels ever conceived. There is the very look of it on the page; the dots, the dashes, the italics, the pointing hands, the massive gaps, the famous or possibly notorious black page. Living in an age which still deferred to the Ancients in its critical canons, however superior it felt to them in other ways, Sterne announced that he would obey neither Mr Horace's rules, nor any other man's rules, but his own. Does this make him an anarchist? But he has anticipated our question, and suggested an answer to it. Look more closely, we are told, and the method in the madness will appear. The digressions and the equivocations will fall into place; even the irony will fall into place. For irony, as Sterne conceives it, has passed from verbal nuance to a still wider range of suggestiveness. It exists now in gesture and mime, as far as the printed page can be adapted to these things.

If this makes Sterne seem a baffling writer, there are ways in which our bearings are easier to find. His hostility to rules is a matter of temperament as well as of style; the nature of his preferences — eccentricity to conformity, sentiment to calculation, spontaneity to decorum, vigour to stylised politeness — is in no way hard to discern. He is more interested than an Augustan would have been in numbering the streaks of the tulip; less obsessively concerned than any of his contemporaries with 'large appearances' and 'general truths'. In some ways he is more strictly a begetter of the novel as we know it today than either Fielding or Richardson; he senses, as perhaps they do not, that the novelist's art will concern itself very particularly with the concrete, the detailed, the revealingly personal and minute. Again and again our attention is directed to small and apparently trifling things, of the kind which most eighteenth-century writers would have dismissed out of hand; to those moments when a man is relaxed or off-guard, and so more likely to reveal himself to a shrewd observer than he would be at moments of public rhetoric, or formal choice. Of course, when we are conscious of drama we act our part; but to the accurate observer it will be an odd remark, a tone of voice, a chance lift of the eyebrows that reveals decisively and beyond argument what we really are. So he turns our attention to those casual or random moments in life, which we all witness, but very few of us understand. And he is interested in the stream of consciousness, as it was later to be called; in the endlessly varied procession of images, reflections and ideas which drift through our minds, often unbidden, often indeed unperceived, but in fascinating counterpoint with our conscious thinking, with the more public spectacle of what we do or say. The discrepancies which he observes at this level provide much of his irony, and not a little of his fun; but they are by no means wholly assimilated to fun or irony, as I shall later attempt to show. More than most writers, Sterne is willing to experiment drastically in the new form he is helping to create. He is willing to come closer to the jumble and chaos of life itself than most writers ever do; to abandon plot and even time sequence if these things do not serve his particular ends. His true successors in the novel are

James Joyce, Virginia Woolf, Aldous Huxley, the radical
experimenters of a period more than one hundred and fifty
years later — though this is not to deny that the nineteenth-
century novelists learned important things from him as well.

If Sterne's methods are complex, his morals are simple: much
simpler than Fielding's, though on much the same track.
Tristram Shandy is in this sense an easy novel to grasp, with a
main lesson so simplified that even the sheep of *Animal Farm*
might be taught it: prudential motive-grinding bad, warm
good nature good. The whole purpose is to make us see Uncle
Toby as Sterne himself does: a simple hero, even at times an
absurd hero, yet the very image of man at his simplest and
finest, if we read him aright. The only sins Sterne really detests
are cruelty and cant, and these he sees more as aberrations of a
bad culture or a bad environment than as deep-seated flaws in
human nature itself.

I think it not unfair to sum up Sterne's moral purpose in this
way. And if we do, we at once see his temperamental polarity
with Swift. In Swift's world, Reason and Nature rule on the
surface, but there is a predictable rottenness at the core. In
Sterne's world, this order is precisely reversed. The surface is
odd and erratic, but the underlying realities are good. Everywhere you look it is the same: the materials for satire exist in
plenty, but the will to satire is nowhere to be found. Almost,
indeed, we are challenged to take a satiric view of Shandy Hall
and its inmates, in order to learn in due time how badly lop-
sided this would be. The test case is Uncle Toby himself — his
imagery full of war, of manoeuvre and bloodshed, his true
reaction to life so tender that he is literally unable to hurt a fly.
But the same holds true of the other characters, if to a lesser
degree. The quirks of Tristram Shandy's Father, the com-
placencies of his Mother, the pomposities of Trim, the self-
centredness of Susannah, the brutal dogmas of Dr Slop — all of
these apparent flaws dwindle in importance as the true nature
of the characters is revealed. Comedy is always more tolerant
than satire, but here it seems to escape from reformative intentions completely; to become almost an act of faith in human
nature as it is. And always in Sterne, the presentation does
much to reconcile us to people who at first sight appear to be
only objects of fun. The propensity of ridicule to overreach itself

D

— to become more important than careful insight, or spontaneous charity, for instance — is exactly one of those things
which Sterne's ridicule sets out to check.

II

A feature of Sterne's peculiar genius is the relationship he
establishes with his readers. This is far closer to friendship, in
the normal sense of that term, than any other novelist ever
comes. It is true that Fielding very often erupts into his novels,
as Dickens was to do afterwards: explaining, exhorting, even
teasing the reader; reminding us, even if we happen to forget
it, that the story is his story, and the characters his characters,
to do with in the end as he will. But Fielding and Dickens were
showmen; their presence in the novels is no more felt as an
intrusion than that of a ringmaster in the circus, or a narrator
in the drama of Ionesco or Brecht. And because they are showmen, their place in their novels is to some degree a formal one:
we feel that we know them, but not as we know someone in life.
The illusion of relationship, of two-way dialogue, is not one they
are concerned to create.

Sterne, however, creates just this illusion of personal contact,
in so far as it is possible for anyone hidden behind the veil of
print to do. 'How could you, Madam, be so inattentive in reading the last chapter?' he demands, or 'Pray reach me my fool's
cap — I fear you sit upon it, Madam — 'tis under the cushion
— I'll put it on'. And the long-suffering lady reader will start
indignantly, the gentleman reader who shares the good-natured
joke at her expense will smile, even two hundred years after
the voice behind the printed page has been stilled. There is
such an immediacy of tone here; such an assumption of living
intimacy, forcing us to respond to it — unless we are determined
to remain wholly godlike and aloof — either with answering
friendship, or with dislike. This, no doubt, is why Sterne's
readers become divided into two sharply contrasted camps.
There are those who close his book after a few chapters, and
take care never to open it again. And there are those who read
on, forgetful of Mr Horace's rules or any other man's rules, their
feelings bordering — with a sentimentality that Sterne himself
would have approved — on affection. For surely friendship in

life itself is like this? — a personal offer, which we accept or reject as we are inclined? And Sterne is wholly aware of the demand he makes, since his entire effectiveness as a novelist depends upon it. 'As you proceed farther with me,' he tells us near the start, 'the slight acquaintance, which is now beginning betwixt us, will grow into familiarity; and that, unless one of us is in fault, will terminate in friendship.' Since this passage goes on to discuss his own method, in ways I shall be returning to later, perhaps I can quote just a little more:

> *O diem praeclarum!* — then nothing which has touched me will be thought trifling in its nature, or tedious in its telling. Therefore, my dear friend and companion, if you should think me somewhat sparing of my narrative on my first setting out — bear with me, — and let me go on, and tell my story in my own way: — Or, if I should seem now and then to trifle upon the road, — or should sometimes put on a fool's cap with a bell to it, for a moment or two as we pass along, — don't fly off, — but rather courteously give me credit for a little more wisdom than appears upon my outside; — and as we jog on, either laugh with me, or at me, or in short, do anything, — only keep your temper.

And of course Sterne's offer of friendship is genuine; it is not a prelude to betrayal, as Swift's so often is, or a technique of manipulation like Gibbon's. He regards friendship very properly as an art, of which the novel itself becomes something of an extension — so that if the liberties he takes with his readers are of a kind which only intimacy can excuse, then the entertainment he offers is also of a peculiarly intimate and satisfying kind.

The friendship between reader and writer is a clue to more aspects of *Tristram Shandy* than one. Reading it is an active, not a passive affair; more than once we are reminded that unless we co-operate with Sterne, we shall never begin to know what he is about.

> As no one, who knows what he is about in good company, would venture to talk all; — so no author, who understands the just boundaries of decorum and good-breeding would presume to think all: The truest respect which you can pay to the reader's understanding, is to halve this matter amicably,

and leave him something to imagine, in his turn, as well as yourself.

We quickly discover that we are to establish friendship with the main actors in Sterne's drama as well as with the author himself. In most novels, again, this is hardly the case. We expect to be formally introduced to the main characters, and then to sit back at a safe distance while we see what they are going to do. We may be told where they were born, where brought up, and what they look like; there may be a brief account of such parts of their history as we need to know. We shall expect to meet them at moments of special significance in their development; most probably at the threshold of some particularly dramatic sequence of events. The whole introduction, in short, will be quite unlike our normal experience in life itself, where we meet people more or less casually, and very seldom at moments of especial significance or high drama. If we get to know them at all well, it is through further meetings, equally haphazard, and only tenuously linked by connections of 'story' or 'plot'. We like or dislike them for reasons that can more often be sensed than described; we may get to know them intimately in the end, but if we do, we shall respond emotionally as well as critically to what they are. And in all this we shall pick up what we know about them gradually, from hints and odd conversations. They will not start an acquaintance with a solemn recital of where they were born and how educated, or what their tastes may be on this or that.

The peculiarity of Sterne's art is to introduce us to his characters with just the haphazardness of life itself; he abandons plot in the normal sense, and even time. Instead, we are conducted through episodes and digressions of the most varying kind. The connecting thread is sometimes hard to discern, but as we read on, certain people and places begin to emerge: vaguely at first from the surrounding muddle, but then with growing clarity and precision, until Sterne's created world seems almost as real to us as our own. The connecting thread turns out, indeed, to be the author himself, whose personality, mediated to us through the friendship that has been established, fills the place left vacant by a more formal pattern. Disguised as his own long-deferred hero, Tristram Shandy, he guides us exuberantly through the maze of digressions and asides, teasing and bantering as he goes: one minute putting shocking ideas into our heads, the next reproving us for having them there. And through all this, we come to know not only him, but the other chief actors on his stage — each with a degree of closeness that affects any sort of moral judgements we shall wish to make. This, I fancy, is why Uncle Toby, Corporal Trim, My Father, My Mother and the rest are so different from any other fictional characters one can recall. It is not for particular episodes, or for particular choices that we remember them; we think of them first as people, and only then for things we remember they have said or done. But our knowledge of them as people grows as we read. The initial strangeness yields to a sense of familiarity where hardly anything surprises, however odd or bizarre. And this, in turn, is the setting in which Sterne's irony exists.

This irony is, therefore, as much involved in paradox as the man. For odd though it sounds, there is a type of self-effacement in the book: of course Sterne is very much present, but he is present as a host may be. No disturbing demands are made upon us, whether for understanding, or for admiration, or for pity. The one demand that he does make is that we should laugh, since the whole life of Tristram Shandy turns out to be a sport. The role Sterne chooses for himself is that of Jester, whose part in society is to tell the truth, but to tell it amusingly; the privilege of truth-telling must always be paid for, and traditionally the Jester pays by the immolation of himself.

So even the disasters that happen to Tristram are made to seem impersonal; they are part of his father's history rather than his own, and in this manner steered from tragedy towards jest. The birth narrative is one long sequence of blows to My Father's theories. The stars are wrong and the place is wrong; the conception is wrong; there is the disastrous accident to his nose, followed by the possibly worse accident to his name. Tristram Shandy comes into the world a doomed soul, at least in his father's eyes, yet all the accidents become frolics; a series of jests played by the Fates for the world's amusement, since his father's theories, for all their crankiness, are more than justified by the event: 'Sport of small accidents Tristram Shandy! that thou art, and ever wilt be!' The point is even underlined, with all the relish of amused detachment:

And here I am, sitting this 12th day of August 1766, in a purple jerkin and yellow pair of slippers, without either wig or cap on, a tragi-comical completion of his prediction.

We cannot doubt that Sterne is speaking for himself at such moments, any more than we doubt it at the end of Book IV:

And so, with this moral for the present, may it please your worships and your reverences, I take my leave of you till this time twelve-month, when (unless this vile cough kills me in the meantime) I'll have another pluck at your beards.

But the man who can write like this is not to be seen only as a trifler, unless we think it easy for a man to trifle with consumption, or to jest with death. Sterne's attitude is as far removed from escapism as it is from self-pity; the word 'courage' does not seem out of place in describing an irony which is both implicated in suffering and absurdity, yet in such assured and resilient mastery of them.

The role of the Jester is often a courageous one, as those who accuse Sterne of trifling are apt to forget; only the extreme Puritan will mistake the ability to jest at serious things for a necessary failure in responsibility. But Sterne's particular offence in Puritan eyes, it need scarcely be said, is to extend the lighthearted irreverence he feels for himself to the solemn and portentous subject of sex. It is entirely characteristic that he should savour, as he so often does, the strange natural irony of the human body which Yeats also drew attention to through one of his jesting *personae*:

> But Love has pitched his mansion in
> The place of excrement . . .

— and which Sir Thomas Browne had attempted to justify, albeit in connection with the Chameleon rather than with man, as one of Nature's economies rather than as one of her jokes:

Again, nature is so far from leaving any one part without its proper action, that she ofttimes imposeth two or three labour upon one, so the pizzle in animals is both official unto urine and to generation. . . .

The Puritan no doubt hates people to laugh at sex—but he may equally hate them to take it seriously; Sterne's ability to laugh is arguably nearer to a healthy seriousness than those ranged against him in their moral purity even begin to see. Certainly he is often very amusing about the human body — and genuinely amusing, as a mere pornographer can never be, since humour and humanity are inseparable in his work. If there must be a moral censure against him, it will have to be that he does not go far enough. His equivocations are sometimes a shade too slyly aware of themselves; they lack the more open and masculine bawdiness of Fielding and Rabelais, where slyness, and the minor concession to prudery that goes with it, is unthinkable. But this, I fancy, is a matter of opinion; and the tone of Sterne's jesting is too distinctive for any word as simple as 'sly' to be wholly appropriate.

The problem posed by this aspect of Sterne's work leads us back to what in some ways is a key question: is his role as Jester consciously chosen, or is it not? Fortunately, the answer is not hard to find. His cap and bells have appeared twice already, even in the brief extracts I have had occasion to quote. And there is an antic disposition as well, to remove any lingering doubts we might have. 'Alas! Poor Yorick!' he writes, with that curious blending of pathos and mockery that is so in keeping with his role. This echo is offered in no arbitrary spirit; it springs from just the balance of incongruities in human grief which Shakespeare himself depicts in the Gravedigger Scene. Even the fantastic jest of Yorick's last moments on earth ('Yorick followed Eugenius with his eyes to the door, — he then closed them, — and never opened them more' ... followed by a completely black page) is, in its mingling of the sentimental and the macabre, very close to the mood of Shakespeare's great clowns. The feeling, surely, is that life itself does not obey the rules of a literary *genre*, but holds laughter and tears closely knit in one pattern. Sterne would have agreed with Aldous Huxley's view that tragi-comedy is much closer to the 'whole truth' about life than either Tragedy or Comedy — the aesthetically purer forms — come on their own. Some of his subtlest explorations are of moments when the tragic and comic do in fact mingle, in a manner which defies us to try to separate, or even distinguish them again.

The description of Le Fever's death may be as good an instance as any. As Sterne shows the desperate straits to which

Uncle Toby is reduced by the last hours of his friend, he does justice to two familiar aspects of human compassion: its intrinsic worth as a human attitude on the one hand, its intrinsic uselessness in the face of such a capricious inevitability as death on the other. Either of these insights in isolation might have led to very bad writing indeed — the first to a mawkish sentimentality maybe, the second to a gloomily embittered cynicism. Sterne, by the deeply serious quality of his jesting, avoids excesses of either kind. Both the sentimental and the cynical are modified by their curious conjunction. A very moving, if somewhat strange realism is achieved.

III

'Realism' is, I fancy, the word towards which these comments have been reaching. At first this may seem paradoxical again, in that Sterne deliberately flouts all the normal conventions whether literary or emotional to which the term 'realism' is normally applied. But just as our introduction to the main characters in *Tristram Shandy*, for all its odd appearance, can be said to be more like the way we get to know people in real life than is usual in novels, so the quality of the irony comes very close to psychological realism when we have once sensed how it works. This irony, which in its simplest form is a mode of comic evaluation, becomes at times an instrument for very acute and penetrating character analysis. It turns out to be Sterne's way of mirroring the odd complexities of real life, and at the same time of reconciling us to the essentially human decencies that these complexities often very thinly conceal. What I have in mind can be best illustrated by a close look at one very well-known passage. The news of Master Bobby's death has just arrived at Shandy Hall, and it is now being announced to the kitchen staff.

— My young master in London is dead! said Obadiah.
— A green sattin night-gown of my mother's which had been twice scoured, was the first idea which Obadiah's exclamation brought into Susannah's head. — Well might Locke write a chapter upon the imperfection of words. — Then, quoth Susannah, we must all go into mourning. — But note a second time: the word *mourning*, notwithstanding

Susannah made use of it herself — failed also of doing its
office; it excited not one single idea, tinged either with grey
or black, — all was green. — The green sattin night-gown
hung there still.

— O 'twill be the death of my poor mistress, cried
Susannah. — My mother's whole wardrobe followed. —
What a procession! her red damask, — her orange tawney,
— her white and yellow lutestrings, — her brown taffeta, —
her bone-laced caps, her bed-gowns, and comfortable under-
petticoats. — Not a rag was left behind. — 'No, — she will
never look up again,' said Susannah.

We had a fat, foolish scullion — my father, I think, kept
her for her simplicity; — she had been all autumn struggling
with a dropsy. — He is dead, said Obadiah, — he is certainly
dead! — So am not I, said the foolish scullion.

— Here is sad news, Trim, cried Susannah, wiping her eyes
as Trim stepp'd into the kitchen, — master Bobby is dead and
buried — the funeral was an interpolation of Susannah's —
we shall all have to go into mourning, said Susannah.

I hope not, said Trim. — You hope not! cried Susannah
earnestly. — The mourning ran not in Trim's head, whatever it did in Susannah's. — I hope — said Trim, explaining
himself, I hope in God the news is not true. — I heard the
letter read with my own ears, said Obadiah; and we shall
have a terrible piece of work of it in stubbing the Ox-moor. —
Oh! he's dead, said Susannah. — As sure, said the scullion,
as I'm alive.

I lament for him from my heart and my soul said Trim,
fetching a sigh. — Poor creature! — poor boy! — poor
gentleman.

— He was alive last Whitsontide! said the coachman —
Whitsontide! alas! cried Trim, extending his right arm, and
falling instantly into the same attitude in which he read the
sermon, — what is Whitsontide, Jonathan (for that was the
coachman's name), or Shrovetide, or any tide or time past, to
this? Are we not here now, continued the corporal (striking
the end of his stick perpendicularly upon the floor, so as to
give an idea of health and stability) — and are we not —
(dropping his hat upon the ground) gone! in a moment! —
'Twas infinitely striking! Susannah burst into a flood of tears.

— We are not stocks and stones. — Jonathan, Obadiah, the cook-maid, all melted. The foolish fat scullion herself, who was scouring a fish-kettle on her knees, was rous'd with it. — The whole kitchen crowded about the corporal.

The accumulation of minute signs and indications is in part a reflection of Sterne's interest in associationism. Locke is actually mentioned in this passage, and recent scholarship has made us sufficiently familiar with Sterne's debt to him. But here, as elsewhere, Sterne's interest is not philosophical but psychological; it is the kind of interest which the novel as an art form will increasingly come to take. Sterne bothers with *minutiae* because he believes that they are the best guide we have to understanding people. In *A Sentimental Journey* he puts it like this: 'I think I can see the precise and distinguishing marks of national characters more in . . . nonsensical *minutiae* than in the most important matters of state.' And again, 'What a large volume of adventures may be grasped with this little span of life, by him who interests his heart in everything.' Public attitudes and rhetorical set-pieces may show a man as he likes to think himself, but his unguarded actions, his incidental indecisions, tell the true observer far more of what he wishes to know. So Sterne in his own *persona* as jester, probes beneath the *personae* of other men; in this particular passage his eye falls upon a number of unconnected trifles: a green satin nightgown, the scouring of a fish kettle, the striking of a stick on the ground, the drop (quite literally) of a hat. Around these disparate items his ironic nuances are generated; the whole tone of the passage is coloured by the eccentricities of punctuation and sentence structure, so wilful in their appearance, so subtle in their achieved effect. In *A Sentimental Journey* Sterne comments on this aspect of his technique as well. If tones and manners have a meaning, as they certainly have, he tells us, then they too contain a world of information for the true observer:

There are certain combined looks of simple subtlety, where whim, and sense, and seriousness, and nonsense, are so blended, that all the languages of Babel set loose together could not express them: they are communicated and caught so instantaneously, that you can scarce say which party the infector . . .

What 'simple subtleties' are there, we may ask, in the passage before us? First of all, there are the gulfs between thought and speech, between feeling and action, which the very convulsions of the syntax seems to reflect. All of the kitchen staff respond to the news more complexly than their words in themselves would show. Susannah, for instance, responds with the outburst: 'O 'twill be the death of my poor mistress!', but already her mind has moved off on to other tracks of its own. What is there in it for me? — and the coveted green satin nightgown floats unbidden into view, to be followed by all her mistress's other garments, in solemn and colourful array. ('The mourning ran not in Trim's head, whatever it did in Susannah's,' as Sterne wickedly says a little further on.) And after Susannah, we see Obadiah and the 'fat foolish scullion', both responding to the news within their limits: Obadiah considering the stubbing of the Ox-moor, which will be extra work for him; the scullion, half-witted and half dead, making the delighted discovery that she, at least, is alive. And as the climax of the piece we see Trim, moving by instinct as he always does to the centre of the stage. 'Alas!' he exclaims, with fitting solemnity, 'fetching a sigh' — and at once, the scene is transformed. The fact of death is to be properly heightened, to be transformed into a public mime. The outcome of Trim's histrionics is remarkable; for whereas the news of the death affected no one, its re-enactment moves the whole kitchen staff to tears. Everyone melts, even the scullion ('We are not stocks and stones'); the scene moves through Trim's relished solemnity to a tableau of grief.

This is what Sterne shows us; but what does he make us feel? Are we to enjoy a sense of cynical detachment, perhaps — to reflect that the pretensions of human nature have been very savagely exposed? Certainly the material could have been handled in this way; it might well have been had Swift had the writing of it, or Aldous Huxley, or any other thoroughgoing satirist. But the passage as we have it is no such thing; remarkably not, when we note how near an approach to satire has been made. All the material a satirist would need has been given us; and if the finished effect is very different from satire, then the quality of Sterne's humanity, as well as of his jesting, is one of the clues we need to discover why.

On a closer look, we are struck far more by the differences

between this passage and formal satire than by the similarities. For whereas a satirist is always judging what he writes about, Sterne is basically simply looking to *see*. What appears to be satiric exaggeration is really a close and indeed sympathetic insight into the truth, the whole truth, of what is going on. For Sterne has developed a deeper insight than most of his predecessors into the sheer oddness and complexity of human response. And whereas a conventional moralist might be shocked by the revelation, Sterne is amused and even heartened by his own report. The striking feature about this passage is its accuracy; for is this not exactly the manner in which people do respond in life, when some unusual news of love or death is brought to them? There may first be a slightly numbed period, in which there is knowledge of what should be felt or what will be felt, but the real response by some natural inhibition is delayed. Meanwhile decencies must be observed, the correct things must be said ('O 'twill be the death of my poor mistress!') — and the mind, shocked from its normal rut, wanders off on its own memories and calculations, whether we like to acknowledge the nature of these or not. It may well be that nine people out of ten will respond, as Susannah does, in clichés; for how else is one to respond, unless perhaps portentously, like Trim? And certainly Susannah is typical enough in savouring the larger-than-life quality of the moment. Just for once she has important news to pass on, to embroider a little, also, for effect. While she is in this position she is 'someone' — just as Trim will more emphatically be, when his more practised sense of occasion comes into play.

The other reactions are equally well observed in their way. The foolish scullion has been struggling with death all winter; soon, she knows, she is fated to succumb. She did not know the dead boy, so has no real grief to respond to; when she hears the news, what could be more natural than her discovery that she, at least, is alive? She is too naïve to conceal her simple pleasure in the discovery, too stupid to distinguish properly between what should and should not be said, as Susannah does.

The final *tour de force* is Trim's rhetoric, and the scene in the kitchen when it finally 'melts'. For is this not again a very accurate representation of life as it is? Very often even real grief does not express itself at once; the words of grief must be spoken, but the less speakable reality bides its time. It is entirely possible that bad art like Trim's ham-acting might precipitate exactly the genuine, if belated, grief that belongs to life itself. For Trim's words, despite such impurities as their heightened sentiment and the obvious relish he takes in them, embody a genuine feeling about death. 'He was alive last Whitsontide' cries the coachman, and 'Whitsontide! alas!' cries Trim — the very concreteness of it at last allows the great commonplace to be felt, although in this still muddled and aesthetically impure way. And the kitchen staff, though enjoying the occasion, are undoubtedly responding to it as well; the tears may not be wholly false, as a superficial observer would be tempted to think.

What Sterne has done, in this passage, is to introduce an important kind of realism into the novel for the first time. He manages to convey, as James Joyce was later to do in *Ulysses*, the rich mixture of motives — sincere and insincere, conscious and unconscious, self-centred and disinterested, tainted and yet still human and honest in their way — which surround the ordinary emotions of ordinary people, in the face of the dramas and inevitabilities of life itself. Psychological realism has entered the novel; and as it enters, it makes the satirist's sneers and exaggerations seem a little crude, a little unbalanced, a little untrue to the facts of human nature as they really are.

For the whole passage is informed by a deep humanity, which is inseparable from the quality of observation that we find. Our final feeling will not be that Susannah and Obadiah, the fat foolish scullion and Trim are all hypocrites, since though we have been given all the information on which such a view could be based, we have been given so much more as well. Sterne's triumph is to show that these are simple, kindly people, for all their strangeness; that simple people are complex, and because complex vulnerable; but that the tensions and contradictions in human nature should not blind us to the grand simple decencies beneath. It is for this reason that he takes the most damaging *minutiae* — the green satin nightgown, the stick and the hat — to savour their ironies; for in the background of such things, it is still simple goodness of heart that he sees.

The resolution to this passage, as of *Tristram Shandy* as a whole, is a comic one. We are confronted with complexity and eccentricity, and challenged to find behind it the simple decency of the uncorrupted human heart. This seems to me a fine kind of achievement, especially in a world as given to xenophobia as our own. Certainly, it defines the manner in which *Tristram Shandy* is a moral work, as well as an endless source of delight to all Sterne's friends. But as usual, the last word had best be left to himself: 'I write a careless kind of a civil, nonsensical, goodhumoured Shandeyan book, which will do all your hearts good. . . . And all your heads too, — provided you understand it.'

CHAPTER 4

GIBBON: DISMISSIVE IRONY

I

GIBBON shares with Swift an effortless mastery of irony in one of its classic forms, the apparent defence of a cause or position which is really a sustained betrayal. His total effect is so different from Swift's, however, that our first task must be an attempt to see why. The relationship between writer and reader is again an important one, but the principle underlying it has undergone a remarkable change. In *Gulliver* it is the reader who is betrayed; in *Decline and Fall* the betrayal is of targets which Gibbon and his readers share. For Gibbon, far from lashing his age for its weaknesses, is concerned to encourage and consolidate it in its strengths. His invitation to the reader is to partnership; we are to join him on terms of true equality, for the re-enactment of manners, beliefs and customs inferior to our own. The moral positives are established by the very force of what is taken for granted; and these positives are less important, it sometimes seems, than the tone and mood in which they are assumed. This tone is a guarantee, in its polished urbanity, of the writer's credentials. And provided that we are not so wanting in taste as to dissent, it is a guarantee of our own credentials as readers as well.

There are no pitfalls, then, for the reader; no traps of the kind into which we might fall because we have failed to test the ground as we go. On the contrary, there is a sustained and gratifying flattery, upon which the entire effectiveness of the irony depends. The vantage point in more ways than one is Olympian; certainly the tone is Olympian, as it was in the work of Gibbon's intellectual master, Hume. Consider for instance the essay on *Miracles*, where the reader is also charmed to heights of urbane dismissal. 'Our most holy religion,' Hume assures us, 'is founded on faith, not on reason; and 'tis a sure

49

method of exposing it to put it to such a trial as it is by no means
fitted to endure.' A century before, the literal sense of this would
have been very generally accepted. Bacon had said, 'We are
obliged to believe the word of God, though our reason be
shocked at it'; Sir Thomas Browne had said, 'Methinks there
be not impossibilities enough in religion for an active faith.' In
neither of these earlier writers was there any ironic intention,
though they were certainly paradoxical, in a realm where irony
is always waiting to pounce. But Hume colours and surrounds
his statement with mockery. Posing as a friend of faith, he
effects a betrayal of it, to which his readers seem every bit as
committed as himself. The tone of voice controls the meaning,
pushing it delicately but inexorably towards the absurd. Against
this tone there can be no appeal, only a drastic rejection of
Hume's invitation to share the joke. But that is to risk the irony
returning like a boomerang against ourselves, since such an
irony not only flatters, but deters.

Gibbon, following Hume in more ways than one, raises this
kind of irony to its highest pitch. The famous Chapters XV and
XVI set a pattern for urbane dismissal which has been often
imitated, but never surpassed. Chapter XV opens gently, with
deference to the 'pure and humble religion' that is now to be
our concern. From the explicit content, there is no reason to
think of the author as anything other than a friend of the faith.
If we detect a latent irony, as we certainly do, there is scarcely
anything in the first few sentences that could be pointed to by
way of confirming the suspicion. Only in the second paragraph
does Gibbon admit, with apparent reluctance, that there are
certain flaws in the early Christians which 'to a careless observer
. . . may seem to cast a shade on the faith which they professed'.
This Iago-like warning against careless observation is the opening of the attack; and before long, the full force of Gibbon's
assault is under way.

This inflexible perseverance (i.e. of the Old Testament
Jews) which appeared so odious or so ridiculous to the
ancient world, assumes a more awful character, since
Providence has deigned to reveal to us the mysterious history
of the chosen people. But the devout and even scrupulous
attachment to the Mosaic religion, so conspicuous among the

Jews who lived under the second temple, becomes still more surprising if it is compared with the stubborn incredulity of their forefathers. When the law was given in thunder from Mount Sinai; when the tides of the ocean and the course of the planets were suspended for the convenience of the Israelites; and when temporal rewards and punishments were the immediate consequences of their piety or disobedience; they perpetually relapsed into rebellion against the visible majesty of their Divine King, placed the idols of the nations in the sanctuary of Jehovah, and imitated every fantastic ceremony that was practised in the tents of the Arabs, or in the cities of Phoenicia. As the protection of Heaven was deservedly withdrawn from the ungrateful race, their faith acquired a proportionable degree of vigour and purity. The contemporaries of Moses and Joshua had beheld with careless indifference the most amazing miracles. Under the pressure of every calamity, the belief of those miracles has preserved the Jews of a later period from the universal contagion of idolatry; and, in contradiction to every known principle of the human mind, that singular people seems to have yielded a stronger and more ready assent to the traditions of their remote ancestors than to the evidence of their own senses.

We are struck at once by Gibbon's relish for words; he savours them as a connoisseur, with an especial delight in ironical overtones. The word 'mysterious' equivocates, being correct in its religious usage, but irresistibly suggesting our more modern meaning: 'odd', and therefore (perhaps) unreliable. The phrases 'more awful', 'still more surprising', 'visible majesty', 'most amazing miracles', are likewise savoured for their power of casting doubt on the position which they seem to exalt. The word 'proportionable' is held in a masterly suspense between its straightforward meaning, and the wholly disproportionate nature of the behaviour towards which it directs attention. Under the guise of homage to the Jewish chronicles, these words and phrases cast wholesale doubts upon their credibility.

The entire passage works in the same kind of way. There is no explicit statement of disbelief. Gibbon poses as a believer, as Hume had done before, making judgements and comments in

E

favour of Jehovah on the supposition that every word is literally true ('As the protection of Heaven was deservedly withdrawn from the ungrateful race' . . . and so on). But Gibbon's defence of the faith, it need scarcely be insisted, makes matters a good deal worse than his open hostility might. To the rational and sceptical mind of the eighteenth century, a number of damaging suggestions are inevitable. If God really did intervene in history like this (and Gibbon is recounting only what is supposed to have happened), then the Jews were the most ungrateful and illogical people who ever walked the face of the earth: and why, indeed, did Jehovah select such a race in the first place? But then again, surely God cannot have acted so? Because if He had, the Jews, however ungrateful and illogical they might be, could scarcely have reversed the appropriate responses to quite this degree? So the ironic trap closes from two directions; either the Jews were illogical or they were deluded. The phrase 'in contradiction to every known principle of the human mind' clinches matters one way or the other, and even suggests that both might be true. Gibbon's elaborate pretence not to notice the overtones he is so skilfully generating, and the damagingly naïve comments which he offers on the story as it stands, become incrementally effective as he proceeds. The treachery of this technique is intensified by his splendidly calculated understatement: 'deigned to reveal', 'the convenience of the Israelites', 'the favour of Heaven' and so on. The language of social condescension is used to describe supposedly epic and cosmic events. Its entire inappropriateness deflates the story in a manner indicating radical disbelief, while at the same time underlining the lack of anything really polite or civilised in the story as it stands.

Behind Gibbon's irony can be felt a certain exuberance, more urbane than Swift's fierce exuberance, but similar in kind. Certainly it is nearer to Swift's exuberance than it is to Fielding's or Sterne's; we sense in it both intellectual pleasure in the sheer destructiveness of the technique, and emotional pleasure in the particular nature of the iconoclasm. Just behind the Olympian detachment of the tone a great deal of energy is being generated: an energy which finds satisfaction in destroying religious faith *per se*, and which is at the same time an active enjoyment of the intellectual sophistication that makes such destructiveness possible.

II

We might conclude, on the strength of this analysis of Gibbon's technique, that the total effect of his irony is negative: the reader is congratulated upon being what he is rather than satirically attacked for his shortcomings, the subject matter is approached in a spirit of fierce hostility that at times seems almost like an end in itself. Is Gibbon not, then, at the opposite pole to a moralist, and wholly unconstructive in his intention?

In fact, of course, he is not; the moral indictment is far more apparent than real. For despite all that has been said about his technique, Gibbon is a humane and enlightened writer, with a very keen moral purpose in mind. The paradoxical fact seems to be that whereas Swift, the satirist, turns out to be largely negative in his moral effect, Gibbon, the cynic and sceptic, is remarkably constructive and sane. The relevant question about irony of Gibbon's type is, 'Is it justified?', and the answer we give must be: 'Yes: with certain reservations, it is.' When we have ceased to take pleasure in the intellectual flexibility of the irony we notice that it is, after all, very hard to argue against. The dislike of Christianity is not merely, or even primarily emotional, but is part of Gibbon's vision of life and history as a whole. As a rationalist, he believes that the human mind can have no certain knowledge of religious truths, and he is therefore justified in exposing the fallacies and fanaticisms of those who think that it can. As a liberal humanist he finds the Old Testament and Early Christian ethic repugnant: a reaction that is shared by very many unbelievers, and that is in a tradition of thought dating back to at least the later part of the seventeenth century (one finds it not only in the deists, but also in a great many of the Anglicans who defended the Christian tradition against them). As a historian, he believes that Reason is the great prerequisite for harmony and order, Superstition with its concomitant emotionalism and intolerance the greatest enemy that any society has to fear. The Christian Religion itself he sees as the chief cause of the break-up of the ancient world — an upsurge of irrational anti-humanistic forces that extinguished the lights of Greece and Rome and became a presiding genius over more than a thousand years of darkness.

The type of irony used in Chapters XV and XVI is not, it

follows, arbitrary or irresponsible, but is wedded to very definite
and salutary moral purposes. By demonstrating the dangers of
irrationalism, both intellectual and moral, it seeks to confirm
readers in their paths of enlightenment. Gibbon's consolidation
with his readers is flattery, but it is not idle flattery; it is an
assertion of principles which he shares with them, and thinks
vitally important if the Age of Reason is to continue. His iconoclasm arises from the intellectual centralities of his age (especially, perhaps, from his reading of Hume) and from his epic
vision of history; there is nothing wanton about it, as the chapter
in Dr Tillyard's *English Epic And Its Background* helps to make
clear.

Gibbon's real aim, we may conclude, is not to castigate his
age for failing to live up to its ideals, but to convince his age
that its ideals are, after all, supremely worth while. *Decline and
Fall* is moral in a deeper sense, perhaps, than satire itself. The
irony is a mode of interpreting and evaluating history; its moral
(if one may borrow from T. S. Eliot for this alien context) is
that darkness itself declares the glory of light.

If we look back on this great work from our present vantage
point, we might decide that it was written at the one moment
in European history when it was at all possible. A few years
later the whole social pattern was to change; the precarious
balance of the Age of Reason was to be swept away, very
possibly for ever. Nor was Gibbon himself insensitive to this. As
an historian he realised very clearly that his own age represented an exception rather than the rule; the whole of recorded
history was 'little more than the register of the crimes, follies,
and misfortunes of mankind'. And the famous passage in his
Autobiography when he offers sober thanks for his own nature,
class and breeding is no idle self-aggrandisement, but a re-
affirmation of the lesson of *Decline and Fall* as a whole. Realising
the extreme vulnerability of reason in human affairs, he did not
think of his irony as a mere underlining of the obvious.

III

An important question now remains to be considered. There
can be little doubt that most writers who have imitated Gibbon
have used his irony with far less vision or sense of responsibility

than he had himself. The very label 'dismissive' which suggests itself as a description is negative in its implications. Is Gibbon's type of irony basically moral, then, so that irresponsible usages must be thought of as an aberration? Or is it basically irresponsible, so that Gibbon's own harnessing of it to a moral vision must be regarded as altogether exceptional?

My own feeling is in favour of the latter view, though it is difficult to dogmatise on this. As a style, Gibbon's irony seems potentially dangerous; it is the style of the clique, the movement, the smart set, the mutual admiration society, the embittered minority. Its positives do not need to be clearly realised, but merely assumed, for the tone to have its characteristic effect. Invariably, it seems, the reader's response is manipulated by an appeal to his baser instincts: love of flattery on the one hand, fear of a humiliation on the other. The tone is admirably suited to dismissing people or opinions on no better grounds than an unsupported feeling of superiority. Even when the end is a good one, we can doubt whether it fully justifies the means. Such a style seems curiously attuned to vanity, smugness, complacency and malice; to the group traits and postures of the semi-civilised.

Most of Gibbon's imitators have been vicious in the use to which they have put him. Lytton Strachy is often cited, and I shall have more to say of him — and of this particular mode of irony — later. And Gibbon himself, of course, is not wholly without blame. By the nature of things, he has a certain insensitivity to the ideals and aspirations of others; an insensitivity which is indistinguishable at times from arrogance. The urbane assurance of his tone is an assertion of superiority which precludes humility; it is an act of judgement which takes for granted the absolute right to judge. There is inevitably, in a style of this kind, a readiness to see through people and things in place of a more costly attempt to see into them. One can almost hear the writer thanking his birth and breeding that he is not as other men are. And some qualities which seem essential to history or biography at its best we shall look for in vain: the sympathy which understands other temperaments and ways of life, the sensitivity which can admire idealism and nobility even in those who are in error, the compassion which embraces the erring and thinks in terms of redemption rather than of censure.

To admit this, however, is not to form an adverse opinion of Gibbon. No conceivable style could contain all the possible virtues or avoid all the possible errors — a very obvious point, yet half of the hostile criticism ever written seems to ignore it. Gibbon, though he has his limitations, and though his tone has proved a vicious instrument in the hands of lesser men, remains one of the greatest of our writers. The civilisation and decorum of the eighteenth century live in his style; the rational and humane judgements implied in his ironic survey remain a most relevant reminder of the dangers, the absurdities of fanaticism. He is, at the same time, a most successful embodiment of that fine eighteenth-century literary ideal, to instruct by pleasing. *Decline and Fall* is still a most readable book: and in this way scores, one cannot help reflecting, over much of the more austerely empirical history that has been written since.

CHAPTER 5

PEACOCK: THE WAND OF ENCHANTMENT

I

In Peacock's satiric novels, the conversations are usually written out as drama and the plots are a narrative thread in between. The characters are nearly all humours, whom we get to know from certain recurring expressions, ideas and gestures, vividly observed from outside. The Honourable Mr Listless in *Nightmare Abbey* is a typical instance of this. With his mannered boredom, his 'upon my honour', his 'laughter is pleasant, but the exertion is too much for me' he stands halfway between the creations of Sheridan in the recent past, and those of the Dickens who was shortly to be. Mr Listless is what E. M. Forster calls a 'flat' character, but he defines himself more sharply than the word 'flat' naturally suggests. The characterisation can be best understood, perhaps, as a kind of symbolism. Tricks of speech and mannerism reverberate against our own experience, helping us to see, as well as hear, the kind of person to whom they must belong. We respond to many people in daily life in rather this way. It is by mannerisms and moods, observed externally and somewhat larger-than-life, that the small-part actors in our own lives exist for us — the lady in the coffee-house with the feathered hat, the old man with the barrel-organ and the monkey (surely the last of his kind?), the girl with the tattooed arms (Scarborough '36, or '37 perhaps), the man with the monocle, laughing with the Ambassador's wife. The world is full of such 'flat' characters, if they *are* flat: characters larger-than-life, and correspondingly larger than time. Our friends and colleagues change with ourselves, but the old man with the barrel-organ, the girl with the tattoos, the lady in the coffee-house with the hat (where *is* she these days?) — they, at least, are always the same.

The permanence is achieved, of course, only by distance;

memory fixes them in its own kind of eternity, as the characters in a favourite novel tend to get fixed. We see them in this manner because we do not get involved with them: or because being involved, it is one particular set of characteristics, or one significant sequence of happenings, which remains in our mind. In Dickens's novels the second of these explanations is more usually the true one, and his humours have a richer life than any, except Shakespeare's, that one can recall. In Peacock, the first explanation comes nearer the truth. The mannerisms, the quirks, the ideas of his characters are part of a pageant, prepared to delight us. We never become involved with them as we do when there is the illusion of 'reality' as well.

The mannerisms, the quirks, the ideas: the ideas above all — yet Peacock is not a novelist of ideas as (say) Aldous Huxley is, and the ideas in his novels are as much a part of the pageant as the characters themselves. For the truth of the ideas, Peacock seems to care very little; it is their quaintness, their picturesqueness, their absurdity that catches his eye. The ideas continually draw us back to their owners, whom they adorn like so many rings and bangles, so many happy extravagances of taste. They draw us back, equally, to the decor most befitting their owners, to the baronial mansion set in rural seclusion, to the festive dinner table, with discourse rare and vintage to crown the feast.

II

These suggestions will be modified, as well as developed, in what follows; meanwhile, Mr Milestone in *Headlong Hall* provides a useful place to begin.

'My dear sir,' said Mr Milestone, 'accord me your permission to wave the wand of enchantment over your grounds. The rocks shall be blown up, the trees shall be cut down, the wilderness and all its goats shall vanish like mist. Pagodas and Chinese bridges, gravel walks and shrubberies, bowling-greens, canals, and clumps of larch, shall rise upon its ruins. One age, sir, has brought to light the treasures of ancient learning; a second has penetrated into the depths of metaphysics; a third has brought to perfection the science of astronomy; but it was reserved for the exclusive genius of the present times, to invent the noble art of picturesque gardening,

which has given, as it were, a new tint to the complexion of
nature, and a new outline to the physiognomy of the universe.'

If we judged by the style alone and not by the content, should
we not ascribe this to an earlier date? — argument piled upon
argument without proper foundation, pseudo-scholarship used
for deflation, formal diction pressed zestfully towards the absurd.
It is all highly boisterous, and the boisterousness is dangerous,
yet the danger is not, after all, what strikes us most. Mr Milestone *is* absurd, but he pleases us; he does no harm (at least at
Headlong), and his vision is undeniably creative in its way.
There is even a kind of innocence in such naked high-minded-
ness; in this quest for perfection through such total defiance
of Nature as she actually is. Our rejection of Mr Milestone's
proposals is more than counterbalanced by our pleasure in Mr
Milestone. Peacock rejoices in the theorist's energy if not in his
theories, and this delight is what his own style, in turn, chiefly
conveys. We feel some of the affection for Mr Milestone, even,
which we feel for Mr Micawber — for so, in his far greater way,
does Dickens delight us, with characters far transcending the
satiric impulse from which they grow.

But the mention of Dickens prompts a qualification; we have
only to recall Mr Micawber, in all his richness, to be reminded
that Peacock's characters never seem particularly 'real'. This
is not because of what they *are*, as I have already indicated: the
stylised qualities can as easily tell for the illusion of reality as
against. It is, rather, because of what happens to them; they
are too protected by their author to merit any emotional involve-
ment from ourselves. The protection works in several different
ways, all of them important; the first of which is the nature of
the plot. Nobody dies, and nobody really suffers; even Scythrop,
who loses two ladies and talks of suicide, finds solace in his
Madeira as the curtain falls. In feasting, in wedding festivities,
most dilemmas resolve themselves; events turn out well for
everyone, or everyone who matters, in the end. The plot, then,
protects the characters, and inside the plot their money protects
them; the decor is always expensive, and poverty, though sometimes mentioned, is kept well at bay. They are protected further,
perhaps still more effectively, by their moral neutrality: though
pleasant and unpleasant, they can scarcely be regarded as

'good' and 'bad'. And they are protected by the conventions of comedy, which in Peacock's handling move very close to farce. Terrible upheavals happen, both physical and spiritual, but everyone survives, with scarcely a bruise. In *Nightmare Abbey* there is a notable collision on a staircase.

Scythrop pursued her, crying, 'Stop, stop, Marionetta — my life, my love!' and was gaining rapidly on her flight, when, at an ill-omened corner, where two corridors ended in an angle at the head of a staircase, he came into sudden and violent contact with Mr Toobad, and they both plunged together to the foot of the stairs, like two billiard-balls into one pocket. This gave the young lady time to escape, and enclose herself in her chamber; while Mr Toobad, rising slowly, and rubbing his knees and shoulders, said, 'You see, my dear Scythrop, in this little incident, one of the innumerable proofs of the temporary supremacy of the devil; for what but a systematic design and concurrent contrivance of evil could have made the angles of time and space coincide in our unfortunate persons at the head of this accursed staircase?'

'Nothing else, certainly,' said Scythrop: 'you are perfectly in the right, Mr Toobad. Evil, and mischief, and misery, and confusion, and vanity, and vexation of spirit, and death, and disease, and assassination, and war, and poverty, and pestilence, and famine, and avarice, and selfishness, and rancour, and jealousy, and spleen, and malevolence, and the disappointments of philanthropy, and the faithlessness of friendship, and the crosses of love — all prove the accuracy of your views, and the truth of your system; and it is not impossible that the infernal interruption of this fall downstairs may throw a colour of evil on the whole of my future existence.'

'My dear boy,' said Mr Toobad, 'you have a fine eye for consequences.'

So saying, he embraced Scythrop, who retired, with a disconsolate step, to dress for dinner; while Mr Toobad stalked across the hall, repeating, 'Woe to the inhabiters of the earth, and of the sea, for the devil is come among you, having great wrath.'

This is splendidly funny, and entirely in keeping with all that has led up to it, but do we even begin to wonder whether Scythrop or Mr Toobad has been hurt? The precipitation of each into his gloomiest philosophising strikes us, rather, as a festive comic release. Everything depends upon the timing, as in a Laurel and Hardy film. Peacock sets out to entertain us, and any moral lessons are very much by the way.

Likewise in *Headlong Hall*, when Mr Cranium is blown off the top of a tower in an explosion; and at the end of *Melincourt*, when Lord Anophel Achthar and Sir Oran Haut-ton in their differing ways run amuck. Likewise, also, the spiritual bruising which Scythrop suffers when both young ladies reject him. Spiritual ills can hurt as much as physical ones but both, in Peacock, submit to the laws of comic farce.

III

Peacock's frivolity is central, therefore, to these works; but is it incompatible with the serious ironic intention which we sometimes discern? The problem is forced upon us by the very nature of Peacock's method, which is to collect a number of individuals with interesting hobby-horses, and to race them against one another in a kind of caucus-race of the mind. The detached amusement with which this race is commented upon suggests a certain superior reasonableness in the author; whose pose may be less Olympian than Gibbon's, yet has an urbane self-assurance of its own. What we appear to be offered is the re-assertion of commonsense over wild intellectualism, a two-sides-to-every-question geniality, steering all sharp exchanges towards the safety of sport. The very setting is attuned to this kind of resolution. In *Headlong Hall* Squire Headlong drinks his Burgundy in rural intactness, his Horatian well-being an ambience where all crankiness is baptised and absorbed. In *Crotchet Castle* the 'schemes for the world's regeneration' evaporate 'in a tumult of voices', as Mr Crotchet's 'matchless claret' has its destined effect.

All of which is abundantly pleasant; and surely too pleasant to be intruded upon by any morose reflections which the sober moralist may entertain? Yet the moralist has his right to be heard, and indeed must be heard, if the right kind of claim for

Peacock is in the end to be made. The 'wand of enchantment' which Mr Milestone flourishes is Peacock's also; he creates a world for our pleasure, more idyllic, for all its irony, than the world as it actually is. We submit to his spell as we read, and are properly grateful; yet if we submit too completely, we may overlook how much is surrendered by the admirably genial tone. The mental sharpness which any totally satisfying irony must have is surrendered; and so is the radicalism from which this irony, in particular, often pretends to spring. Peacock's characters are not 'good' or 'bad' in any serious sense, as I have already noted; they are morally neutral in themselves, whatever the implications for good or ill in their ideas. They are more-or-less eccentric, more-or-less loveable cranks; or alternatively, more-or-less eccentric, more-or-less loveable cynics, resisting crankiness in the name of common sense, good humour and port. Peacock's own *persona* veers in different novels between the two: in Mr Hilary of *Nightmare Abbey* he puts himself in the latter camp, but in Dr Folliott of *Crotchet Castle* and the Reverend Dr Opimian of *Gryll Grange* (both part *personae*) he moves somewhat the other way. A revealing remark about Dr Folliott is made by Lady Clarinda: 'He is of an admirable temper, and says rude things in a pleasant, half-earnest manner, that no-body can take offense with.' This 'manner' is one which Peacock clearly admired; yet how much complacency, how much insensitivity, how much intransigent reaction, must it have sanctioned in its time?

The setting is attuned, then, to Peacock's temperament; and so is his characteristic handling of ideas. He hardens ideas towards absurdity, as politicians harden one another's policies in election year. There is little regard for truth, and none for fairness. To make the ideas amusing, and therefore impossible, is the sole intent.

The damage sustained by the ideas has already been touched on; they are made to sound like part of a Christmas game. They need, for Peacock's purpose, to be both simplified and arrested: simplified so that original notions sound wildly eccentric; and arrested so that one simplified idea can clash with its opposite to the greatest effect. The result falls far short, one need scarcely add, of synthesis; and still further short of the point where any meaningful action might occur. It guarantees that no synthesis

or action will ever be possible — not, that is to say, while
Peacock's geniality can keep its hold.

In itself, the technique can be amusing, and not unsubtle —
as in this exchange in *Nightmare Abbey*, when Scythrop and his
father clash over a choice of bride (Mr Glowry speaks first).

'Sir, I have pledged my honour to the contract — the
honour of the Glowries of Nightmare Abbey: and now, sir,
what is to be done?'

'Indeed, sir, I cannot say. I claim, on this occasion, that
liberty of action which is the co-natal prerogative of every
rational being.'

'Liberty of action, sir? there is no such thing as liberty of
action. We are all slaves and puppets of a blind and un-
pathetic necessity.'

'Very true, sir; but liberty of action, between individuals,
consists in their being differently influenced, or modified, by
the same universal necessity; so that the results are un-
consentaneous, and their respective necessitated volitions
clash and fly off in a tangent.'

'Your logic is good, sir; but you are aware, too, that one
individual may be a medium of adhibiting to another a mode
or form of necessity, which may have more or less influence
in the production of consentaneity; and, therefore, sir, if you
do not comply with my wishes in this instance (you have
had your own way in everything else), I shall be under the
necessity of disinheriting you, though I shall do it with tears
in my eyes.' Having said these words, he vanished suddenly,
in the dread of Scythrop's logic.

Ostensibly, this is an intellectual discussion depending on
logic; obliquely, it is a clash of wills, conveyed to us precisely
through the exuberant irrelevance of the ideas. The fun is
beautifully managed, with Peacock's usual side-glances at
transcendental long-windedness, yet the ideas are totally
sacrificed to the humour of the situation itself. And why not,
when Peacock writes as amusingly as this? — except that one
would like to be sure that the author realises the limits, as well
as the possibilities, of his technique. Our suspicion is that he
does not realise the limits; that he mistakes his skill in having
fun with ideas for serious satire against the ideas themselves.

He misunderstands, it sometimes seems, his actual target — which is not a variety of ideas, but one kind of person: the person who talks rather than acts, and is superficial in his talk. The various incarnations by which Shelley and Coleridge are pursued through his writings are always amusing; but does he realise that they are not Shelley and Coleridge? Does he see that they are, rather, undergraduates talking Shelley and Coleridge? — talking fluently and pretentiously, and with all the major ideas just slightly askew?

Did Peacock realise, in fact, that Shelley really was an exceptional man, for all his absurdities, and that Coleridge (to use Mill's tribute) was one of the two great seminal minds of his age? This matter is clearly important, for though there is nothing objectionable in caricature recognised as caricature, there is certainly something objectionable in caricature parading as satiric truth. And Peacock himself may not have known this; there is no evidence that he understood the nature of a truly original or speculative mind. He had little understanding of which questions were really worth asking, or of which kinds of enquiry might lead towards truth. He had no insight into which kinds of originality might be productive. The charlatan and the scientist, to him, were entirely the same.

Mr Cranium in *Headlong Hall* is an interesting instance; Mr Cranium's theory, it will be remembered, is that our behaviour is largely determined by bumps. He lectures on this theme with amusing pedantry, and what he says, one agrees, is almost self-evidently absurd. Yet *is* it as absurd as we think it? — or is it the kind of absurdity which might be a growing pain for truth? Mr Cranium was wrong about bumps, and human behaviour cannot be related to them; it can, however, be related to genes, though Mr Cranium was naturally in no position to know about these. His search for some physical link was, however, inherently plausible. Might we not see him in retrospect as a transitional figure between magic and science — a necessary link, even, between the astrologer, and the molecular biologist of today?

My contention is not that there are no Mr Craniums in the world we live in, for clearly there are, and every bit as silly as Peacock makes out. It is, rather, that there are also geniuses who superficially resemble Mr Cranium, and that Peacock makes no distinction whatever between the two. In *Nightmare Abbey* the scientific butt is Mr Asterias; and of course Mr Asterias *is* very funny, with his theory that all life evolved from the water, and his search for mermaids and tritons as a missing link. But would Peacock have seen a Mr Asterias in Darwin? It is virtually certain that he would. In *Crotchet Castle* Mr Firedamp's remedy for malaria is remarkably funny, and it is no doubt unfortunate, for Peacock at least, that it also turned out to be true. And Mr Toogood's political theories are 'the strangest of the lot', as Captain Fitzchrome points out: 'He wants to parcel out the world into squares like a chess-board, with a community on each, raising every thing for one another.'

If Peacock had lived in the twentieth century, Freud would have been a godsend to him, while Professor Fleming's early experiments with penicillin would have exhibited just the kind of absurdity he relished most. And this, really, is why a moral point about him cannot be evaded: he makes his cranks representative of the men who shape destiny, as cosy reactionaries nearly always do.

IV

I have suggested that Peacock failed to distinguish between genius and crankiness. He failed also, from his own point of view more disastrously, to distinguish between complacency and common sense. You have only to compare him with Johnson, whom he sometimes paraphrased and obviously admired, to make this failure almost embarrassingly clear. In the writings of Johnson there is always a vital distinction between ills such as death, which we must learn to accept, however painfully, and ills such as poverty, against which we must never cease to campaign. From the former we can learn fortitude, from the latter justice; and the two together form part of a true 'common-sense'. Common sense, as Johnson conceives it, is a kind of wisdom: a distillation of human experience over the ages, a codification of all that is fine. To turn from this concept to Peacock's is to turn from human greatness to the smug complacency which 'commonsense' usually is. Peacock sees little difference, as facts that must be accepted, between death and poverty; since both are part of the world we live in, to protest

against either would be somewhat absurd. His acceptance of
class distinctions is everywhere apparent, in the early and more
'radical' works like *Melincourt*, as well as in *Crotchet Castle* and
Gryll Grange, where resistance to social change has turned into
a major theme. And with the acceptance of class distinctions,
there is acceptance of the social *status quo*. In *Melincourt*, it is
true, a corrupt clergyman is satirised for his attacks on education, but in *Crotchet Castle* the pendulum has swung the other way.
This time it is Lord Brougham who is satirised, for his efforts
to spread education to the workers. It has dawned upon Peacock that if you educate people they might get ideas above their
station. They might even be disruptive to the people who have
educated them: and this, Peacock's brand of radicalism cannot
be expected to endorse.

Exactly here, I think, we have a clue to our ambivalence
about Peacock: I speak for myself, of course, but I fancy that
many modern readers might feel the same. The more realistic
he is, the less we like him; for the more realistic he is, the more
conscious we become of basic assumptions with which it is
impossible to agree. The nearer he moves, however, to idyll
and fantasy, the greater his hold on our imagination, and
indeed on our affection, becomes. As a realist he is reactionary,
and his tone, when it fails to be genial, can sound harsh and
false. As a writer of idyll and fantasy, he is a great entertainer;
and the entertainment has its own pleasantness, its own validity,
its own proper tone.

V

I want in conclusion to develop this distinction, and to
suggest that Peacock is a reactionary writer whom his greatest
opponents can still, however, enjoy. Even in *Melincourt*, reactionary habits of mind proliferate, despite the attack on
slavery, which Peacock vigorously and honestly launched. The
Anti-Saccarine Fête, it will be remembered, is part of a boycott; sugar is a West Indian product, and Mr Forester sees the
boycott as a means of resisting slavery from home. But the
Fête, though launched as a boycott, turns into a feast; and
the manner in which even Mr Forester thinks of it suggests something less than wholehearted commitment to a cause. When ills

nearer home are mentioned, the radical impulses appear to have expended themselves. The chapters on Desmond and his family are a *locus classicus* for anyone wishing to assimilate benevolence to the political right. Desmond is driven by poverty nearly to desperation, but is rescued by the private charity of a benefactress — in this case, by the heroine of the book. The payment for charity is, of course, heartfelt gratitude; and this Desmond offers, in company with the wife and children who have been rescued along with himself. Mr Forester's approval of the whole episode is also Peacock's, and his words are worth quoting in full.

I am no revolutionist. I am no advocate for violent and arbitrary changes in the state of society. I care not in what proportions property is divided (though I think there are certain limits which it ought never to pass, and approve the wisdom of the American laws in restricting the fortune of a private citizen to twenty thousand a year), provided the rich can be made to know that they are but stewards of the poor, that they are not to be the monopolisers of solitary spoil, but the distributors of general possession; that they are responsible for that distribution to every principle of general justice, to every tie of moral obligation, to every feeling of human sympathy: that they are bound to cultivate simple habits in themselves, and to encourage most such arts of industry and peace, as are most compatible with the health and liberty of others.

How, one wonders, can this not be ironic? But in Peacock no irony is intended, not even, I think (though I am less sure of this) in the very peculiar parenthesis about 'the wisdom of the American laws'. Mr Forester is no revolutionist, certainly, as he admits: he is, rather, the exponent of that brand of optimistic Toryism which can afford to be good-humoured and genial, as long as 'simple habits' are not interpreted in too austere a sense. A radical's irony would be certain to be at the opposite pole to this with Oscar Wilde: 'the virtues of the poor may be readily admitted, and are much to be regretted.' Has any radical ever been able to consider the gratitude of the poor without dismay?

Crotchet Castle is altogether the harshest and least pleasing of Peacock's novels, no doubt because here the threat to benevolent

F

Toryism is most pressingly felt. 'I am out of all patience with this march of the mind,' announces Dr Folliott. 'My cook must read his rubbish in bed; and as might naturally be expected, she dropped suddenly fast asleep, overturned the candle, and set the curtains in a blaze.' 'His rubbish' is Lord Brougham's *Observations on Education of the People*, and the effect on the cook ('naturally to be expected,' says Mr Folliott) combines the literal and symbolic dangers of education in one. Lady Clarinda, the heroine of *Crotchet Castle*, is strangely egotistical and cynical; her wit has the glitter and hardness of Restoration Comedy, yet Peacock seems to endorse it in the course of the tale. The element of farce in this novel becomes more violent. For once, someone is actually killed in the course of a brawl, but since he is only a robber, and a lower-class robber at that, we are made to feel that his death hardly counts. The attack on America, moreover, is surprisingly lacking in the urbanity we have come to expect. We are reminded, naturally enough, of *Martin Chuzzlewit*, but the similar content merely underlines the dissimilar tone. Dickens's satire originated in disappointed idealism; Peacock's is more like the stay-at-home's 'I told you so'.

In the early novels Peacock's serenity rested in the unchanging pattern of English life; given this, radicalism was a luxury he could well afford. Only later, when social change turned out to be in full flood, did he see the threat contained in it to all that he valued most. The ideas he had played with so amusingly seemed somehow less funny; they had taken hold — or some of them had — and the very world where one could laugh at them was being destroyed. In *Crotchet Castle* Peacock seems just to have made this discovery, and there is a corresponding rawness in his tone. But by the time *Gryll Grange* was written, much later in his life, he had assimilated the change, and was able to wave his wand of enchantment once again. This last novel is both his mellowest and his most purely delightful, even though his reactionary sympathies are here most openly displayed. And this, if I am right, is because he has returned from realism, or near realism, to fantasy. Once more, the mood of idyllic seclusion is fully established; the mood of Dr Opimian, indulging in his country retreat the four tastes which were so much Peacock's own: 'a good library, a good dinner, a pleasant garden, and rural walks.' Dr Opimian is not so much a benevolent Tory as a reconciled Canute; confronting the incoming tide which cannot be halted, he enjoys present good fortune all the more fully in such time as is left. His views on science are famous, and one hundred years later sound less eccentric, perhaps, than they may have done at the time:

> Science is one thing, and wisdom is another. Science is an edged tool, with which men play like children, and cut their own fingers. If you look at the results which science has brought in its train, you will find them to consist almost wholly in elements of mischief. See how much belongs to the word Explosion alone, of which the ancients knew nothing. ... See collisions and wrecks and every mode of disaster by land and by sea, resulting chiefly from the insanity for speed, in those who for the most part have nothing to do at the end of the race, which they run as if they were so many Mercuries speeding with messages from Jupiter.... Look at our scientific machinery, which has destroyed domestic manufacture, which has substituted rottenness for strength in the thing made, and physical degradation in crowded towns for healthy and comfortable country life in the makers. The day would fail, if I should attempt to enumerate the evils which science has inflicted on mankind. I almost think it is the ultimate destiny of science to exterminate the human race.

Whereas the doctrine of regress was once, for Peacock, one eccentric extreme to be played off against its opposite, it now speaks fairly directly for himself. And there are other interestingly prophetic passages in this last of the novels: Dr Opimian already foresees the pattern of Britain's declining influence in a changing world

> ... the time will come when by mere force of numbers, the black race will predominate, and exterminate the white.

But alas for radicalism — and alas for the hope that Peacock's England might submit gracefully to the drift of world events. In the face of the threat, all Dr Opimian's reactionary prejudices float to the surface: the inferiority of foreigners (especially coloured foreigners) and the inferiority of peasants, both self-contained categories, whose emergence from obscurity can be expected to cause nothing but harm.

Yet geniality in *Gryll Grange* has re-established itself; and not least in the plot, with its total defiance of these gloomy forebodings about the great world outside. In the plot, nothing is changed: the old order is arrested at its most idyllic point, and celebrated in strains of high romance. The main frame of the novel presents us, in fact, with a choice of two idylls; the Horatian contentment of Dr Opimian in his rural seclusion, and the fairy-tale contentment of Mr Falconer, secure and studious in his 'enchanted palace', with seven chaste young ladies to order his life. The idyll of Mr Falconer, longingly though Peacock toys with it, is the one that has to yield. Peacock will believe, himself, in the bare possibility, but he knows that it is 'too good for this world'. The world will disbelieve in Mr Falconer's purity; and Mr Falconer's seven virgins *are* lower class, despite the superior education they have had. This 'superior education' is, at a more realistic level, the problem: it has unfitted the seven young ladies for their normal station, so what is a novelist responsible for them to do? If they are not to devote themselves chastely to Mr Falconer they must find other employment; but Peacock finds it hard to see what this could possibly be. Fortunately, when realism is powerless, idyll comes to the rescue. Seven virtuous young men of the virgins' own class appear, rugged and healthy, admiring and true. These young men know that the young ladies are too good for them, but are prepared to marry and cherish them just the same. 'They are so like young ladies,' as one of them puts it, 'they daze us, like.' Any italics that a modern reader is tempted to insert here are entirely his own.

With the intervention of the seven providential peasants, the other complications of personal relationship are also solved. The novel can move to its last major statement in the Aristophanic Comedy, a showing forth of the truth that for nearly two thousand years nothing has changed but for the worse. Modern music, modern cities, modern inventions, all conspire against us, in a shadowy regress which only mirth and present laughter can hold at bay.

And is this not a fitting apotheosis for Peacock himself, as well as for the last of his works? If irony cannot stop ideas and customs from changing, at least it can extract humour from them in the present that we have. To enjoy the present, to

swallow up foreboding in geniality, to feast and to celebrate —
these are Peacock's gifts as a writer, the wand of enchantment
which he, like his own Mr Milestone, has. And in his hands, too,
the wand is a genuine magic, whether we respond to its owner's
vision or not. For why should we not respond, even though our
own vision may be a different one? If a man has reasonable
taste and reasonable wealth; if he loves the good things of life,
yet is by temperament reclusive; if he enjoys the play of ideas,
but mistrusts their meanings; if he can forget the encroachments
of change, and lay social conscience by: is this not a possible
way for him to live, even today?

If, like Peacock, he can also amuse and entertain us, making
some part of his good fortune vicariously ours, there seems every
reason to accept unchurlishly what he gives.

CHAPTER 6

THACKERAY: AN IRONY AGAINST HEROES

I

In February 1847, when *Vanity Fair* had just started to appear, Thackeray wrote in a letter to Mark Lemon, the editor of *Punch*:

> A few years ago I should have sneered at the idea of setting up as a teacher at all ... but I have got to believe in the business, and in many other things since then. And our profession seems to me as serious as the Parson's own.

Vanity Fair marked, indeed, the significant turning point in Thackeray's career. His earlier journalism had been brilliant if ephemeral, a variety of topics discussed under a variety of names. The papers on Snobbery had been very successful, and there had been one novel, *Barry Lyndon*, a satiric piece somewhat in the tradition of *Jonathan Wild*. No great impact on the general reading public had yet been made, however, and it was not until the first episodes of *Vanity Fair* were issued that his journey towards fame really began.

The foundations had been laid earlier, as we should expect. Thackeray's training as a book reviewer had already given him great insight into the techniques of fiction; had prepared him, perhaps, for assimilating Fielding's influence to very different purposes of his own. His personal sufferings, moreover, had deepened his seriousness over a number of years; after the death of a daughter and the madness of his wife, brilliant iconoclasm no longer seemed an end in itself. *Vanity Fair* was conceived as early as 1845, as a series of chapters called *Pen and Pencil Sketches of English Society*. At the time, Thackeray could not find a publisher for it, and the original manuscript (now preserved in the Pierpont Morgan Library) was laid aside. By March 1846, however, Bradbury and Evans had accepted the project and Thackeray was free to resume work on it towards the end of the year. For the original title he substituted *Vanity Fair*, and the famous subtitle 'A Novel Without A Hero' is mentioned in letters as early as March 1846. Publication was in serial form between January 1847 and July 1848, the parts running concurrently, for the most part, with Dickens's *Dombey and Son*.

Almost immediately, Thackeray found himself raised to fame, though with an element of notoriety as well. There were friendly paragraphs in *Fraser's Magazine*, in *The Scotsman* and in *The North British Review*; in July 1847 *Sun* hailed him as 'the Fielding of the nineteenth century'. In January 1848, even more significantly, there was a long panegyric in the *Edinburgh Review*, and Thackeray wrote to a friend:

> There is no use denying the matter or blinking it now. I am become a sort of great man in my way — all but at the top of the tree: indeed there if the truth were known and having a great fight up there with Dickens.

But while this praise was going on, other reviewers and readers were denouncing the book, with something of the violence later to be lavished on Swinburne, Ibsen and Zola. Harriet Martineau left *Vanity Fair* unfinished because of 'the moral disgust it occasions'; in the *Quarterly Review* Miss Rigby called it 'one of the most distressing books we have read for many a long year'. Robert Bell in *Fraser's Magazine* and John Forster in *The Examiner* were appalled by Thackeray's vision of evil. On the Continent, one anonymous reviewer in 1848 enquired: 'Is it advisable to raise so ruthlessly the veil which hides the rottenness pervading modern society?' Even Ruskin was sufficiently disturbed to record that Thackeray settled 'like a meat fly on whatever one had got for dinner and made one sick of it'.

Against these attacks Thackeray defended himself, as many novelists have done since, in the name of 'realism'. Life was not heroic in his view of it, and the novel seemed pre-eminently the place for asserting this. In a letter to David Masson in May 1851 he wrote:

> The art of novels *is* to represent Nature: to convey as strongly as possible the sentiment of reality — in a tragedy or a poem or a lofty drama you aim at producing different emotions; the figures moving, and their words sounding,

heroically: but in a drawing-room drama a coat is a coat, and a poker a poker; and must be nothing else according to my ethics, not an embroidered tunic, nor a great red-hot instrument like a Pantomime weapon.

The Preface to *Pendennis*, published a year before this in 1850, offers what is perhaps the classic reply to those who argue that a novel should not disturb us with sordid or unpleasant themes:

If truth is not always pleasant, at any rate truth is best.

It soon became apparent that not only the early reviewers, but many discriminating creative minds, were on Thackeray's side. Charlotte Brontë, one of his earliest and fiercest admirers, had this to say:

I see in him an intellect profounder and more unique than his contemporaries have yet recognised; because I regard him as the first social regenerator of the day — as the very master of that working corps who would restore to rectitude the warped system of things.

In 1857, George Eliot added her tribute:

I am not conscious of being in any way a disciple of his, unless it constitute discipleship to think him, as I suppose the majority of people with any intellect do, on the whole the most powerful of living novelists.

Trollope, writing of the literary scene in his autobiography, said: 'I do not hesitate to name Thackeray the first'; Henry James placed Thackeray among the novelists whom he thought of 'primarily as great consciences and great minds'; Hardy thought him one of the masters of artistic form. E. M. Forster also has high praise for *Vanity Fair* in *Aspects of the Novel*, where he finds Becky an outstanding example of a round character, such as those achieved by Tolstoy, Dostoevsky and the truly great masters of the novel form.

Academic criticism in the first half of the twentieth century was less enthusiastic, and for a time Thackeray's high reputation seemed to have been eclipsed. Since 1950, however, the dedicated work of Gordon Ray and the two Tillotsons has done much to restore him to full critical esteem. It is possible again in the 1960s to write of him as a great ironist without feeling that any apology for doing so must be made. *Vanity Fair* remains, to my mind, his masterpiece, and it is with this work that the following comments will be concerned.

II

'A novel without a hero' has a very modern sound. We have become familiar in recent years with novels in which the hero is valued for his lack of any qualities to which the word 'heroic' could plausibly be applied. The anti-hero of the 1950s may, however, be little more than a product of semantic confusion; have novels with 'heroic' heroes ever been anything but unusual? Ever since the novel disentangled itself from the romance tradition, there has been no reason why the central character should be 'heroic' in the epic sense. Jane Austen's *Northanger Abbey* begins with the confession: 'No-one who had ever seen Catherine Morland in her infancy, would have supposed her born to be an heroine.' This is said with tongue in cheek, since against extravagantly romantic ideas of a heroine Jane Austen is suggesting that a quite ordinary person might deserve the deepest imaginative attention we have to give. Her teasing draws attention, however, to the confusion caused by using the word 'hero' as a synonym for 'central character', and usefully evades the unreal paradox of an 'anti-hero'. We are reminded that though the chief character in a novel may not always exemplify outstanding courage, or dignity, or dependability, at least he should have claims on our understanding and interest. Today, the anti-heroes of Wain and Amis, Braine and Sillitoe certainly pass a test of this kind; they hold our attention just *because* their deflation as individuals speaks to the condition of us all. But Thackeray, also, claimed the right to prefer a deflated hero to an idealised one. He believed that this was part of the truth that a novelist has a special duty to tell.

There is, however, a further nuance in Thackeray's subtitle, which we should not overlook. Though George Osborne is far from being really heroic in the romantic sense, he is always regarded as such by Amelia. She worships the ground he treads on, making him the excuse for increasingly serious moral evasions of her own. With this in mind, no doubt, Thackeray half-playfully deflates his heroine as well: 'As she was not a heroine there is no need to describe her person.' Later in the novel, when he is speaking of Becky Sharp, his irony veers another way: 'If this is a novel without a hero, at least let us lay claim to a heroine. . . .' Readers may be uncertain how to take this: the tone and context are satiric, but the direction of the satire is less clear than it looks. Becky may be very unlike a heroine of the kind that Victorian young ladies had come to expect, but she does have qualities of courage, independence, resilience, even magnanimity, beyond those of any other character in the book. Like Milton's Satan she can lay claim to these traditionally epic virtues, though in a context where they are fated to be always anti-social, and often sour. Our ambivalence towards Becky's virtues is germane to many of the novel's complex effects, and we are forced to wonder whether Thackeray really might regard her as his heroine, even though he pretends to treat this view with conventional scorn.

I shall return to this matter later, and argue that though there is some truth in such a view, it is only enough to trap us if we try to take it too far. My present point is simply that Thackeray claims, as a novelist, the right to be a total realist, and that realism meant, for him, coming to terms with a radically unheroic world.

III

I have started from the novel's subtitle, and from the problem connected with that, but wherever one starts, enigmas begin to crowd in. *Vanity Fair* is surely one of the world's most devious novels, devious in its characterisation, its irony, its explicit moralising, its exuberance, its tone. Few novels demand more continuing alertness from the reader, or offer more intellectual and moral stimulation in return. In part, at least, this deviousness can be seen to relate to Thackeray's own life. As Gordon Ray has shown in his admirable biography, Thackeray knew Vanity Fair from the inside, with all the insight of a man engaged in its ways, yet deeply ill at ease. One remembers his complex dissatisfactions with his lot. He regretted his nationality, thinking that he would have written better in some other language — an illusion which his own achievement surely exposes, even if we invoke no other names for the defence. He regretted his century, imagining that he would have been more at home in the eighteenth: but would Swift and Sterne have disgusted him as they sometimes did if this were true? He regretted his occasional poverty, and the restless bohemianism which followed the tragedy of his married life, but this was the very material of his art: without such experiences, he might have remained a clever and savage journalist to the end of his days.

Such dissatisfactions led to the iconoclasm of his earlier days, but they paved the way, too, for his compassion. He said himself, on one occasion, that he was created with 'a sense of the ugly, the odd, of the meanly false, of the desperately wicked'. The intensity with which he always responded to the human comedy pushed him towards a more radical criticism of society than perhaps he intended. He acquired, as Walter Bagehot noted, a heightened sense of human inequalities, of the diversity of criticism to which the unprotected and poor are especially exposed. One sees how readily his temperamental restlessness responded to the restlessness of Vanity Fair itself — to its noise and bustle, its surface gaiety, its instinctive cruelty, its truthlessness and faithlessness, its occasional courage and resilience, its desolating lack of heart's ease.

Such considerations lead us very naturally towards Thackeray's pervasive ambivalence of tone. Where does he stand in relationship to his characters, and to their world? Does he come to them chiefly as friend or foe? The explicit indications of attitude, which are numerous enough, and to some readers offensive, do not take us very far. In the opening pages — beautifully and hauntingly written, like so much that is to follow them — he presents himself as a puppet-master, the sole creator of his characters, and their destiny. By the laws of art, this is self-evidently true: all writers do invent their characters, and decide what their fate is to be. By the laws of great art, however, it is a half-truth at best. The greater the writer, the more likely he is to find other laws taking a hand; to find as Richardson did in *Clarissa*, and Tolstoy in *Anna Karenina*, that he cannot deal with his own characters as simply as he may wish. *Vanity Fair* turns out to be a novel where the puppet-master is, after all, bound by the iron discipline of his own greatness. The characters come alive, and their creator cannot blacken or praise them superficially without his readers detecting and resenting the lie; they come alive in the real world of human morality, where every complexity of sensitive response must be allowed for, whether the creator fully approves of such complexity or not. As E. M. Forster has pointed out, Becky Sharp is an outstanding example of a 'round' character; she defies any rule of characterisation that simple logic might prescribe, and becomes as familiar and unpredictable as if we had known her all our lives. Thackeray, of course, knew when his characters came alive as well as we do, and his role of puppet-master is only one of the various *personae* he adopts. Sometimes, he claims the puppet-master's privilege of knowing his characters' secret thoughts, and telling us what these are. But at other times he is reticent, as one would be in life; we are never shown Amelia's deepest moments of grief, though we know the torment they must be. And very occasionally — though on particularly important occasions, as it turns out — he throws open the enigma of life itself as part of his art: who *can* be sure when Becky is telling the truth?

The reader of *Vanity Fair* soon finds other evidence to belie the notion that artifice and contrivance are all. To an unusual degree we have the sense of a real world going on all round the main characters, full of diversity and colour, full of characters who appear and disappear, enacting at the edge of our consciousness the same patterns of sin and anxiety which hold the centre of the stage. This use of surrounding detail and seeming irrelevance to reinforce the main structure of the book reminds us of Sterne; as, to a lesser extent, does the fluidity of the time-scale that Thackeray adopts. Though there is nothing as obviously eccentric as the digressions and flash-backs of *Tristram Shandy*, we find that Thackeray's narrative does shift backwards and forwards in time in a way not always easy to chart. The effect is of a 'real world' into which the novelist's memory dips rather than of an artificial world which he creates as he goes along. Later in the novel, Thackeray represents himself as a man who learns of all the main events by hearsay. The omniscient narrator, the preacher in cap-and-bells, gives way to this further *persona*, middle-aged, curious and detached.

To learn caution about Thackeray's role as puppet-master is to learn caution about the explicit moral judgements of which the novel is full. Some modern critics have blamed Thackeray for saying too much, but this is surely a naïve misunderstanding of his technique. The tradition of commenting upon characters goes back at least to Fielding, but even in *Tom Jones* we are kept continuously on the alert. Are we really to admire Master Blifil's honesty as we are told we should, and to look forward to the hanging of Tom at the end? Fielding adopts the pose of a conventional moralist as a challenge, forcing us to match our personal wits and sense of values against his own. In *Vanity Fair* Thackeray pursues a similar strategy, with ironic overtones even subtler in their range. We are reminded of Fielding's influence in the knowing, man-of-the-world asides; in the ferocity, the gusto almost, with which various kinds of hypocrisy are exposed. There is even something of Sterne in Thackeray's willingness to act the fool, to claim the cap-and-bells as his own. But the prevailing tone of *Vanity Fair* is very different from Fielding's, and *a fortiori* from Sterne's. There is a lack of warmth about it in certain moods: if Thackeray had invented Tom Jones he would surely have found his hero more difficult than Fielding did to forgive, while Uncle Toby one cannot imagine him inventing at all. For though Thackeray's iconoclasm is in part exuberant, it also has a tinge of bitterness; it is nearer than Fielding and Sterne ever are to despair. Very readily the teasing and flamboyance give way, at moments of strain, to the tone of the preacher, no longer in cap-and-bells, but solemn and prophetic now in his own right. The title of the novel is taken from Bunyan, and though Thackeray has nothing of Bunyan's clear-cut doctrine to depend upon, he shares the occasional mood of a Wisdom writer; religious judgements are inescapably present, though not directly expressed. In the introductory note 'Before the Curtain', we are warned of the melancholy induced by Vanity Fair — a melancholy which gives rise to, and shades into, compassion for the suffering and transience of man. Behind the ostensible warmth of tone, which we can never rely on, there is warmth of a deeper and costlier kind. We are involved in the fate of the characters we laugh at, not distanced from them; what happens to them in the end we really must know.

Obviously, then, Thackeray's tone is a complex affair; its local nuances can never be isolated from the whole. We are always left wondering what to make of it, whether it really is as simple, or as moderately simple, as it is dressed out to seem. There is the rather arch playfulness, for instance, that surrounds both Becky and Amelia: is this simply a sentimental evasiveness on Thackeray's part, or does it serve some more devious end? On the surface, the archness is tender towards Amelia, sharp (like her name) towards Becky; yet its eventual effect is to diminish Amelia, while making Becky appear interesting, and even great. Around Amelia, Thackeray deliberately creates a cloying tone, apparently in order to confirm the complacency of his readers, yet really to create in them a growing unease: what *are* these virtues we are being so cosily invited to admire? How *can* we respond with this degree of whimsy to an adult? Around Becky, however, the same tone plays with very different effect. Throughout the novel, she is referred to as 'our little schemer', very much as one might speak of a naughty but not wholly unsympathetic child. In the period when her fortunes are at low ebb, and she sinks to being an extremely seedy (though still resilient) adventuress, Thackeray writes about her almost in the tone of *The Rose And The Ring*:

> So our little wanderer went about setting up her tent in various cities of Europe, as restless as Ulysses or Bampfylde Moore Carew. Her taste for disrespectability grew more and more remarkable. She became a perfect Bohemian ere long, herding with people whom it would make your hair stand on end to meet.

The effect of this is so odd that one is tempted to regard such archness here, if not elsewhere, as an aesthetic flaw. The implication is presumably that Becky lived for a time as a courtesan, yet the tone seems designed to deflect attention away from the actual fact. We have only to imagine Shakespeare writing about Cleopatra as a little schemer whose plots would make our hair stand on end to see how far from serious the passage is.

Nevertheless, too much can be made of such blemishes; certainly they exist in the novel, but they should not blind us to the extreme subtlety of the ironic strategy as a whole. I have mentioned the archness of tone at the start because modern readers are especially likely to need guidance on this: they will be alienated by it more immediately than most Victorians would have been, but they may fail to realise that usually, if not always, this is precisely what Thackeray intends. In what follows, I shall assume that he is one of the most sophisticated of our ironists, and that nearly every effect is very exactly and maturely contrived.

IV

When we look more closely at Thackeray's leading actors, his subtlety soon begins to emerge. Criticism of their personal characters comes very easily to him — too easily, we are immediately forced to suspect. There are Becky's lies and Sir Rawdon's meanness, Mr Osborne's anger and Mrs Bute's treachery — all very wicked, surely?, as the author takes every opportunity to assert. Such comment is, we sense, a very surface affair; a kind of thin ice, on which we are too effusively invited to skate. Social and religious comments are less explicitly stated, yet they are certainly implied, and with mounting insistence as the full pressure of the novel comes to be felt. It occurs to us, after a time, that these deeper implications may run counter to the simpler personal ones that are paraded on the surface; that things may be very much less simple than they seem. Consider, for example, the contrast between Becky and Amelia, around which so much of the action is built. The destinies of the two girls are clearly to be intertwined, the one a conventional heroine (though Thackeray denies her the name), the other a villainess specially designed to make our hair stand on end. As Amelia withdraws from school into her world of money and privilege, Becky is thrown out into the battle of life, with nothing but her wits on her side. We see the girls both trying to catch husbands, the one aided by her mother's socially acceptable stratagems and a good dowry, the other almost fatally handicapped by the lack of these things. At Waterloo we see them with the husbands they have eventually won, Becky triumphant now because of her inborn resilience, Amelia beginning to sink under the deeper handicap of her inner nature — her lack of any real intelligence or talent, or of the courage and will-power needed when life turns sour. Towards the end of the novel there are further reversals, and the two girls, both older and sadder, both soiled by life, neither much wiser, work out the underlying

logic of their lives. Becky has to live now without the husband
she has loved in her way, Amelia has to live with the second
husband she has accepted just slightly too late. During the
action the two women are compared in a great many ways. We
see them both as mothers, Amelia too indulgent, as we would
expect, Becky too detached. At times, Becky seems a very false
friend to Amelia; she behaves very badly at Waterloo, and
becomes one of the many people that Amelia has to fear. The
actual harm she does is less, however, than it appears; there is
no planned malice in it, since this is not a sin she has it in her to
commit, and George's character would be the same whatever
she did. There is also an evening of accounts later on: if Becky
rather contemptuously harms Amelia by flirting with her husband before Waterloo, she equally contemptuously does her a
good turn as the novel is nearing its end. The second act — the
use of George's old letter to disillusion Amelia about his
memory — is as finely ambivalent as many of the other decisive
actions in the book. At one earlier point Becky has reflected that
she could crush Amelia by producing George's letter, but she
has had too much casual good-nature to put this to the test.
When she eventually does produce the letter it is in order to
help Amelia, yet her emotions must have included a certain
triumph; her motives must have been characteristically mixed.

In the contrast between Becky and Amelia, the moral characters of the two girls are always involved. At a very deep level,
Thackeray is critical of them both. The notion that his attitude
to either can be taken at face value can survive only for a reader
of the most superficial kind. In a letter written to his mother in
July 1847 Thackeray had this to say about Amelia (no doubt
slightly overstating the truth):

> My object is not to make a perfect character or anything like
> it. Don't you see how odious all the people are in the book
> (with the exception of Dobbin) — behind whom all there lies
> a dark moral I hope. What I want is to make a set of people
> living without God in the world (only that is a cant phrase)
> greedy, pompous, mean perfectly self-satisfied for the most
> part and at ease about their superior virtue.

Just after the novel was finished, he told Robert Bell in
another letter:

I want to leave everybody dissatisfied and unhappy at the end of the story — we ought all to be with our own and all other stories.

Undoubtedly in making these comments Thackeray was sincere, but like all critical comments they are necessarily less subtle than the force of the novel as a whole. For the moment, I should like to concentrate a little on the strategy of characterisation which underlies such intentions. On the face of it, Amelia is the virtuous girl of the two, sweet and gentle, though with a helplessness that soon begins to cloy. 'The charming sweet thing' is a first impression most people have of her, modulating to 'the poor sweet thing' fairly soon. At school she has many friends among the girls, but when the battle of life is entered upon nearly all women, including her mother, come to view her with contempt. To men she remains an object of courteous attention, but hardly an obvious choice (except to Dobbin, who loves her) as a wife. Thackeray himself appears to sympathise with her, and he does in fact establish her tenderness as the virtue it is. But adverse judgements, often rather slyly foisted off on 'the world', begin to mount. Her love of George is imperceptive and self-indulgent. She blinds herself to his faults and (more seriously perhaps) refuses to see that he does not love her; duty and dignity are thrown overboard in the pursuit. When she wins George, she has little wit or liveliness to offer in return for the sacrifice which he sees himself as having made. As the novel progresses her future is increasingly overshadowed by fears, and we sense that she is destined to be a casualty in the battle of life.

Her virtues also turn out to be more tainted than they at first appear. Her great claim to virtue is the passiveness of self-sacrifice, yet is self-sacrifice, as she practises it, not an insidious self-indulgence in disguise? As a mother she is weakly and harmfully indulgent, as a daughter she fails her parents in their years of need. When George is alive, her love for him is self-willed and self-regarding; when he is dead, the myth of her marriage becomes an evasion of Dobbin's love.

Becky, in contrast, is ostensibly bad, yet her heroic qualities shine out against Amelia's faults. She is sparkling, clever and resilient; from her earliest years she has had to live by her wits, and if the world is against her, is this not mainly because she inherited neither status nor wealth? Her anti-social qualities are at least as much the effect of the world's dealings with her as their cause. Thackeray goes out of his way to blacken her character in his opening pages, as though he entirely shares the standards by which she is judged. As she flings Dr Johnson's 'Dixionary' at the feet of good, silly Miss Jemima, we see her convulsed with hatred and rage; when the coach moves off, 'the young lady's countenance, which had before worn an almost livid look of hatred, assumed a smile that perhaps was scarcely more agreeable'. During her stay at the Sedleys' she is accused of envy and covetousness, malice and pride; it seems as though all the deadly sins must be laid at her door. We hear of the time when she was caught 'stealing jam' at eight years of age, as if faults which would be venial in a well-to-do child must be accounted mortal in her.

As the action of the novel unfolds, it is true that her sins become more substantial. She wounds Amelia, ruins Raggles, plays fast and loose with a great many friends and admirers, treats her husband (as she does everyone else) with good-natured contempt, though after her fashion she loves him. Her thoughtlessness as a mother is hard to forgive; when Thackeray says 'she had no soft maternal heart, this unlucky girl' for once he is not exaggerating the truth. She lives always as a parasite and sometimes, if we take the hints, as a harlot. At the end, it is even suggested that she becomes a murderess — and though this is only malicious gossip and almost certainly untrue, Thackeray's 'Who *can* tell?' echoes uncomfortably in our ears.

Despite all this, it is clear that Thackeray overstates the conventional case against Becky knowingly and deliberately, as the case against Tom Jones was overstated by Fielding. When we ask how we come to detect this, and in any way at all to be on Becky's side, the answer takes us nearer to the heart of the book. In one sense, it may be simply that Becky's courage and resilience are admirable in themselves, whether they are applied for good or ill; in this familiar sense Thackeray may be of his heroine's party without knowing it — or more likely, knowing it slightly better than he would wish. Another possibility is that our sympathy with Becky is sentimental or indulgent and little more. Some critics, indeed, have written as though this were true of Thackeray himself: his 'sentimentality' can be dissociated, they suggest, from his 'irony', and regarded as a balance on the other side. When bitter censoriousness has brought Becky down, good-natured sentimentality brings her up again; tears and laughter alternate like April weather, and the author is simply a creature of his moods. Such a view is, I am suggesting, extremely superficial, but where Becky is concerned there may be a particular reason why it appeals. Criminals always *are* easier to sympathise with from a distance, in literature as in life; Becky is undeniably a character more easy to forgive when she is safely contained in the pages of a book.

None of this, however, does more than scratch the surface of the problem, for surely we do admire Becky, and legitimately, however glad we are to be outside the range of her wiles? The fact is that she *belongs* to Vanity Fair, both as its true reflection, and as its victim; for both of which reasons, she very resoundingly serves it right. Like Jonson's Volpone, she is a fitting scourge for the world which created her — fitting aesthetically, in the way of poetic justice, and fitting morally, in that much of her evil is effective only against those who share her taint. Dobbin is largely immune to her, since he is neither a trifler, a hypocrite nor a snob. The other characters are all vulnerable in one or other of these ways, and we notice that those who judge her most harshly are frequently the ones who have least earned such a right.

The right to judge is, of course, the crux, for Vanity Fair is a social place, and no critique of individual characters can be conducted in a void. What Thackeray comes near to suggesting, like Bunyan before him, is that a society based upon privilege and money is rotten in some fundamental sense. The very concepts of Christian morality become, in such a context, an evasion; an attempt to visit upon the underprivileged and the unprotected sins which more properly belong to society at large. In a world of class and privilege, the simple ideas of 'lying' and 'stealing', when applied by the haves to the have-nots, will clearly not do. An ideal validity they may have, but in the world as we know it they are turned into a mockery of themselves. How far Thackeray was aware of these implications, or wished to be aware of them, it is hard to say. In the novel, he places both his readers and himself in Vanity Fair. We are all tainted with the Crawley hypocrisy, whether of Mrs Bute or Miss Crawley, of Sir Rawdon or of Becky herself. Exactly here, however (and surely this is intended, too?), a further temptation is put in our way. To be all tarred with the same brush, and to be brought to realise that we are, can be a relief as well as a challenge. Need we really do more than the next man in the way of penance, if we have done no more than he in the way of guilt? To judge ourselves guilty, and read on, is less uncomfortable than setting about a wonderful mending of the world. All satirists suffer from this possible evasion of their challenge, but some perhaps suffer less than others — and a few might be tempted to take the same escape route themselves. In 1848, the year of Revolution as well as the year of *Vanity Fair*, Thackeray confessed himself a Republican but not a Chartist. He had no wish to be associated with the hated 'levellers', yet his picture of society is remarkably in tune with theirs. The poison of 'snobbery' had always fascinated him, but whereas his earlier satire was boisterous and comic, the satire of *Vanity Fair* reaches more unerringly towards the roots. The Bute Crawleys are supposed to be Christian, but their plots against Rawdon and Becky are evil in a purely competitive sense. Miss Crawley imagines herself to be a liberal and a Republican, but she is as parasitic as Becky herself (they are truly birds of a feather), though at the other end of the moneyed scale. Almost every sin in Vanity Fair can be traced, beyond personal weakness, to the fundamental laws of money and class; to fawn upon the rich and kick the poor is a Christian law of the land. The poison in Vanity Fair infects the bottom rungs of the social ladder as well as the top: Mrs Sedley's servants join in the hunt against Becky when she has fallen from grace, her own servants turn against her when Rawdon has stormed off and they sense that her social position is at an end. The poor have more than their chains to lose in Vanity Fair, they have their opportunities for hurting one another as well. If Thackeray went less far than the Marxists in political analysis of the scene he depicts, it may have been (to give him the benefit of the doubt) because his view of human nature was correspondingly gloomier than theirs.

The whole institution of marriage is bound up with these attitudes, as Thackeray is also concerned to bring home. When

Mrs Sedley is shocked by Becky's stratagems, after her husband has explained them to her, her shock is not to do with prudery but with class. How dare a hired governess of dubious parentage 'look up to such a magnificent personage as the collector of Boggley Wollah?' The cruel realism of this becomes still more detestable when it mingles with conscious snobbery and insensitivity — as it does in George Osborne, when he also conspires against Becky's attempts to steer quietly to port in Joseph Sedley's arms. Thackeray's savagery in such passages has been sometimes overlooked, one suspects, by readers who deplore his 'prudery' without realising how realistic about sex he can also be. He was reticent about physical love, as all Victorians were, but in *Vanity Fair* there are franknesses that can shock us even now. Becky, for instance, is not a sensual woman at all; given wealth and social position, she would have managed without sexual adventures fairly well. She is willing to marry Joseph Sedley for all his absurdity; and our very revulsion from this, if we experience revulsion, may be only a sentimental lack of realism about marriage of our own. In Vanity Fair, as Thackeray depicts it, sex is as little reverenced or respected as anything else. On the one hand, it is a subject for endless gossip and malice; a common frailty in which we are all likely to be caught out unless we take sufficient care (but if we are caught Heaven help us, since Vanity Fair is understanding but in no way forgiving about those who fall by the way). And on the other hand, it is a powerful asset to a mother looking round for a good catch for her daughter. Though the weaklings of the world like Amelia may think only of love, a mother will think rather of physical attractiveness and charm. These are the true assets she has to trade with in the marriage market — assets almost as substantial as the dowry itself, though who doubts that money speaks a little louder in the end?

In all such matters Thackeray reports faithfully and even ferociously what the world is like, with a directness that speaks very strikingly across a hundred years of sexual emancipation to ourselves. He is willing to show how far from being pure-minded young soldiers are when they joke together, courteous though their attentions to an Amelia may be; he is willing to depict the cynicism of Mr Osborne, who will readily see George amuse himself with any woman he fancies, as long as he is not mad enough to want to make her his wife. Boys will be boys, says Mr Osborne in effect, but 'unless I see Amelia's ten thousand down, you don't marry her' . . . 'And that's flat'. A modern reader is often tempted, I think, to treat this as bitter satire, rather than as the very minimal realism which it is. What Thackeray is saying, surely, is that the Flesh has very little chance indeed of triumphing when the time comes for it to do battle with the World.

Our sympathy with Becky, to return to this, is so closely connected with, as to be almost inseparable from, the context of Thackeray's social realism. Even while conventional judgements are being made against her, a social background is movingly, if less noisily, sketched. We hear of 'the dismal precocity of poverty' without surprise. In the contrast with Amelia, it is at once apparent that whereas the one girl is cushioned, the other must fight to survive. Their quest for a husband is similar, but Becky, with no mother to help her, must risk the insults and misunderstandings attendant upon doing everything for herself. And this, really, is why we are on her side: not because we idealise her ruthless scheming, or foolishly imagine that we should get along rather well with her ourselves, but because we see the need for what she does. In a society using Christian values almost wholly perversely, resilience and energy are forced to know themselves, in a Becky, as conventional sins. For this reason too we forgive her, for we see how little right society has to judge her as it does. She is indeed its reflection, and interesting to us largely because she has the courage and energy, though so heavily handicapped, to play its game. We notice that though she employs hypocrisy, she is never taken in by it herself; she does not make her sin a virtue, and is to this degree preferable to those who do. She is never revengeful or consciously hard-hearted; she is able (a really saving grace) to laugh at herself exactly as though she were someone else.

Reflecting upon this, we see the deeper purposes Thackeray must have in mind. To a much larger extent than we would expect, Becky's judgements on people are the novelist's own. When she writes a letter to Amelia, for instance, mocking the uncouth and canting inmates of Queen's Crawley, Thackeray assures us that it is the wicked Becky speaking, and not himself:

'Otherwise you might fancy that it was I who was sneering . . .
I who laughed . . . whereas the laughter comes from one who
has no reverence except for prosperity, and no eye for anything
beyond success.' But clearly this dissociation of himself from
Becky is largely false, and the irony is of the two-edged kind we
find throughout. Given that Thackeray himself judges with
compassion, and that this quality is one that Becky, by the
nature of things, does not have, the judgements she makes of
Queen's Crawley are substantially the same as his own. Because
she sees the standards by which the world actually lives in such
sharp contrast with the standards by which it professes to live,
she can judge as well as exploit it in its chosen terms. For, indeed, she belongs to Vanity Fair herself, and reform, whether
for herself or for it, is very far from her thought. She glories in
the world's game with all the superior energy and intelligence
that she can command. It may even be fair, if one thinks in these
terms, that the comparatively innocent should have to suffer
along with the rest. Old Raggles might seem an innocent victim,
but is he not as corrupt and open to punishment as anyone else?
By thrift he assembles his nest-egg, and by trust he loses it; yet
his trust is tainted with snobbery, the mark of Vanity Fair is
on it for us to see.

The obverse of this is that Becky's character rises in our
esteem as that of her victims sinks. How could her gaiety and
courage have expressed themselves in any more worthy way?
Had she been born to position or power, she would have risen
nobly to the role. '"It isn't difficult to be a gentleman's wife,"
Rebecca thought. "I think I could be a good woman if I had
five thousand a year."' And so, as the world judges, she could
have been. Who would more charmingly distribute charity
than a privileged Becky, or more graciously accept in return
the world's esteem? She could have been a Queen, we are told, if
she had been born to it; and it is apparent enough that she could.

Lacking, however, these natural advantages, Becky knows
that the appearance of respectability and wealth must be sought
for instead. And since Vanity Fair is as much pleased with the
appearance as with the reality, until such time as the discrepancy is seen through and the hunt can begin, Becky has all her
intuitive understanding of its values on her side. The appearance can be maintained, it is true, only by exceptional effort;

the world's homage is bought at a price, and those who cannot pay cash must know how to charm, and flatter, and amuse. For long periods Becky creates and maintains the required appearance; her resourcefulness and gaiety seem never-ending, though she knows (as Lord Steyne brutally confirms to her) that she is living in a house built of straw. And she lifts Rawdon up to apparent affluence and comfort with herself. Though others suffer as she does so, and have to suffer, she is a good wife to Rawdon from the first. It is not the least of the novel's ironies that she loses her husband without really deserving to (though the circumstances leading up to this are surrounded with characteristic enigma); and that this last rebuff is the bitterest of all, the rebuff she needs most courage to survive.

At this point in the novel we surely pity her; and our attitude has by now become a most searching moral comment upon ourselves. Of course we have to judge as well as pity, but have we, as readers, earned the right to judge? Have we even any pity that rings true, or that Becky will need or be prepared to accept if it does? Again and again Thackeray reminds us that we, too, belong to Vanity Fair. To condemn Becky easily is a *a fortiori* to condemn ourselves; how are we to make any judgement without resorting to hypocrisies deeper and more shameful than her own? The imaginative power of Thackeray's vision forces the reality of this dilemma upon us: some further dimension must be sought before we can be sure that we have the right. Should it be the religious dimension, perhaps, to which the word 'vanity' directs us? Or the political one, to which the whole analysis of class and money appears to point?

As I have already insisted, we can by no means be sure how far Thackeray would have committed himself in such ways. He was no religious mystic, though he catches the profound melancholy of the contemplative; nor was he a political agitator, though the moral of *Vanity Fair* might have seemed obvious to Karl Marx. Most of his explicit comments reinforce the notion that he is criticising human individuals rather than the structure of society as a whole, yet the novel's pattern, I have tried to show, prevents us from leaving the matter comfortably at this.

Perhaps Thackeray never did decide how far the poison at work in Vanity Fair is a social sin, which decisive social action might remove, and how far it is a personal flaw, an ineradicable vanity in the heart of man. The lack of a clear-cut answer may account in part for his restlessness, which we always sense behind the apparently easy elegance of the style. Religious and political solutions can, however, be a form of glibness themselves. Can we expect Thackeray to offer a clearer answer to such problems than we have worked out for ourselves? For at least a hundred years now the Western mind has been discovering enigmas and doubts. In extending our understanding and compassion, Thackeray does the work a novelist is chiefly concerned to do.

V

This brings us to the novel's true greatness, to its claim to be one of the undoubtedly major novels that we have. It was Charlotte Brontë, one of Thackeray's earliest admirers, who said:

> It is 'sentiment' in my sense of the term — sentiment jealously hidden, but genuine, which extracts the venom from that formidable Thackeray, and converts what might be corrosive poison into purifying elixir.
>
> If Thackeray did not cherish in his large heart deep feeling for his kind, he would delight to exterminate: as it is, I believe, he wishes only to reform.

The 'deep feeling' and 'corrosive poison' are not opposites, but simply different sides of a unified response to life. We sense the capacity for the former in Thackeray's great sonorous phrases about vanity: 'Yes, this is Vanity Fair; not a moral place certainly; nor a merry one, though very noisy'; we sense it in the sympathy we are made to feel for nearly all of the characters, even when — and perhaps especially when — we have also seen them at their worst. Mr Osborne's selfishness and tyranny are strongly realised, yet his suffering when George dies is none the less powerful and real. Thackeray is able to make us feel pity for a man like ourselves even as we probe the bitter impurities of grief:

> And it is hard to say which pang it was tore the proud father's heart more keenly — that his son should have gone out of the reach of forgiveness, or that the apology which his own pride expected should have escaped him.

Mr Sedley also becomes, in his ruin, a broken and pathetic figure; even Miss Crawley comes to an end which we feel to be worse than she deserves.

The most remarkable example of Thackeray's compassion, however, is surely to be found in his dealings with Amelia. The strategy of her characterisation is at least as subtle as Becky's, though there are somewhat different ends in view. In writing of Amelia earlier, I stressed the main intention of Thackeray's irony: he tries to trap us into an easy and arch indulgence towards her in order to shatter this, later, with a very damaging moral critique. But this is half the story only, and not the half that matters most. It is in keeping with the subtlety we expect from a major novelist that our disillusionment with Amelia should contain a further trap of its own. The swing from simple indulgence to simple censure is easy to make; too easy if morality is to be very much more than a game. By shifting the tone of his irony in various puzzling ways, Thackeray invites us not only to see the causes of judgement, but to probe their validity. With Amelia as with Becky, in fact, we are made to look beyond conventional judgements to that true situation — more costly to contemplate — which we so often miss. When Thackeray rebukes our easy sentimentality towards Amelia, he is clearing the way not for cynicism, but for pity of a truer kind. Cynicism indeed is not the opposite to sentimentality but its twin, another kind of shallowness which we too easily swing towards when rebuked. We discover that though sentimental indulgence is a travesty of compassion, clear-sighted judgement ought to be simply a stepping-stone on the way. What Thackeray makes us see is that Amelia is an incurably neurotic woman, destined to unhappiness whether things go well with her or ill. The contrast between herself and Becky is to some degree a contrast between robust mental health and mental defeat. Becky survives even the gravest hardships and rebuffs, Amelia remains fearful even when she achieves, or seems to achieve, her heart's desire. The comments Thackeray makes upon her are always delicately poised. Soon after her marriage — far too soon — we read:

> Her heart tried to persist in asserting that George Osborne was worthy and faithful, though she knew otherwise.

Amelia's 'knowledge' is really, of course, a fear: it is the presentiment of evil which always besets her, as a measure, perhaps, of her own inadequacy. It is also, however, a justified fear; one senses that she is the kind of person whose fears create situations in which they are most likely to be fulfilled. Though her fears are described as knowledge, moreover, and though paranoia converts fears into 'knowledge' in this way, this is not a knowledge by which she chooses to live. Her fears are true, in a manner which only culpable self-deception could fail to see, yet after George's death Amelia suppresses them, building instead a myth of his absolute devotion by which to live. This, in turn, becomes a mode of evasion, both of her responsibilities as a daughter and as a mother, and of the ever-present challenge of Dobbin's love. The suggestions clustering around this situation are typical of Thackeray's complex sense of reality. Even apart from the obvious weakness of Amelia's conduct, its underlying selfishness is relentlessly exposed. She never really considers Dobbin, or anyone else apart from herself — and this despite the fact that self-sacrifice is the virtue always attributed to her, the virtue that she would claim for herself. Further ironies open out from such perceptions. Is Dobbin's fidelity to the living but unresponsive Amelia entirely different from Amelia's fidelity to the dead George? Might not Dobbin's love, unbeknown to Amelia, be the one experience that could have quietened her fears and given her peace?

Our awareness of these cross-currents is beautifully stage-managed; and represents one of Thackeray's most interesting challenges to ourselves. The material for censoriousness is offered in abundance, but is censoriousness the most human response we can make? Not, surely, if we think of life as it is, with all its perversities; with all its intolerable perplexities and burdens, especially for the lonely and weak. Most of the judgements just suggested against Amelia are touched with glibness: true in a sense they may be, but the whole truth is a bigger and more saddening affair. The kind of love Amelia lavishes on George may be excessive, but had he been worthy of it, the situation could have been transformed. If Amelia had had the good luck to fall in love with Dobbin, her particular virtues might have been productive, not sour, her lack of intelligence and talent might have mattered scarcely at all. One might blame her, perhaps, for preferring George's good looks to Dobbin's plainness (and indeed if there is a sensualist in the book, Amelia rather than Becky fills the role). But life is like that after all; since we cannot fall in love to order, can Amelia's evasiveness about Dobbin be wholly and honestly blamed? It may also be that certain types of tenderness, of self-sacrifice and reticence, can take root only in such soil as Amelia provides. When Mr Sedley on his death-bed repents of the harshness he and his wife have shown towards Amelia, he may be recognising a true flaw in their treatment of her (surely he is), and not simply indulging a last nostalgia in the moment of death.

We rush too easily into censoriousness when reading novels, as Thackeray well knew; the luxury of catching fictional characters out in errors can be very readily mistaken for unusual moral maturity in ourselves. Compassion is better than censure, in literature as in life; by involving us as he does with his characters, Thackeray makes this more than usually plain. It is just when we want to judge most harshly that he allows his stress to fall another way — on the perversity of circumstances and the shortness of time, on the need for forgiveness which embraces us all. The most memorable moments in the novel are those when this insight comes to the surface, and the deep currents of feeling crystallise in phrases we are never likely to forget. The tormented striving, the enigma, the restlessness give way to a grander sense of human solitude and need. Things go wrong for this character or that beyond any deserving, and we see him confronting the world bewildered and alone. There is the poignant moment just before Waterloo, when George comes in late to Amelia after his flirtation with Becky, to be with her, as it turns out, for the last time:

> Two fair arms closed tenderly round his neck as he stooped down. 'I am awake, George,' the poor child said, with a sob fit to break the little heart that nestled so closely by his own.

And there are other moments, no less pure and heart-rending, that we remember: Mr Sedley's confession to his wife of his loss of money, in words as desolating as they are brief:

> 'We're ruined, Mary. We've got the world to begin over again, dear.'

and little Rawdon Crawley's reaction when the mother whom he once idolised boxes his ears before Lord Steyne:

'It is not because it hurts me,' little Rawdon gasped out — 'only — only' — sobs and tears wound up the sentence in a storm. It was the little boy's heart that was bleeding. 'Why mayn't I hear her singing? Why don't she ever sing to me — as she does to that bald-headed man with the large teeth?'

We remember, too, Becky's own reflections, characteristically tough, yet hardly less poignant for that, when during her later wanderings she thinks again of the husband she has lost:

'If he'd been here' she said, 'these cowards would never have dared to insult me.' She thought about 'him' with great sadness, and perhaps longing — about his honest, stupid, constant kindness and fidelity, his never-ceasing obedience, his good-humour; his bravery and courage. Very likely she cried, for she was particularly lively, and had put on a little extra rouge when she came down to dinner.

To all of us in Vanity Fair, the weak and the strong, the proud and the humble, the good and the bad, there come such moments, when after the bustle and gaiety, the hoping and working, the striving and fearing, we find ourselves downcast and alone. At such moments, in Thackeray's depiction of them, all the irony and cynicism, the hatred of worldliness and scorn of fools, gives way to this note of a deeper compassion:

Ah! *Vanitas Vanitatum!* which of us is happy in this world? Which of us has his desire? or, having it, is satisfied?—, Come children, let us shut up the box and the puppets, for our play is played out.

CHAPTER 7

MARK TWAIN: *HUCKLEBERRY FINN* AND THE WHOLE TRUTH

I

IF Shakespeare's 'fatal Cleopatra' was the quibble, Mark Twain's was the practical joke, or so his readers at times are tempted to think. 'How could he?' we wonder, as we move towards the end of *Huckleberry Finn*. It is not only that our sense of Jim's dignity is outraged as he is sacrificed to Tom Sawyer's nigger-minstrel antics, nor is it merely reluctance to concede that Huck's exquisite sense of values, tested and proved throughout the novel, can fail once more before Tom's adolescent and unreflecting romanticism. What worries us most of all, I think, is the suspicion that a great work of art is being sold out to a schoolboy sense of fun. Tom himself might conceivably turn Jim's predicament into a farce. He hasn't lived through the experience of the raft, morally he is less sensitive than Huck. He knows, moreover, that Jim is already freed, so that his attitude is at least understandable in human terms. But how can Huck and Jim accept the situation as they do? How, above all, can Mark Twain? We look back at that most famous and disregarded of warnings from writer to reader at the beginning ('Persons attempting to find a motive in this narrative will be prosecuted; persons attempting to find a moral in it will be banished; persons attempting to find a plot in it will be shot'), and wonder.

The ending has not, however, lacked its distinguished defenders. T. S. Eliot and Lionel Trilling have both found the return from Huck's world to Tom Sawyer's structurally appropriate. 'It is right,' says Eliot, 'that the mood of the book should bring us back to the beginning'; 'a certain formal aptness,' comments Trilling. Leo Marx, in an interesting recent essay, has taken them both to task for this. What really counts in a novel, he thinks, is not structural but moral appropriateness, and in this the end of *Huckleberry Finn* is lacking. It is here that I tend for my own part to differ from him, as to some extent from all the critics I have read on the work. Lionel Trilling's general moral claim for *Huckleberry Finn* is that it tells the truth, and to my mind this claim extends to the ending not in the somewhat desultory way he suggests, but as part of the logic and texture of the whole book. The raft, paradoxically idyllic though life on it seems, has to tie up somewhere; and if one honestly favours the whole truth, the return to land at the end, with its lessening tension and its gradual descent from clear-cut decencies and responsibilities to the more muddled ones of everyday life is the only ending that will really, over a long period, ring true.

But this is to jump ahead: best to start, perhaps, from the irony, which is the clearest clue to Mark Twain's intentions that we have, providing a far firmer unity for the work than it gets from the pleasantly picaresque and rambling plot. Twain's sense of the incongruous rubs shoulders with the practical joke at many points, but it also ranges through much of the spectrum of irony, sometimes seeming most at home as it approaches the tragic. 'Everything human is pathetic,' as Twain himself once wrote. 'The secret source of humour itself is not joy but sorrow. There is no humour in heaven.' Ernest Hemingway, taking his cue perhaps from this, has gone to the extreme of seeing *Huckleberry Finn* as a novel moved by its own powerful insights in one direction, and wrested away again only by the deliberate sabotage of the author. 'If you read it,' he says, 'you must stop where the nigger Jim is stolen by the boys. This is the real end. The rest is cheating.' Yet the true state of affairs, I believe, is that Mark Twain followed the fluctuations of human fortune more subtly than this or any similar view allows. His irony approaches both the comic and the tragic, as most truly great irony does, but it finally rests in neither. Its essential insight can be more usefully linked with the 'whole fortune' of Huck and his father, as Jim tells it at dead of night, using a hair ball out of the fourth stomach of an ox.

   Yo' ole father doan' know, yit, what he's a-gwyne to do. Sometimes he spec he'll go 'way, en den agin he spec he'll stay. De bes' way is to res' easy en let de ole man take his own way. Dey's two angels hoverin' roun' 'bout him. One uv' em is white en shiny, en t'other one is black. De white one gits him to go right, a little while, den de black one sail in en bust it all up. A body can't tell, yit, which one gwyne to fetch him at de las'. But you is all right. You gwyne to have considable trouble in yo' life, en considable joy. Sometimes you gwyne to git hurt, en sometimes you gwyne to git sick; but every time you's gwyne to git well agin. . . .

Mark Twain, like Jim's hair ball, responds to life as a gamble, with good and bad endlessly struggling together, neither actually winning, but neither cancelling the other out. The two angels hover, and there is no telling which will come to fetch us at the last. The fate of Huck's father is dubious, but Huck himself? If he takes the rough along with the smooth all will be well with him, though death in one form or another will be waiting at the last. As a philosophy of life we are normally inclined, I believe, to think of such ideas as naïve, and one of Twain's triumphs is to show how much better they stand up to actual experience than the more sophisticated beliefs of Miss Watson and the widow. Throughout *Huckleberry Finn* good and evil are shown co-existing in Nature as well as in man. The squirrel Huck sees as a natural friend, the snake as a natural enemy: why? — because the one he can live with, embracing its faults with his tolerance, and the other he can't. There is an acceptance of fact here which is not only part of Huck's unsentimental common sense, but part too of the common sense of Mark Twain himself manipulating the irony. Most human minds gravitate towards either optimism or pessimism; there is a constant temptation to think that either good or bad will 'win' in the end. Mark Twain, like Huck, does not share this view — which is why his irony never settles in either a comic or a tragic mould, and why his ending is deliberately less conclusive than either would require.

Doubts about the ending of *Huckleberry Finn* cluster around another misconception, not dissimilar to the one of Hemingway I have been considering. This is the very common error of regarding the novel as a simple contrast between *two* worlds — the one civilised, insensitive and corrupt, the other uncivilised, sensitive and humane. The widow, 'dismal, regular and decent' as Huck calls her, is seen as typical of the former, Huck himself and Jim as typical of the latter. Tom Sawyer, while having many fine qualities, belongs basically to the widow's world; and Twain's irony is taken to be the playing off of the genuine against the conventional, the good, if one likes, against the bad.

Now though this is true in that the values achieved on the raft are used for an ironic survey of society at large, I am convinced that to put the matter so simply is misleading. For one thing it overlooks, as most criticism does, the importance of the Duke, the King and Huck's father. These are all much further away from the 'respectable' folk than Huck himself is, yet they are the most decisively evil characters in the book. One has only to recall them to be aware that Jim stands less hope of mercy from this group than he does from Miss Watson and Tom, and that a straight choice of 'outsider' against 'insider' is not at all what is being presented. Nor is this all. The eventual freeing of Jim comes about not through the journey on the raft, but through a change of heart in his former owner. The method by which it happens is muddled, the insights behind it are less pure, to put the matter mildly, than those of the raft, yet the fact of freedom comes from Miss Watson's dying request, and from the camp of the respectable. In allowing this, Mark Twain is not 'selling out' the rest of the novel, as some commentators assume, but simply being faithful to the realism which makes us trust him all along. Respectable morality, though muddled and sometimes cruel, does have certain ideals behind it: the ideals, indeed, which Huck himself embodies in a purer form, outside society, and paradoxically in defiance of it. The world of the widow and of Miss Watson might be blinkered, and provided with blind eyes for all occasions; it might recoil with horror from its own more Christian ideals when despite every precaution it catches sight of them. But it is myopic rather than totally blind, thoughtlessly rather than wilfully cruel. Miss Watson's request in her will is the beginning, maybe, of a challenge to the system of slavery from inside; a moment without which no purer moral protest, however noble, would stand much hope of eventually winning the majority to its side. If we think historically, we shall see that her dying decision to free Jim, despite the fact that he has sinned both against herself and against the economic system by escaping,

H

may be as important a landmark on the road to emancipation as the dangerous quest for freedom on the raft itself. Actual humane progress does come about, whether we like it or not, through muddled insights, muddled kindliness, muddled actions as much as from the straightforward vindication of ideals. Twain's ending draws attention to this, too, and it is part of the whole truth he has to tell.

At the end, the values of the raft are assimilated to the pattern of life seen steadily and as a whole. Could Mark Twain really have shown Huck and Jim simply winning through to freedom, without violating history and contriving an ending we should have doubted? Could any conceivable ending, on the other hand, have really betrayed the realities of the raft, in such a way that we should retrospectively doubt them? The final balance is one in which we see what has been achieved on the raft as real rather than illusory, yet exceptional rather than normative. And this, I am sure, is what the author intended.

For consider the journey itself. During the course of it, Huck and Jim are living in a very special world, from which almost all the distinctive data of human living have been removed. There is no sex on the raft, no politics, no formal worship, no money, no status. There are no traditional sanctions, either. Huck is unimpressed by dead people, including Moses; even his Conscience turns out to be a Trojan Horse smuggled in by the enemy, not a genuine moral inheritance from the past. There is, however, in this apparent vacuum, and in the strenuous business of survival which occupies it, a fundamental human decency at work which is the ground for all good manifestations of sex, politics, worship, money, status, wherever they occur. In being driven outside society, Huck and Jim are given an occasion to transcend it. Their tenderness and affection for one another is the condition of all good relationships, private or public; their sensitivity to the grandeur and mystery of nature and to the suffering of men is the condition for all true reverence; their deep sense of responsibility, and their natural dignity, are a condition for all uses of money and status that can ever deserve respect. In the world of the raft, they represent a type of pre-morality; a decency outside civilisation, which is both a seed for all that grows good inside it, and a touchstone for all that turns bad. To achieve the raft, Huck has to renounce everything — his father, his money, even his official life; Jim, to achieve it, has to be betrayed even by his owner, and to be driven to complete isolation. In the ensuing events, totally exiled from humanity, the two of them achieve the highest type of relationship of which humanity is capable. The paradox involved in this is not overlooked; it is, indeed, the impetus of much of the irony. Yet Huck and Jim are not mistaken for, or presented as, a norm. Their morality cannot exist permanently without social contexts, and when it returns to these it will be unable, perhaps, to exist as purely and unambiguously as it does on the raft. At the end, they return to the world where their values, never articulate at the best of times, will become clouded again by the mesh of actuality. When this happens, the raft will remain as a memory, and as a leaven. And this, in fact, is what happens. We are left with the assurance that there is, in man, a power for good as well as bad and that good is worth fighting for; we are not left with the assurance that the power for good is normally or easily followed, or that it will necessarily win.

II

But at this point we must approach Mark Twain's irony more directly. At one end of the scale, as we know, there are the practical jokes — the simple incongruities of fooling people which are usually associated with Tom Sawyer, though Huck can be his uneasy partner at times. Tom Sawyer has often been called a 'romantic', and so he is, if one uses the word to mean, not necessarily with disrespect, the adolescent and the immature. In a fairly obvious way, he is a distinguished example of a type familiar in British boys' books of the period — healthy, good natured, full of animal spirits, a born leader of men. He flirts with the terrible as he does with Becky Thatcher, courting death and glory without being entirely aware of what he is doing, and without therefore being entirely serious. His immaturity is ironically underlined, yet Mark Twain sympathises with Tom in important ways. He likes his boisterousness, his courage, his lively fancy, his sentimentality, his *joie de vivre*. Tom is the sort of lad that Dr Arnold would also have been happy with at Rugby; a Christian boy? — hardly; a Christian gentleman? — yes, given time, that is just what he will be. His unreflecting, limited but not uncostly decency is a pre-eminently respectable virtue; unlikely, as Huck knows, to engage in such eccentric enormities as nigger emancipation, especially at this stage of history, but to be relied on nonetheless for goodwill to all men in so far as expediency and the general good permit. His immaturity is of the type which, properly nurtured, passes unscathed through adolescence into manhood, protecting the ruling class by and large, with all its gifts, its virtues and its opportunities, from producing too many radicals, intellectuals, artists and others disruptive of the *status quo*. He is a good empire-building type; an adventurous extrovert, as Mark Twain himself was; far more fit than Huck to be running the world, and far more likely to be doing so. Even his naughtiness exists, as one critic has pointed out, only inside the limits that he knows are expected of him. And his make-believe, like his jesting, goes to show that though his fancy is lively, his imagination — and especially his moral imagination — is dulled and conventional. Moral imagination — the response to people and to events with direct insight and sympathy — is exactly, of course, the quality in which Huck excels. This is why Huck is never wholly at ease with Tom, though he naturally looks up to him. It is also why Huck is peculiarly fitted to see the deepest moral truths, though he is at the same time peculiarly unfitted to articulate them, or to set about making them prevail.

Practical joking, and its implications, is only the start of our enquiry. Mark Twain's sense of the discrepancies between one world and another goes beyond the gulf between schoolboy fantasy and reality; the more basic gulf between Tom and Huck is the clue that leads towards the heart of the matter. Consider, for example, the following passage, in which two essentially adult worlds are held in sharp contrast.

Then Miss Watson she took me in the closet and prayed, but nothing come of it. She told me to pray every day, and whatever I asked for I would get it. But it warn't so. I tried it. Once I got a fish-line, but no hooks. It warn't any good to me without hooks. I tried for the hooks three or four times, but somehow I couldn't make it work. By and by, one day, I asked Miss Watson to try for me, but she said I was a fool. She never told me why, and I couldn't make it out no way.

I set down, one time, back in the woods, and had a long think about it. I says to myself, if a body can get anything they pray for, why don't Deacon Winn get back the money he lost on pork? Why can't the widow get back her silver snuff-box that was stole? Why can't Miss Watson fat up? No, says I to myself, there ain't nothing in it. I went and told the widow about it, and she said the thing a body could get by praying for it was 'spiritual gifts'. This was too many for me, but she told me what she meant — I must help other people, and do everything I could for other people, and look out for them all the time, and never think about myself. This was including Miss Watson, as I took it. I went out in the woods and turned it over in my mind a long time, but I couldn't see no advantage about it — except for the other people — so at last I reckoned I wouldn't worry about it any more, but just let it go. Sometimes the widow would take me on one side and talk about Providence in a way to make a body's mouth water; but maybe next day Miss Watson would take hold and knock it all down again. I judged I could see that there was two Providences, and a poor chap would stand considerable show with the widow's Providence, but if Miss Watson's got him there warn't no help for him any more. I thought it all out, and reckoned I would belong to the widow's, if he wanted me, though I couldn't make out how he was a-going to be any better off then than what he was before, seeing I was so ignorant and so kind of low-down and ornery.

The irony here is not generated by Huck's conscious attitude. When he sees through people himself, as he often does, it is only after 'thinking it all out', and then with a shrewd and charitable insight far removed from any tone that would lead to irony, or that an ironist himself could adopt. Though Huck tells the story, in other words, the irony comes directly from the author behind Huck; it is a communication to the reader in which the narrator has no share. Where, then, is the irony aimed? Are the widow and Miss Watson its targets? To some extent, yes; their piety is unreflecting, and their dealings with Huck are less than intelligent. Yet they mean well, as Huck correctly allows, and their belief in prayer and in Providence is not entirely

discredited, though it is damaged, by Huck's reflections. Might
the irony, then, be at the expense of Huck? On a superficial reading we are tempted to think so, and it is here that Mark Twain's
most basic moral trap exists for the reader: if we think that Huck
is the victim, we are in fact the victims ourselves. For Mark
Twain is neither here nor elsewhere a civilised man glancing
with superior amusement at ignorance — his is not the irony
of a Gibbon, or a Lytton Strachey; nor is he an indulgent
father smiling at the errors of a favourite child — still less is it
the irony of a Lamb. Though at first sight Huck's reasoning is
deceptively schoolboyish, a moment's reflection reveals not its
folly, but its wisdom. For one thing, he pays the widow and
Miss Watson the compliment of taking them seriously, even
though what they say sounds to him like nonsense. He has the
humility and readiness to learn without which any education,
however sophisticated, cannot be more than a sham. But then
again, he has shrewdness and independence of judgement, the
qualities which are at the root of his remarkable moral honesty
and intelligence. Testing what he has been told against his own
experience of life and his own observation of people, he finds
grave reasons for doubting it. These doubts are anything but
ill-informed cynicism; they have a seriousness which places the
traditional piety of Miss Watson and the widow very exactly,
and it must be admitted very damagingly, for what they are.
Huck's own 'religious' awareness is governed by things he
knows — the mysterious grandeur of the river, the stars in the
night sky, the age-old folk-lore of good and bad omens, which
fit in with his sense of the splendours and uncertainties of life
better than doctrines of prayer that he can't make to work,
and tales of Providence, Heaven and Hell that relate to no
experiences he has had.

Huck is serious and honest, then; he is also kind and gentle.
It is these latter qualities which make the word 'wisdom' rather
than 'common sense' seem appropriate. He is sure that Miss
Watson and the widow are doing their best to educate him, and
he has no wish to hurt them by arguing. Whenever he can, he
gives them the benefit of the doubt. Prayer does work, perhaps,
for some folk, but not for the likes of him. This possibility he
accepts unselfconsciously and without bitterness. The fact that
he does so is part of the irony, but his obtuseness at this level,

unlike that of (say) Gulliver, reflects nothing but credit on
himself.

What one sees in this passage, more than anything else, is
Huck's selflessness and humanity, all the richer for the paradoxical form they take. For though he applies tests of self-
interest to prayer and Providence, and is quick to see that
Miss Watson herself is less disinterested than she might think,
it is his good sense, not his greed, that is proved. His real
selflessness can be easily seen in the readiness with which he
accepts himself as 'low-down and ornery' without, however,
making this an excuse for bitterness or irresponsibility, and in the
fine natural courtesy towards others which he invariably has. A
similar important paradox inheres in his lies. 'I never seen
anybody but lied, one time or another', he comments, but his
own lies are always related to a deeper honesty: fidelity to fact
and to good sense as he sees them. His lies, are, in fact, worked
out in the face of much he is asked to believe, evasive action
taken not because he is wilful or stupid, but because he is
generous and alive. They are a technique for surviving in a
largely immoral world with as little unpleasantness for himself
and for everyone else as possible. Jim, who shares Huck's
predicament, shares his attitude to lying. His greeting to Huck
when he first meets him during the escape, and thinks he must
be a ghost, is a splendid example of the type of lie which includes
in almost equal measure an instinct for survival, a deference to
fact however unexpected, genuine courtesy even to one as
beyond the pale as a ghost, and a sense that one outcast ought to
be able to appeal to the sympathy and goodwill of another,
even if naked truth isn't wholly expedient. 'Doan' hurt me —
don't! I hain't ever done no harm to a ghos'. I alwuz liked dead
people, en done all I could for 'em. You go en git in de river
agin, whah you b'longs, en doan' do nuffin to Ole Jim, 'at 'uz
alwuz yo' fren'.'

What, then, characterises this irony most? It does not score
points against people as its main aim, and is wholly untainted
with the assumption of superiority. At root, it is a juxtaposing
of two or more real worlds at points where they do not, and
cannot, meet. Both worlds exist, and though Huck's is the
more virtuous, that of Miss Watson and the widow is the more
usual. The irony offers a rich realism, the 'whole truth', as I am

calling it; but the whole truth shot through with a moral awareness without which such a description of it would not be deserved, and with a charity rare among writers who use irony at all.

III

The inevitable question concerning Mark Twain's values now presents itself. How far is *Huckleberry Finn* the expression of a clear preference, either for radicalism or for the noble savage? The answer is not clear-cut. If one tries Mark Twain out with some radical causes of the present day, he can sometimes seem reactionary. He would have been anti-apartheid, of course; if his irony is committed to any obvious 'cause' it is that. But he might well have been for hanging rather than against it, on the familiar grounds, abundantly clear in his work, that reformers interested only in kindness overlooked the grim realities of human evil, against which society must protect itself strongly, even ruthlessly, to survive. Huck's charity, it is true, transcends this, by way of an equally ruthless honesty on the other side. Confronted with the murderers trapped on the boat, he reflects: 'I began to think how dreadful it was, even for murderers, to be in such a fix. I says to myself, there ain't no telling but I might come to be a murderer myself, yet, and then how would I like it?' And when the Duke and the King have perpetrated every possible treachery against both himself and Jim, he can still spare them compassion in their own misery and suffering. But Mark Twain himself, on the whole, feels that murderers and others like them deserve what they get; as to the do-gooders like the new judge who thinks he can reform Huck's father by kindness, they come in for frequent satiric treatment at his hands.

Mark Twain takes evil seriously, in other words, and he believes that strong social law is necessary to combat it, even though law will be tainted with the defects of the class who make it. This becomes more obvious when one thinks of the really anti-social figures in *Huckleberry Finn*. Huck's father, the Duke and the King are all failures, who stand outside society not because they are too honest for it, like Huck, or unjustly discriminated against by it, like Jim, but simply because they are lazy, vicious, and by nature parasitic. The passage in which

Huck's father fulminates against the Government for tolerating an educated 'nigger' is irony of the straightforwardly boomerang kind, and of him, as of the other scoundrels in the book, there is no good word to be said. Though Huck understands and pities them, and sees himself partly in the same boat, he certainly does not approve of them, and he is nothing like them himself. In an important sense, they represent what happens when the respectable virtues are rejected outright — the good like duty, justice, responsibility along with the bad — and for Twain the last state is clearly worse than the first.

Huck himself, and to a great extent Jim, are wholly different from this. They represent not the rejection of society's highest values, but their fulfilment. The irony here is that society rejects Huck for being too good; by living up to its own ideals he becomes unfamiliar, and offers a challenge which can easily be mistaken for something stupid, or sceptical, or subversive. On the raft, Huck and Jim become what Lionel Trilling has called a 'community of saints'; yet their values come not from the civilised society which is supposed to encourage saints, but from the older incentive of a common danger, a common humanity, a common predicament.

It is here that the most penetrating ironic effects take place. The fact that Huck thinks himself worse, rather than better, than his fellows leads to the major irony that from first to last he sees the help he gives Jim as a sin; and the notion of selling Jim back into bondage can repeatedly present itself as a prompting to repentance and virtue. There are the harrowing moments when he wavers; and the final victory when he says 'All right, I'll go to Hell then' is all the more powerful for being unrecognised by Huck himself as savouring of either paradox or irony.

Nor should one underestimate the nature of Huck's stand at this moment. A large part of the country's economy depended on slavery, and one knows for a fact that even tender consciences have difficulty in seeing very clearly when this is so. Again and again the point is underlined. The question is asked, 'Anyone hurt?', and Huck answers, quite naturally, 'No mum; one nigger killed.' The doctor towards the end of the tale assumes that recapturing a runaway slave is a more pressing moral duty than attending to a patient. Huck himself is horrified to think that Tom Sawyer might have degenerated into a 'nigger stealer', and is relieved to discover that this is not so. All of this may be slightly exaggerated for purposes of the irony, but truth can sometimes defy a satirist to improve upon it for his purpose. The depth to which an economic condition causes moral blindness is deeper, at any rate, than Huck's conscious moralising can reach. Huck really thinks he *is* being wicked, and the irony here cuts straight from writer to reader, by-passing Huck himself, though enhancing his stature.

One can see, from this central point, what Mark Twain is really doing. Though he rejects ideals that strike him as facile or dangerous, he holds passionately to the conviction that underlies all true radical feeling: namely, that all men should be treated as equally human, irrespective of the natural or man-made barriers of colour, class, belief or what you will. That men are not equally good he acknowledges, and that some are too bad to be tolerated he also admits. But that a man should be despised simply for being brought up in poverty, like Huck, or for being the wrong colour, like Jim, fills him with outrage. In presenting the pair of them as the salt of the earth he is making a most profoundly radical point. He is also doing more. The decency of Huck and Jim offers some hope for the human species itself: an original virtue, perhaps, constantly departed from, and paradoxically exiled, yet ultimately not to be eradicated from the human heart.

The episode I now want to consider is the very famous one, felt by many readers to be the high point of the novel's greatness. Huck, having been separated from Jim in a fog, and been mourned by him as dead, returns, and plays a joke of Tom Sawyer's kind. (It is very similar, in fact, to the one played by Tom Sawyer on Aunt Polly in the earlier book.) Jim's honest joy at seeing him again he puts down to drink: he hasn't been away, he says, Jim must have imagined it all. So great is Jim's trust in Huck, that he sits thinking for five minutes, and then decides to believe Huck before the evidence of his own senses. 'Well, den, I reck'n I did dream it, Huck; but dog my cats ef it ain't de powerfullest dream I ever see.' Huck allows Jim to give an account of the 'dream', together with an ingenious interpretation, and at the end, by pointing out certain things which do not fit in, makes Jim realise that he has been fooled. The episode continues as follows.

MARK TWAIN 109

Jim looked at the trash, and then looked at me, and back at the trash again. He had got the dream fixed so strong in his head that he couldn't seem to shake it loose and get the facts back into its place again, right away. But when he did get the thing straightened around, he looked at me steady, without ever smiling, and says:

'What do dey stan' for? I's gwyne to tell you. When I got all wore out wid work, en wid de callin' for you, en went to sleep, my heart wuz mos' broke bekase you wuz los', en I didn' k'yer no mo' what become er me en de raf'. En when I wake up en fine you back agin', all safe en soun', de tears come en I could a got down on my knees en kiss' yo' foot I's so thankful. En all you wuz thinkin' 'bout wuz how you could make a fool uv ole Jim wid a lie. Dat truck dah is *trash*; en trash is what people is dat puts dirt on de head er dey fren's en makes 'em ashamed'.

Then he got up slow, and walked to the wigwam, and went in there, without saying anything but that. But that was enough. It made me feel so mean I could almost kissed *his* foot to get him to take it back.

It was fifteen minutes before I could work myself up to go and humble myself to a nigger — but I done it, and I warn't sorry for it afterwards, neither. I didn't do him no more mean tricks, and I wouldn't done that one if I'd a knowed it would make him feel that way.

Almost any comment on this is bound to be clumsy; it is one of the most memorable moments in literature. In Tom Sawyer's world, a joke of this type would be more or less in order; personal relationships matter less, affections, emotions, sensibility are all blunted or suppressed to the necessary degree. Here, on the raft, it is supremely wrong, as Huck comes to *feel*, as usual without entirely understanding why. In fact, the lies he has told Jim are not his type of lies, and his moral imagination has for once let him down. The law of the raft has been broken, and personal affection sacrificed to a cheap, though not malicious, victory on points. The behaviour of Huck and Jim at this moment, free as it is of the sentimentality or the embarrassment which normally surrounds and inhibits such feelings, is both moving and authentic. The values of the raft here reach a moment of undeniable and unforgettable reality.

IV

Mark Twain's irony, I have insisted, is a direct communication between the writer and reader. No one at all in the novel, including Huck, knows that the raft is a place of virtue; it is the secret communication of the irony. Mark Twain's greatness as a writer can be demonstrated from the skill with which he uses Huck's obtuseness about his own worth as part of his own technique, yet enhances rather than damages him as a person in so doing. It can also be shown from the lack of any arbitrary traps in his work of the Swiftian kind. The reader is challenged wholly at the level of moral response; failure to perceive the direction of the irony is indistinguishable from failure to perceive Huck's virtue. The irony is, indeed, a forcing into the consciousness of readers more educated than Huck himself the reality, as he embodies them, of their own ideals.

The end of the novel, I have contended, is the final insight that Twain has to offer, the final twist of his technique towards truth. It is right, psychologically and historically as well as structurally, that Tom Sawyer should come into the ascendant again; he is, after all, a leader, and Huck and Jim will naturally start trusting him again more than they trust themselves. We can be sure, however, that whatever happens to Huck, as the long process of 'civilising' him starts afresh, he will be a good man. The values which Twain's irony have been establishing will stand more chance of survival because he is in the world, even though they will never have an unambiguous victory. There will be a redemptive possibility at the heart of what Mark Twain elsewhere calls the 'damned human race', underlying the cruelty, the muddle and the squalor. Naïve cynicism, like naïve idealism, will not after all have the last word.

For the rest? Goodness might not have a sure triumph, Mark Twain seems to imply, but it has some claim on the universe nonetheless. Huck's enjoyment of life, his honesty, his reverence and charity deserve to be respected; whatever happens he will somehow be all right, as Jim says when telling his fortune. The claim might be solely by way of our own human moral sense; the Mississippi itself will flow on, caring little who worships and enjoys it and who does not. Yet Huck and Jim, with whatever indifference the river might return their worship, remain undefeated, and one feels it is right that they should. This, too, is part of Mark Twain's feeling for life; a reason why Hemingway is wrong to say he cheats at the end, why Dr Leavis, Lionel Trilling and others are right to find him one of the great writers of moral health.

CHAPTER 8

SAMUEL BUTLER: THE HONEST SCEPTIC

I

BUTLER is something of a puzzle, like all major ironists. Are we to regard him as a classic satirist, in the line of Swift? That *Erewhon* is closely modelled on *Gulliver* scarcely needs to be said. Both works set out as traveller's tales, but soon unmask themselves as satiric fantasy. The appearance of realism is a fraud, intended only to cover some preliminary sleight-of-hand. What the opening scenes leave us with as the fantasy gets under way are two flesh-and-blood heroes, whose physical courage we already admire, but whose mental and moral courage has still to be tested. Are the views of these heroes in any way the same as their author's? They may or may not be, and the satire is largely a challenge to us to find out. Certainly Mr Higgs[1] leads us a remarkable dance, as Gulliver did before him. The fact that he is also a more rounded character than Gulliver does not necessarily make it easier for us to grasp what Butler is about.

But Butler's affinity with Swift goes further than this. There is a high degree of technical virtuosity in his work; a curious and distinctive energy of tone, running at times to flamboyance, which co-exists with a serious and even embittered content. And there is an iconoclasm which lashes out at traditions that have been valued beyond their true worth, or for the wrong reasons, or in simple defiance of the *Zeitgeist*. His main irony was reserved for the Christian Religion and the Victorian Family; for the very foundations of middle-class respectability, as it seemed to his age. But he was the last man to be trapped into alliances with others simply because they had some ideas in common with himself. His irony struck out also at the scientists and the

[1] The hero of *Erewhon* is unnamed, but in *Erewhon Revisited* he turns out to be Mr Higgs. I shall call him this throughout, for the sake of convenience.

progressive humanists. As Basil Willey has pointed out, he alienated almost every main party of his age in turn.

In all these ways, there is an obvious link with Swift. But in at least one way, and it is an important one, Butler differs decisively. For whereas Swift was a genuine rebel for all his Toryism, Butler's rebelliousness was of a curiously restricted kind. His views on religion were radical enough, as indeed were his views on sex. But on some matters he was at least as *bourgeois* as the class he normally attacked. Arguably he was even more *bourgeois*, since his strong regard for money, security and success was similar in kind to that of his middle-class contemporaries, and eccentric only in being so honestly, not to say blatantly, proclaimed.

The problems posed by this are distinctly odd. Many of Butler's beliefs are of the kind which we would expect to attract satire in their own right. Can he really be serious, we wonder, when he writes about money? Is his attitude to liberal Christianity really as ruthlessly dismissive as it sounds? Doubts about Butler's intentions extend to some of the most famous chapters in his work; and there is nothing unusual about this in itself. All ironists like to baffle us, to test our mental and moral agility as we read. But Butler, we feel, is sometimes caught in the ironic trap himself. The nuances of irony run ahead of the ironic intentions; the virtuosity escapes from any purpose that could be clearly and exactly expressed. There are moments when Theobald Pontifex himself seems to peer out at us through the ironic thickets. Is it possible that Butler might himself have been, just for short periods, of his father's party without knowing it?

I shall be returning to these disturbing questions later, but want first to say a little about Butler's life. With most satirists, this would be a dubious procedure to adopt. If a writer's life is really as dull as Butler's seems to have been, is this in any way relevant to a critic? Normally, I would be inclined to say 'no', but Butler's life *is* his art to an unusual degree. 'A man of five and thirty,' says Ernest Pontifex in *The Way Of All Flesh*, 'should no more regret not having had a happier childhood than he should regret not having been born a prince of the blood.' If Butler had acted upon this precept himself, hardly any of his creative work would have been done. Again and again his own childhood provides material for his work. Whole episodes are taken from real life into the novels with a minimum of alteration; *The Way Of All Flesh* comes as near to direct autobiography, in places, as any novel of its stature one can recall. Butler's awful Father and Mother, his still more awful Sister Harriet, are mediated to us in the portraits of the Pontifex family. And his own early upbringing is described, in all its gruesomeness, in the history of Ernest. There is a special emphasis on the two aspects of Butler's childhood that rankled most, his training for the Ministry of the Church, and the total ignorance of sexual matters in which he was kept. Ernest Pontifex comes off worse than his creator, it is true. Ernest is trapped first into Holy Orders and later into Holy Matrimony, with a spell in prison for Indecent Assault sandwiched between, whereas Butler managed to avoid all these hazards. But we are left in no doubt that one trained in this way went in danger of such a fate; and which of us today would doubt that he did? Ernest also manages to lose all of his money through trust in a plausible rogue, and here Butler was describing his own experience more or less directly. The same thing had happened to him, and a very great shock it had been.

The rest of Butler's private life also finds its way into his work in one form or another. There was his platonic friendship with Miss Savage, characterised as it was by tepid alternations between affection and fear rather than by the more dramatic polarity of love and hate. Miss Savage was intelligent, emancipated and deliciously naughty; her ideas struck Butler as an antidote to everything he disliked most in Victorian family life. In *The Way Of All Flesh* he translated her into the fairy-godmother figure of Aunt Alethea, who offers Ernest the benefit of lighthearted honesty while she lives, and a very considerable fortune after her death. But Aunt Alethea was beautiful as well as intelligent, whereas Miss Savage was inescapably ugly. And whereas Aunt Alethea in the novel is kept well in hand, Miss Savage in real life proved much less easy to manage. Sometimes she would be so excessively intelligent, emancipated and naughty all at once, that Butler's initial admiration would yield to an almost unbearable sense of strain. There was always, moreover, the terrible possibility that she might be trying to trap him into marriage, despite the acknowledged unorthodoxy of their views. This constant threat both terrified Butler and filled him with obscurely morbid feelings of guilt.

If Miss Savage provided satisfaction for Butler's intellectual needs, his animal ones were taken care of by a French lady, with far fewer complications or regrets. His sexual appetites were always strong; he seems to have regarded them as an end in themselves rather than as the basis for a stable relationship. Today, we might suspect behind his aversion to marriage some deep-seated fear of responsibility; I shall suggest later that this fear certainly exists in his works, whether it formed part of his personal life or not. It is worth pointing out, however, that frank acceptance of sexual freedom at this period demanded a certain courage, whatever unconscious fears we may choose to speculate upon as its cause. This courage is, of course, part of Butler's strength as a writer; it would be wrong to suggest that this aspect of Butler's life was any serious liability to his art. What one can say, perhaps, is that his male friendships take an unhappier turn, when he translates them into the novels, than his female ones. There were two strongly romantic friendships with young men that we know about, and these no doubt provided the emotional inspiration for Towneley in *The Way Of All Flesh* and George in *Erewhon Revisited*. But Towneley and George are by common consent among the least successful of his characters. It seems that when he allowed himself to be sentimental he lost not only his capacity for irony, but even the most basic sense of proportion.

This brief account of Butler's life is unlikely to surprise or dismay a modern reader; neither, however, is it likely to interest him very much. Our usual complaint will be that the pattern is too normal to excite us, the character we discern behind the pattern too timid to have a very general appeal. Surely a great many shy, intelligent people respond to life in very much this way? But the word 'timid' is the one we have to pause on. Certainly it seems justified when we look at his hesitations and fears, the consistent refusal of responsibility in his private affairs. But does it explain the risks he took in writing as he did? Does it explain (and of course it does not) the obvious stature of his work? His Victorian readers were constantly being shocked by him, and the capacity to shock, the vocation to shock one might call it, was always strong within him. For over and around

I

everything else that he did, here was one compulsion which would not be denied, much though he must sometimes have resented it; the compulsion which makes him seem to us so typically a Victorian writer, however deep his rebellion against Victorianism went. It was the compulsion, in short, to tell the truth. He was one of those men whose instinct for peace and quiet is not stronger, in the last resort, than the courage of his convictions. We might perhaps call it a George Washington Complex, in that it certainly exists but has not yet been christened by the psychologists, as far as I know. Butler seems to have realised that honesty was the only policy for him, whether it was also the best policy or not. This was the key quality which redeemed him from mediocrity as a man, just as it turned him as a writer into one of the greatest ironists we have had.

We can now approach the central oddity about Butler's satire, towards which all I have so far said has been pointing. And it is simply this: that his irony is classically satiric, but he is in no normal sense of the word an idealist. He feels little disgust for the sinful; what he appears to feel for them is contempt, not unmixed with fear. And the 'sinful' are not defined in any narrowly Victorian way, as we have already seen. His indignation is never called out by the fallible body as Swift's so often was; still less is it called out, as Carlyle's was, by the honestly doubting mind. What it does spring from is his unswerving belief in ordinary truth and honesty; a belief which most Victorians would have endorsed in theory, but which in practice — or in Butler's practice, at any rate — filled most of them with dismay. How well he knew his own contemporaries when he threw at them the famous taunt: 'equally horrified at hearing the Christian religion doubted or seeing it practised'. And how well such a vision of an age does, after all, lead on to satire, from the unbelieving and sceptical mind as well as from the idealistic and devout.

Butler's achievement was to generate in defence of normal honesty an intensity usually reserved for some more remarkable crusade; his whole talent was to direct against excessive idealism the satiric *animus* very often devoted to its cause. His notion of 'honesty', however, was more than a theoretical one. It included the down-to-earth conviction that most of us have little honest right to censure our neighbours, and still less honest right to dictate to them. His *saeva indignatio* is reserved almost exclusively for those who sin against these practical extensions of honest good sense: for the tyrants and hypocrites, whom all satirists abhor, and all societies can be depended upon to produce. In this important way, he is far more like Fielding and Twain than he is like Swift—while also being less vital and robust than they were; more given to earnestness, though in causes that earnestness is usually inclined to deplore.

I have suggested that Butler's honesty becomes hard to distinguish from rebellion against all forms of authority. Does this put him in the same camp as the primitivists, we have to ask, or even as the Romantics themselves? Certainly he believes in individual freedom, as they did. He shares their conviction that most of our ills can be traced to false forms of authority or restraint. His prime hatred, like theirs, is for all sorts and conditions of Father Figures; for priests and judges naturally, but for actual Fathers still more; for Canon Butler archetypally and most of all.

Despite these similarities, however, his practical sympathies fall very much outside those any primitivist or romantic would have. For whereas the primitivist views human nature with optimism, Butler's vision was less idealised and enchanted by far. And whereas the Romantic leaps very happily into abstractions, Butler's feet remained firmly on the ground. He had no yearning for revolutionary clean sweeps, no myth of a New Heaven and a New Earth shortly to be revealed. The freedoms he craved were on a homelier and more domestic scale: elbow room to be himself without interference; protection from the whims of idealists; an end to the endless babble of hypocrisy and cant. His real demand is not that we should change or redeem ourselves, but that we should honestly recognise ourselves for what we are. Looking round him, he sees a society which worships Christ with its lips but ignores him in its hearts; which denounces Mammon with its lips, but spends nine-tenths of its life in his service. And what he wants is that we should be honest about this. Why not ignore Christ if you disbelieve in him, is his challenge? Why not be respectful about Mammon, if you run your society wholly to his rules?

Butler's true indignation is not that of a Christian who sees his beliefs betrayed by its other adherents. It is the still deeper

indignation of a Non-Christian who sees Christians betraying
the one belief of any value they are supposed to uphold. In
theory the Church stood for honesty, as Butler himself did; in
practice, this was the very last virtue it was accustomed to have.
For surely, he felt, an honest Christian is a lapsed one? Surely
an honest Christendom would be a Christendom announcing
its final collapse? But the collapse of Christendom appeared
to be as far away as ever; and meanwhile an honest unbeliever
had to live in the shadow of creeds that were incredible, and of
morals that no clearsighted moralist could endorse. To make
matters worse, Butler believed that one should give worship of
an honest kind in one's life, both to God and to Mammon; but
to a God much less personal than the Christian one; to a
Mammon restored almost to innocence by the resolute refusal
of cant.

And so one can see how rebelliousness and conservatism met
in this rather remarkable man. For his rebelliousness was in the
cause of a quiet life — which was exactly what an honest man
was denied by the nineteenth-century society to which he
belonged. The mood of his satire can be best summed up in a
series of heartfelt negatives: not to be interfered with in his
private affairs; not to be dominated by tyrants; not to be
pestered by hypocrites; not to be forced to say he believed things
he did not believe; not to be forced to pretend he was not a
sexual being when he was; not to have to set the human ideal
too high, and then have to bemoan its unattainability; not
to have to pretend he disapproved of money when in common
with ninety-nine out of a hundred of his fellow men he thought
it the prime requirement for a happy life. What he wanted,
more positively, was to be normal and decent, respectable and
honest, but in a *human* way; not in the forced and strained
manner that Christianity has managed to impose. Surely it
should be possible, he is always implying, to cultivate religious
and sexual frankness, to live a basically good-natured life
without having too many damned ideals? Of course it was not
possible in the late nineteenth century, just as it is not possible
to any very great degree today. But if it is a little more possible
now than it was for Butler, we ought to honour him as a pioneer
of the change. Whether we agree with his personal ideas about
sex and religion or not, most of us are probably in favour of the

freedom to have personal ideas on these matters, for which he fought.

Enough has been said to establish the basic seriousness of Butler's ideas. But what are we to make of his naughtiness? It was G. D. H. Cole who drew attention to Butler's naughtiness, in an admirable little study of the man. And this may be just the clue needed to lead us to the heart of his ironic technique. One cannot imagine Prometheus defying Zeus in a mood of naughtiness; one cannot conceive of Blake finding anything naughty in his own very frank views about sex. No thorough-going radical will ever feel naughty in quite this way; it is the mood rather of the schoolboy, who has decided to break the rules and knows that it is manly to do so, but knows also that he might be caught, and this gives added spice to his revolt. Butler's tone is often coloured by just such an adolescent note of conscious rebellion. Stylistically it is a sparkling quality, but morally it may well be a flaw; a curious lack of *final* conviction about the causes for which he chooses to crusade. His attitude towards smoking is one slight, but revealing example of this. Again and again he writes of smoking as a vice, which he likes to indulge in even though — and perhaps half because — Mrs Grundy will be annoyed. Whereas Tennyson and a great many other Victorians would puff away at their pipes and give the matter scarcely a thought, Butler is always slightly on the defensive: he knows that it is against the rules, but is determined to stand up for himself if he is caught. This slight concession to convention, which is the other side no doubt of his refusal of thoroughgoing radicalism, becomes much more serious when the father/son relationship is in question. For once again the main force of the protest is a negative one; he hates the abuse of authority, but seems much less certain of the distance to which authority may legitimately go. In *The Way Of All Flesh* we are never in doubt about what to make of Theobald Pontifex; every judgement offered against him is wholly justified from any sane viewpoint one can conceive. The trouble sets in when Butler has to turn to the other side of the picture, and represent Ernest himself as a father. Ernest solves his problems of parent-hood by giving his children away to some 'poor people' living 'near the waterfront', whom he admires as his social inferiors, and thinks more capable of bringing the children up properly than he is himself. Certainly this could be described as an abdication of parental tyranny; and since Ernest's marriage was breaking up, we may have to look upon it as a special case. But Ernest does not atone for Theobald's mistakes by any positive paternal successes of his own. There are no insights into a successful family life to balance the very acute insights into a disastrous one that have gone before.

When we turn to *Erewhon Revisited*, we find an even odder failure to visualise family problems concretely. Mr Higgs returns to Erewhon after an absence of twenty years to discover that he has there an illegitimate son called George. The moment the situation becomes clear, he discovers that George, and George's mother, are united in the highest affection and concern for him. It is not merely that there are no reproaches. The original sexual act is justified on the plea that anything which brought so admirable a son into the world must have been good. And the son himself turns out to be a model of perfection: more handsome, more courageous, more virtuous than any other man, including the legitimate son of Mr Higgs's marriage to another Erewhonian — the one who went off with him in the balloon. Mr Higgs therefore has the pleasure of conceiving a son, the pleasure of discovering him twenty years later, the pleasure of finding him everything a father could wish, and the pleasure of having not known he even existed in the period between. If this is Butler's formula for getting the best of all possible worlds, one has to admire its thoroughness. But if he is offering this as a correct alternative to parental tyranny, then one has to admit that it simply will not do.

II

A weakness on the positive side must, then, be acknowledged. When it is, I do not think that the criticism of Victorian family life has been in any way invalidated. Butler may not be able to visualise an ideal family, but his insights into a bad one have seldom if ever been surpassed.

It is now possible to turn to *Erewhon* and *The Way Of All Flesh*, two of the major literary delights of their age. 'Erewhon' is 'Nowhere' spelt backwards, or very nearly: at one point the reversal is wrong, as a very cursory glance will show. Why did

Butler allow this flaw in his reversal? Perhaps 'Erehwon' did
not look right to him, and we are dealing only with a trifling
aesthetic preference. But perhaps he did not want the word
exactly reversed; neatness and predictability are precisely the
qualities that any ironist will mistrust. The twist in the title
may remind us, whether it was consciously designed to do so
or not, that irony is as full of unexpected turnings as a maze.
At the very moment when we are sure we are nearing the centre
we might be half way up a *cul-de-sac*, or wandering in a path that
takes us back again to the start.

From the opening pages of *Erewhon* Butler keeps us on the
alert, as Swift did in *Gulliver*. The careful precision of the narrative, the homely good sense of the hero, conceal purposes that
are only slowly to be revealed. Erewhon itself is a highly ambivalent land; sometimes full of outrageous abuses, which
boomerang on ourselves when we laugh at them; sometimes full
of simple honesty of the kind we normally try to evade. The
Erewhonians hold, for instance, that sickness is a crime, for
which men deserve to be punished. Can they really be serious,
we wonder? But in wondering this we become vulnerable ourselves, in ways we have not foreseen. Again, they hold that
'unalloyed virtue is not a thing to be immoderately indulged in',
and actually have a Deformatory — as we learn in *Erewhon
Revisited* — to which over-virtuous children are sent for correc-
tion. Do they really mean it this time, we ask again? And the
answer here is that they do and they don't: Butler is exaggerating, of course, in the Deformatory, but maybe the Erewhonians
are simply being more honest than ourselves? The satiric
technique in the first example is modelled on Swift, but in the
second it is nearer to Shaw and to Wilde. Sometimes Butler
uses exaggerations of an obviously monstrous kind, that remind
us of the *Modest Proposal*. But sometimes his delight is in epigrams which sound cynical, proposals which sound outrageous,
but only because our sense of the cynical and the outrageous
has itself been perverted by cant.

A central problem in *Erewhon*, as in *Gulliver* before it and
Orwell's *1984* after, is what we are to make of the narrator. Is
Butler identified with Mr Higgs in any way at all, or does he use
him only as a satiric convenience? Gulliver, Mr Higgs and
Winston Smith all come to bad ends, it will be remembered.

Gulliver turns into a misanthropist, Winston Smith into a slave; Mr Higgs comes out in the last chapter with a modest proposal for converting the Erewhonians to Christianity which suggests that he has taken a moral turn for the worse, to put things mildly. In *Gulliver* and *1984* a very real problem is presented by the ending. We want to know — indeed we must know — how far the pessimism of the final twist is seriously meant, and how far it is simply a last exaggeration for effect. In *Erewhon*, however, it seems clear that the second of these two explanations is correct. Butler is allowing himself one final outrageous flourish, since religion has always been Mr Higgs's vulnerable point; but fundamentally his hero remains the same. This draws our attention, nonetheless, to the degree to which Mr Higgs *is*, by and large, a rounded character of the kind that readers of nineteenth-century novels had come to expect. I would go further, and say that his consistency as a character for the greater part of the work is necessary to the particular ironic tricks Butler has to play. The fact is that Butler admires Mr Higgs to some degree, and puts a great deal of his own rugged honesty into the making of him. The one decisive point where Mr Higgs differs from his creator is in not being especially intelligent. It is this which delivers him over to conventional ethics and religion, thereby allowing Butler to get on with the main task of his satire: which is, I take it, to show that cant and cruelty can exist not only in bad men, but in good men as well, if they happen to have been trained in a certain way.

What manner of man is Mr Higgs? He is a patriot, an individualist, an explorer; an honest and decent man within limits, and not without a certain simple dignity. He is good-natured rather than the reverse, but his good nature is always at the mercy of his religion; and this in turn is far more at the mercy of concealed self-interest than he even begins to perceive. Intellectually he is dogged, persistent, honest again within limits. But his whole cast of mind is narrowly conventional; beyond a certain point he seems unable to question what he has been taught. He has no compunction about killing animals, which may suggest a lack of reverence for life — though on the other hand, it may suggest only a practical man's unsentimental good sense. Morally he is fairly well content with himself, but admits to certain 'faults' which trouble him from time

to time. These, we are left in no doubt, are sexual; and ironically, his attempts to compensate for them by converting a few
heathen to Christianity lead him into far worse faults, humanly
speaking, than the ones he is trying to atone for.

Right at the start we find him pondering on the possibility of
converting Chowbok, in a passage I should like to quote.

> I had set my heart upon making him a real convert to the
> Christian religion, which he had already embraced out-
> wardly, though I cannot think that it had taken deep root in
> his impenetrably stupid nature. I used to catechise him by
> our camp fire, and explain to him the mysteries of the Trinity
> and of original sin, with which I was myself familiar, having
> been the grandson of an archdeacon on my mother's side,
> to say nothing of the fact that my father was a clergyman of
> the English Church. I was therefore sufficiently qualified for
> the task, and was the more inclined to it, over and above my
> real desire to save the unhappy creature from an eternity of
> torture, by recollecting the promise of St James, that if any-
> one converted a sinner (as Chowbok surely was) he should
> hide a multitude of sins. I reflected, therefore, that the
> conversion of Chowbok might in some degree compensate for
> irregularities and shortcomings in my own previous life, the
> remembrance of which had been more than once unpleasant
> to me during my recent experience.

These amusingly two-edged reflections are later intensified —
but also I think distorted — in his grandiose plans for converting
the Erewhonians as a tribe.

Already, the main lines of Mr Higgs's character are apparent;
he is a good man, but very much a slave to convention. His
decency is often strong enough — and this is one of the important trump cards that Butler keeps up his sleeve — to lead
him in the right direction even when his reasoning is wildly and
tellingly astray. The main satiric intention, however, is to
show how a man of this kind can be led into absurdity by his
own beliefs. The passage quoted above is only a preliminary
glimpse of the extent to which a bad religion has led his good
sense astray. His stupidity at such moments is all the more
damaging to his religious beliefs because he is, essentially, a man
of goodwill. There can be no question of religion having made

him a better man than he would otherwise have been. His inherited values are so obviously less good than those he would have arrived at unaided.

Mr Higgs's obtuseness is a quality Butler can also use, when it has once been established, as a challenge to his readers. We are invited to think faster and straighter for ourselves, if we can. Fairly early in the work Mr Higgs discovers that his watch is an object of disapproval, and that all the other watches in Erewhon seem to have been destroyed. Naturally he is amazed by this, and at a loss to guess what the reasons might be. His own reflections are perplexed and cumbersome, but the reader is given a chance, or some sort of chance, to arrive at the truth independently. There are clues in Mr Higgs's account which he is blind to himself; there is the challenge of a cultural pattern different from our own, yet working to laws which intelligence might manage to deduce from the clues. Later on we are told the full meaning, in the celebrated chapters on machines. But an opportunity is offered us to guess as much as we can in advance; to pitch our wits against Butler's own, if we can.

This is the challenge; but certain doubts about it are bound to arise. Is it possible for us to guess exactly what Butler has in mind? The implications of his fable may be larger than the solution; and if so, he is playing slightly less than fair. In the instance I have chosen, I would give him the benefit of the doubt. His speculations about machines are highly original, yet a mind prepared to speculate freely, and given the clues, might well get far nearer the truth than Mr Higgs himself is likely to do. But there is another major issue in Erewhon where the implications Butler confronts us with are still more confusing, and the doubts about his own control of them become a matter of major critical concern. I am thinking of the famous Chapters XI and XII, to which I should now like to turn in more detail.

Chapter XI is an account of a number of trials which Mr Higgs hears in an Erewhonian Court of Law. Let me start with a brief summary of these. The first case is that of a man who has recently lost his wife. He is accused of 'misfortune', which is the underlying charge in all the judicial proceedings in Erewhon. The defence his counsel tries to establish is that he never really loved his wife, so that her death was not really a misfortune at all. But this breaks down, since witness after witness establishes that they were a devoted couple, and that the man is indeed heartbroken at his loss. In sentencing him to three months' hard labour, the Judge comments: 'You have suffered a great loss. Nature attaches a severe penalty to such offences, and human law must emphasise the decrees of nature.' The next case is that of a youth who has been 'swindled out of a large property during his minority by a guardian', and the Judge's words to him are no less severe. 'People have no right to be young, inexperienced, greatly in awe of their guardians, and without independent professional advice. If by such indiscretions they outrage the moral sense of their friends, they must expect to suffer accordingly.'

The third and most famous case is that of a man who is 'accused of pulmonary consumption — an offense which was punished with death until quite recently'. This time, the Judge is especially savage. The law, he says, exists to safeguard the community, and a man so dangerous to his fellows as this man is can expect little in the way of understanding or compassion. Already there has been a long criminal history, of 'aggravated bronchitis' and fourteen other illnesses 'of a more or less hateful character'. 'It is intolerable,' the Judge goes on, 'that an example of such terrible enormity should be allowed to go at large unpunished.' The judicial tirade continues predictably, until it nears its peroration in the telling phrase: 'You may say that it is your misfortune to be criminal; I answer that it is your crime to be unfortunate.' The sentence is life imprisonment, with an exhortation to repentance thrown in. 'During that period I would earnestly entreat you to repent of the wrongs you have done already, and to entirely reform the constitution of your whole body.' As a special act of clemency, some help towards this is to be given. 'I shall therefore order that you receive two tablespoonfuls of castor oil daily, until the pleasure of the Court be further known.'

This is an outline of Chapter XI; and what is Butler's intention in all this? A few obvious bearings can be taken. The phrases 'decrees of nature', 'moral sense' and so on are cant, of the kind which covers any judicial severity a country might have. And the main absurdity exists in two separate, but closely connected attitudes: the first, that misfortune should be regarded as intrinsically criminal; and the second, that illness should be treated in a way likely to aggravate rather than alleviate its social dangers.

But after this, the difficulties start to crowd in. Butler's great discovery, of which he was justly proud, was the analogy between crime and disease. His satiric purpose is in essence a simple one; we are to be startled, by these Erewhonian applications of judicial severity, into a radical reappraisal of our own.

But the analogy is far richer in implications than it at first seems. It may be that we ought to make a conscious selection of Butler's intended meanings, and reject any others that might get in their way. Yet this is by no means easy to do, when we are brought to a point. Butler's earliest readers often imagined him to be condoning all forms of crime. His meaning, they thought, was that a man might no more be able to help robbing a bank or murdering his wife than catching smallpox. If you read him like this, of course he seems to be talking nonsense, and the early readers were right to be annoyed. But Butler's real intention is clearly different from this. His analogy is concerned not with the causes of crime, but with its treatment. The Erewhonian severity towards illness is both inhuman and inexpedient, and it is at *this* point that the analogy with our own criminal law exists. The Erewhonian system seeks neither the causes nor the cures of disease. It sees diseases as a social menace, which they are, but attempts to prevent them in ways calculated to make them a great deal worse. There may be some trifling successes from such an approach — as when Mr Higgs himself loses a cold more quickly than he has ever done before in his life. But real illnesses are not so easily deterred. Fear of the law, and of the social disapproval which necessarily accompanies the law, leads those who have diseases to conceal them for as long as they can. During this period, they no doubt infect many fellow citizens who would otherwise escape. And since doctors have been driven underground with the utmost ruthlessness, the only ways in which a real cure might be found are proscribed. As to the unfortunate wretches who are put into jail, the likelihood of their being 'reformed' is self-evidently absurd.

Self-evidently absurd — but is it? Butler is by no means finished yet, since in Chapter XII we are allowed to hear

Mr Higgs's reflections on what he has seen. These take us on to new and more complex ground, where it becomes less easy to find our way. Mr Higgs has been 'rather unhappy' about the justice he has witnessed, but he is by no means contemptuous of it. As we have seen, he is a conservative at heart; his natural instinct is to make the best of whatever institutions happen to exist.

'They had no misgivings about what they were doing [he reflects of the Erewhonians]. There did not seem to be a person in the whole court who had the smallest doubt but that all was exactly as it should be. This universal unsuspecting confidence was imparted by sympathy to myself, in spite of all my training in opinions so widely different. So it is with most of us; that which we observe to be taken as a matter of course by those around us, we take as a matter of course ourselves. And after all, it is our duty to do this, save upon grave questions.'

After expressing a few further doubts about the Erewhonian methods, Mr Higgs moves on to consider the underlying principle of punishing people for their misfortunes. Here, his sympathies are entirely with the system.

I write with great diffidence, but it seems to me that there is no unfairness in punishing people for their misfortunes, or rewarding them for their sheer good luck; it is the normal condition of human life that this should be done, and no right-minded person will complain of being subjected to the common treatment. . . .
What is the offence of a lamb that we should rear it, and tend it, and lull it into security, for the express purpose of killing it? Its offence is the misfortune of being something which society wants to eat, and which cannot defend itself. This is ample. Who shall limit the right of society except society itself? And what consideration for the individual is tolerable unless society be the gainer thereby? Wherefore should a man be so richly rewarded for having been son to a millionaire, were it not clearly provable that the common welfare is thus better furthered? We cannot seriously detract from a man's merit in having been the son of a rich father

without imperilling our own tenure of things which we do
not wish to jeopardize; if this were otherwise we should not
let him keep his money for a single hour; we would have it
ourselves at once. For property *is* robbery; but then, we are
all robbers or would-be robbers together, and have found it
essential to organise our thieving, as we have found it
necessary to organise our lust and our revenge. Property,
marriage, the law; as the bed to the river, so rule and convention to the instinct; and woe to him who tampers with the
banks while the flood is flowing.

Mr Higgs goes on to consider the manner in which our own
society protects itself from certain menaces — from the maniac
by locking him up, from the serpent by killing it 'simply for
being the thing which it is'. And yet, he continues, surely the
case of the man suffering from consumption is different?
Though everyone in the Court accepted its verdict — the
Judge, the bystanders, even the prisoner himself — nevertheless custom has in this instance blinded them to things 'which
one would have thought would have been apparent even to a
child'. The law, he adds, is less 'barbarous' now than it used to
be, in that the sentence of death is passed less often; but in
broad outline it remains the same.

There are still further twists of the irony before Butler is
through, but this is enough to be going on with. The whole
passage I have been quoting is interestingly poised. What Butler
is dealing with here is a problem very familiar to modern liberals;
a theme to which E. M. Forster and Angus Wilson, among
other important twentieth-century writers, have returned in
their novels many times. It is the problem of the limits of
tolerance in a society; the point at which those who are felt to
be a danger to the majority have to be suppressed rather than
permitted, for the good of the whole. Clearly, you can arrange
these different cases in a hierarchy, beginning with those
whom most societies tolerate (though not the Erewhonian
society): cripples, invalids, the poor, and the generally unfortunate. From here, one passes to more controversial cases, who are
tolerated in some societies but not in others — racial and religious minorities, political and sexual ones. Then come the
cases where any society has to take steps to preserve itself, but

the nature of these steps may be very revealing of the degree of civilisation it has attained: criminals on the one hand, dangerous lunatics on the other. And finally, there are such non-human forms of life as lambs and serpents, which we either prey upon for our own animal needs, or recognise as natural enemies and kill.

The problems arising in this area are classic ones: is tolerance of any or all of these classes humane and civilised, or is it merely sentimental and weak? Is tolerance expedient, when it is properly considered, or does it merely expose the normal majority to hazards they would be better without? At what point does the odd-man-out cease to deserve our sympathy, and start to become as alien and dangerous as the serpent? At what point *can* the problem of minorities be solved by the criminal law, and at what point does the attempt to do this merely aggravate the problem it is trying to remove? Is it right to suggest that tolerance is always the most civilised attitude, or must each case be considered separately, in terms of the nature and extent of the threat?

When we read Chapter XII with these questions in mind, we can see that Mr Higgs has been caught up in more analogies than he can comfortably handle. He appears to regard all minorities as posing a similar problem: namely that they are unfortunate, and neither nature nor society can side with misfortune for very long. At a fairly obvious level, we can say that this is the ironic point the chapter exists to make. Butler wants to show a sincere but somewhat stupid man, not in-humane yet too conventional to accept any sweeping revisions of his views, caught up in a new and challenging instance of the criminal law. Mr Higgs is trying to justify the unjustifiable: and in doing so, he indulges in exactly the well-meant but mistaken analogies which defenders of reaction in this country normally employ.

That much we can say with confidence; but it is far from being the whole story. For if we take this chapter simply as a satiric nudge towards radicalism, we overlook points at which Mr Higgs may be right — or perhaps one should say, points at which Butler thinks he may be right. When he says that *some* conventions are necessary in society unless the floods are to arise and sweep us all away, of course we have to agree with

him. And the disturbing underlying principle of all this, that
misfortune always is punished in one way or another and
success rewarded, is not to be laughed off as a merely reactionary whim. Mr Higgs may have hit here on exactly that
sense of ruthlessness in life itself which some radicals, at any
rate, fatally overlook. In his careful and plodding way, he sees
law and convention as a necessary part of social survival; and
he sees that pleas for tolerance can readily turn into pleas for
anarchy, unless some firm grip on reality is retained. What we
have to see, I think, is that Mr Higgs's cautious conservatism is
not to be wholly despised. The temptation to rush straight into
radical extremes in opposition to it may itself be another facet
of the ironic trap.

For this chapter now has its next surprise in store, when
Mr Higgs goes on to describe the views of an 'energetic
minority' who hold rather extreme opinions about 'the treatment of criminals'. These 'malcontents', as they are called, are
held in great odium by the generality of the public, 'and are
considered subverters of all morality whatever'. Their opinions
include such notions as these: 'that illness is the inevitable result
of certain antecedent causes, which, in the great majority of
cases, were beyond the control of the individual', and that 'the
greater part of illness which exists in their country is brought
about by the insane manner in which it is treated'. The malcontents, in short, express exactly the radical view towards
which the irony seems to have been pointing. When we find
Mr Higgs contemptuous of them, we are inclined to think this
a further irony at his expense. And so it is, up to a point; yet
another proof that he is as obtuse as the rest of his class, for all
his good-humoured attempts to be fair. But there is one further
twist to come, when Mr Higgs tells us (and is this just another
piece of blindness, or is it something which happens to be true?)
that the malcontents themselves are motivated by expediency
rather than by compassion.

'But the main argument on which they rely is that of
economy . . . they think that the more medicinal and humane
treatment of the diseased of which they are advocates would
in the long run be much cheaper to the country; but I did
not gather that these reformers were opposed to meeting some

of the more violent forms of illness with the cat-of-nine-tails, or with death; for they saw no so effectual way of checking them; they would therefore both flog and hang, but they would do so pitifully.'

By this time, we can take the passage in any of several ways. It may be a final demonstration of Mr Higgs's obtuseness — in that he repeats the ordinary gibes at reformers without reflecting on whether they are true or not, yet manages unknown to himself to reveal that the reformers' case *is* expedient as well as humane when properly understood. But on the other hand, Mr Higgs may be right here in detecting hidden, and less reputable motives in those whose reforming zeal takes them to extremes. Or again, Butler may regard the willingness of the malcontents to 'flog and hang pitifully' as a saving grace. As one who was himself on their side, he might have wanted to make clear that they were not wholly sentimental or unrealistic in their approach.

How, then, are we to sum up? The ironic gymnastics are as subtle as anything I can think of outside Swift; Butler has thrown us into the middle of a most vital debate, and shocked us into reflecting upon it from points of view more fundamental than might otherwise occur to us. The very difficulty of knowing *exactly* where he stands may be part of the strategy; though it is also possible that he became slightly muddled himself. The analogies are, after all, hard to control; a satirist might always find his sheer virtuosity introducing suggestions that are not strictly compatible with his main purpose, or even with one another.

What we have to do perhaps is to simplify again, and remind ourselves that some things, at least, are very clear. The main force of the irony is directed at the insane way in which the Erewhonians treat disease; and by implication, at the insane way in which we British deal with crime. Mr Higgs's role is mainly that of showing the mental limitations of his class — though as I have stressed, Butler sees certain virtues in him as well, and may not be wholeheartedly on the other side.

When this is allowed, I fancy that two final comments might usefully be made. One is that Butler *may* be thinking mainly of our treatment of sexual 'crimes', and the whole trial of the man with pulmonary consumption may have been conceived with this in mind. The combination of moral savagery with penal ineptness reminds us irresistibly of the comments judges are still likely to make when dealing with sexual offenders. This possibility becomes much more likely when we compare Chapter XI of *Erewhon* with the equally famous chapter in *The Way Of All Flesh* where Ernest is imprisoned for Indecent Assault. The words of the Judge there are very similar, both in their tone and in the totally misguided view of sexuality which they imply. Certainly this is a matter on which Butler felt strongly, and it may help us to take our bearings if we keep it in mind.

My final comment hinges on Mr Higgs's reflections, in an earlier chapter, on the social disapproval felt in Erewhon towards disease. 'Indeed, that dislike or even disgust should be felt by the fortunate for the unfortunate, or at any rate for those who have been discovered to have met with any of the more serious and less familiar misfortunes, is not only natural, but desirable for any society, whether of man or brute.' Here, again, we detect a peculiarly two-edged quality in the irony. Mr Higgs is 'explaining' the Erewhonian ethos, in a manner which appears objective, but really suggests a want of sensibility in himself. The irony rebounds upon any reader who tries to dissociate himself from Mr Higgs, since whether we like it or not — this is the force of the challenge — we *do* act on some such belief, in our dealings with criminals for instance, or with the poor. But there is a further complication in the fact that what Mr Higgs says is in some ways true. As an evolutionist, Butler knew that Nature itself has few liberal sentiments, but picks for survival only those species which are fitted to endure. As a social realist, he knew that money and success are important; much of his irony is an attempt to make us admit just how actually important they are. It would be too easy to regard Mr Higgs as simply wrong at this point. Perhaps it is better to say that he hits here, with peculiar and disturbing honesty, on the insight that nature and society *do* favour the fortunate and successful, almost with the force of a law. Civilisation, however, may depend on other laws, not as directly traceable to natural or social expediency as Mr Higgs seems to think. It may involve our overcoming our natural distaste for the underdog, and allowing humanity and tolerance to prevail in our dealings with him. This, of course, Butler also firmly believed, and it is one of the reasons why we admire him. But he was too firmly rooted in realities to exaggerate his case. We might say, in fact, that his very lack of idealism or fanaticism acts as a brake on the irony when it threatens to sweep us to extremes. Butler is always governed at such moments by a sense of proportion; far more so than Swift, or than most writers who use irony in this way.

III

I have concentrated attention on two chapters of *Erewhon*, not only because they are justly famous in themselves, but because they exemplify the type of problem Butler very often sets, in one context or another. His irony at the expense of religion is a frequent feature of his work. The chapters on the Musical Banks of Erewhon, and the College of Unreason, offer a powerful critique of theological thinking. Butler actually anticipates Orwell in defining doublethink: the technique whereby you believe and live with impossibilities, but without any consciousness of being insincere. For him, this is the normal language and mentality of the Church. In *Erewhon Revisited* his central satiric purpose is to show how the Christian faith might have evolved to its present form, in an age before science had come on the scene. Start with an admittedly unusual historical event; add to this twenty years of oral hearsay and embroidery; stir in the shrewdness of a Hanky or a Panky, or any other aspirants to priestly power; season well with human wishes and fears: the end product, Butler tells us, as both Hobbes and Hume had done before, is an Authoritarian Faith of the kind we are all too familiar with in Christianity itself. *Erewhon Revisited* pursues this theme with amusing audacity; the parallels between Sunchildism and Christianity are too close to be anything other than intended, for as usual Butler's serious purpose is coloured by the consciously naughty delight of a little blasphemy. The Sunchild Sayings turn out to be a corrupt version of scriptural texts which Mr Higgs had himself taught the Erewhonians twenty years before. As usual, Butler plays at least two games at once. The fact that the texts have become more or less reversed in twenty years indicates the kind of value an oral tradition might be supposed to have. At the same time, the texts have been reversed in a direction which Butler takes to be a sensible one. The Sunchild Text 'When the righteous man turneth away from the righteousness which he hath committed, and doeth that which is a little naughty or wrong, he will generally be found to have gained in amiability what he hath lost in righteousness' is one to which he would have cheerfully assented.

The serious purpose of *Erewhon*, then, is a biting satire on revealed religion. But towards the end Mr Higgs says — and here Butler certainly appears to be speaking for himself as well — that the Church itself might be preferable to the new scientific humanists as a cultural guardian of the future. It almost looks as though the liberal Christianity which Butler satirised in *The Fair Haven* has at last developed real attractions for him. It is not that he believes any of it, of course; he remained an uncompromising agnostic up to the hour of his death. It is, however, that he sees an even worse human possibility in terms of a purely mechanical and scientific world. The Book of The Machines in *Erewhon* had already explored, in a manner that anticipates twentieth-century science fiction at its best, the revolution that machines might bring about when they come fully into their own. And after *Erewhon*, Butler's bitter quarrel with Darwin increased his mistrust of scientists as the possible arbiters of the future. Even on this key matter of Christianity, then, Butler's views are not without a certain characteristic ambivalence. But here, even more than in his theories of criminality, our main bearings are clear enough. Butler disliked and mistrusted Christianity with all his heart, as the main originator of tyranny and hypocrisy in his age.

Butler's masterpiece is *The Way Of All Flesh*, about which a few words must certainly be said. *The Way Of All Flesh* is not a consistent satire like *Erewhon* and *Erewhon Revisited*. It is, rather, a realistic novel with satiric overtones close to the surface. One could, if one wished, be very severe with it as a novel. The characterisation is often poor; Butler's presentation of Towneley is as revealing as it is uncritical — there is no doubt that a good-looking, moneyed, good-natured but fundamentally carefree young man represented his own ideal of perfection, for better or worse. And the narrator is a tiresome character; a know-all, who manipulates the novel heavy-handedly, telling us far more about Ernest's future fortunes than we ought at any stage to know.

Other flaws of this kind could be mentioned; if the novel had to stand solely on its plot, or its minor characters, its chances of survival would be small. But of course this is not the final test we have to apply. *The Way Of All Flesh* really stands or falls on its wit, and on the very humane and serious insights underlying the wit. As such, it seems to me the equal of anything left by Shaw, and at least as certain to give continuing pleasure as a minor classic.

The mention of Shaw is no arbitrary one; for Shaw was a great admirer of Butler, and very much in his debt. Take, for instance, the following witticism from *The Way Of All Flesh*, which could be matched hundreds of times over from the book. 'There are two classes of people in this world, those who sin, and those who are sinned against; if a man must belong to either he had better belong to the first than the second.'

The irony here is of the kind which Shaw and Wilde were also masters of, in their very different ways. It consists in saying something which you know will sound outrageous, yet which you mean — or very nearly mean — as it stands. The appearance is one of cynicism, but the intention when it is grasped is serious, and even morally sound. What Butler does is simply to give shock treatment to a threadbare platitude. By reversing it, he announces not a universal truth, but at least something more useful and amusing than the original.

The main body of the novel is a study of parental tyranny, and its consequences on the youth and early manhood of the victim. The details are beautifully observed, and the moral will seem to most modern readers definitive. Butler's attitude to his theme is expressed sometimes in the elegant, almost self-mocking wit of a moment like this: 'And he brooded over the bliss of Melchisedek who had been born an orphan, without father, without mother, and without descent.' But beneath the surface, there is savage bitterness which sometimes emerges from the ironic surroundings with all the nakedness of direct statement: 'The only thing to do with them (i.e. Ernest's parents) was to humour them and make the best of them till they died — and be thankful when they did so.' Most of the novel is remarkably free, however, of such obvious savagery. Its tone can be gauged from the following delightful passage, which occurs when Ernest has been imprisoned for Indecent Assault, but has at last managed, as if in compensation, to lose his faith.

And how should he best persuade his fellow-countrymen to leave off believing in this supernatural element? Looking at the matter from a practical point of view, he thought the Archbishop of Canterbury afforded the most promising key to the situation. It lay between him and the Pope. The Pope was perhaps best in theory, but in practice the Archbishop of Canterbury would do sufficiently well. If he could only manage to sprinkle a pinch of salt, as it were, on the Archbishop's tail, he might convert the whole Church of England to free thought by a *coup de main*. There must be an amount of cogency which even an Archbishop — an Archbishop whose perceptions had never been quickened by imprisonment for assault — would not be able to withstand. When brought face to face with the facts, as he, Ernest, could arrange them, his Grace would have no resource but to admit them; being an honourable man he would at once resign his Archbishoprick, and Christianity would become extinct in England within a few months' time.

The irony faces two directions, as ever. Of course to some degree it is at Ernest's expense; his naïveté, itself the result of his upbringing, is constantly delivering him into false calculations like this. But the irony is also at the expense of the Church, for Butler really did think that a modicum of honesty would bring about its total collapse. Whether such a view indicates that he was more honest than most of us, as he would have thought himself, or merely that in religious matters he was more insensitive, we must each decide for ourselves. *The Way Of All Flesh* remains an amusing novel, even for those who have doubts about its truth.

Where does Butler's reputation stand today? One disadvantage he suffers from is that so much that he fought for has been won. It takes some effort of historical sympathy to see how daring and important it was to express seventy or eighty years ago ideas which we like to think of as commonplaces. But another disadvantage is that many modern readers resist him just as strenuously as his own contemporaries did; truth-telling as Butler conceived it never has been popular, and one doubts if it ever will be.

On top of this, Butler was no good friend to himself. His serious reputation was damaged by the crankiness of some of his strongest enthusiasms and views. He quarrelled violently with Darwin without having the necessary scientific training; he erupted into the field of classical studies with speculations about Homer which appeared at the time, and still do, somewhat absurd. To make matters worse, he imagined insults against himself when none was intended, and paraded imaginary persecutions before a bored and often hostile world. All of this combined to make it easy for his contemporaries to ignore him. Posterity, however, has not been alienated to the same extent. Basil Willey has recently treated Butler's evolutionary views with respect; Bernard Shaw, Malcolm Muggeridge and G. D. H. Cole are other distinguished writers — interestingly different from one another as well as from Butler himself — who have found him worthy of detailed and sympathetic appraisal. Over and above this, I am convinced that all readers with a taste for satire will sooner or later discover the peculiar flavour of his work. *Erewhon* and *The Way Of All Flesh* may not be major classics, but they are assured of their own lasting niche in the satiric canon.

CHAPTER 9

OSCAR WILDE: IRONY OF A SOCIALIST AESTHETE

I

'I LIVE in terror,' wrote Wilde, 'of not being misunderstood.' As it turned out, he need not have worried. His contemporaries liked or disliked him largely for the wrong reasons, the earlier twentieth century reacted decisively against him. Even today, with two major films on their rounds in Britain and television programmes innumerable, he remains curiously hard to understand. As a humorist he set out to amuse, as a successful humorist he paid the price of being taken less than seriously. The normal English attitude to humour is notoriously odd. Most of us look on it as a national asset, in wartime it becomes almost a mystique. But there is a puritanism in the English tradition which prevents the more boisterous and flamboyant types of laughter from flourishing unchecked; Mrs Grundy will have her say in the name of the national genius as well. And there is a pharisaism which is always ready to be revenged, if the moment offers, on laughter directed too openly at itself. At the best, the humorist is likely to find himself cast in the role of jester, whom no one really listens to, despite his unusual privilege of telling the truth. Should the serious ideas underlying his jests become too apparent, he might even be turned on, by a public which values laughter, but not more than it values its own dignity and peace of mind.

If the public attitude to humour is odd, so, in other ways, is that of the university critics. Most 'comedy' as the term is now understood keeps entertainment firmly under the thumb of instruction. Laughter by itself is not enough, there must be a moral purpose as well. Ben Jonson passes easily enough, so, it goes without saying, does Jane Austen. But what of Restoration Comedy? Or Sterne? 'Irresponsible trifling' suggests a voice,

and at once there are doubts. Nor does 'wit', when the Metaphysical and Augustan types have been exempted, fare much
better. The very term in *Scrutiny* circles is a tainted one, at best
associated with Bloomsbury, at worst with the *fin de siècle* and
with Wilde most of all.

My own sympathies are not all against the *Scrutiny* view;
there were various possibilities of cruelty in the '90s (when are
there not?) which Wilde's type of wit could easily be made to
serve. Yet Wilde himself was one of the kindest and sanest of
men, in addition to being a prince of entertainers; and laughter,
though sometimes a scourge, can be relaxation or good fellowship, tonic or simple delight as well. Wilde's laughter, moreover,
had its serious side, as his first hearers often knew to their cost.
The challenge today is to discern what sort of seriousness it was
which prompted some of his contemporaries to a notable
revenge, yet in the 1960s often seems hard to detect at all.

For Wilde's serious ideas have been misunderstood as well as
his laughter. And I am thinking now not of the consciously
'serious' moments in his plays, where something is very obviously wrong, but of the values and insights behind his wit
itself. He stood unashamedly for aestheticism, asserting this now
unfashionable doctrine in a series of amusing paradoxes which
we are the more ready to write off as flippancies in proportion
as we fail to take seriously their underlying idea. When Blake
writes, 'I tell you, no virtue can exist without breaking these
Ten Commandments', the paradox is accepted as a challenge
from somewhere higher, not lower than the normal morality
it outrages; certainly it is not taken at face value, exuberant
though the tone might be. When Wilde makes outrageous
paradoxes of the same *genre* the usual response is one of simple
shock. He was a jester by choice, a victim by destiny. The
ironic *persona* of such a man is harder to penetrate than of one
whose moral earnestness is a fierce energy burning through his
style.

Wilde's values, I shall suggest, were not dissimilar to Blake's,
though his life, or what public hostility chose to make of it, was
less edifying, and his talents were inferior. He is an example,
maybe an extreme one, of a writer whose insight belonged by
and large to the camp of moral health, but whose creative gifts
were limited to fields where moral health is always liable to

suspicion. When he tried for seriousness as an artist he failed;
as an entertainer he was more morally clearsighted than is
usually allowed.

II

We must start, then, with his theories. There are a large
number of ways of treating the complex relationship between
art and life, and every age is aware of several at once. But it so
happens that certain important aspects of the relationship which
Wilde saw very clearly are seen today hardly at all. *The Decay
Of Lying* and *The Critic As Artist* are not much read in the 1960s,
yet they make at least four important observations on the
differences between art and life which are as valid now as they
ever were. The characteristic fault of present-day criticism is a
brand of moral realism which comes close to confusing fictional
characters with ideas, and creative art with morality. Wilde's
essays still pose to temptations of this kind a number of correc-
tives. 'All art is immoral', he said, and again 'all art is absolutely useless'. These dicta, at first sight the most suspect of his
'flippancies', must be considered together with certain comple-
mentary passages, such as that in which he declares: 'It is the
function of literature to create, from the rough material of
actual existence, a new world that will be more marvellous,
more enduring, and more true than the world that common
eyes look upon, and through which common natures seek to
realise their perfection.' One must be on guard here, as so often,
against apparently disquieting overtones. Though he sounds
like an aristocrat, Wilde's socialism is quite genuine: 'common
nature' is no sneer at the *vulgus profanum*, but a courteous
acceptance of the cultural potential of Everyman. What Wilde
means is that Art is primarily concerned, by the laws of its
making, with perfection, and that it is therefore said to be
immoral by those who prefer squalor to beauty, or who sense
an absolute gulf between respectable behaviour and the artist's
insights. He also means that the artist is not a preacher but a
maker, and that what he makes, being nearer to ideal than to
everyday experience, will be entirely useless for exhortation,
propaganda, or in any manner that a utilitarian would
understand.

The difficulty here, which Wilde purposely creates in order

to be challenging, is one of terminology. In a deep sense he thought that Art *is* what we should normally call 'moral': that it is to do, that is, with order and beauty in perception and conduct, and with the ambition to make life itself a shaped and satisfying whole. He chose, however, to call this 'aesthetic' rather than 'moral', handing the latter word over to those most fond of using it, and to his mind the least entitled to do so, the puritans and kill-joys with whom he warred. The abandonment of the word 'moral' was meant to shock, but not to be taken at face value. Wilde's whole wit is a series of shocks to normal responses, intended to offer the delight of emancipation culminating in the delight of extended insight. If we remain at the literal level, we are mistaking genuine irony for flippancy. The temptation to make this error is precisely the technique upon which the irony depends and falling for the temptation is, therefore, a failure of intelligence in reading.

The strategy of Wilde's terminology is easier to grasp when one remembers two more of the main distinctions he sees between Art and Life. Art is more ordered than life, he believes, and more beautiful. The supreme secret of beauty is form; which in men manifests itself as conduct, in nature as harmony, in art as style. Now man and nature are always changing. The sunset no sooner appears than it starts to fade; the colours alter as we watch them. Only in art is the beauty which natural scenery and conduct no more than hint at given shape, significance, and the prospect of permanence; only the artist can give to the beauty he sees a form that moves it towards its own ideal and preserves it from erosions of change. His shaping intelligence heightens the meaning of beauty; the medium he works in is more enduring than both the occasion of his art, and himself.

Wilde's perception that art is more ordered than life is reinforced, then, by awareness that it is more permanent; it comes as near to the immortal and the immutable as anything in a turning world ever will. This insight came to him, we need hardly remind ourselves, from Keats's Odes, mediated through the Pre-Raphaelite sensibility and already decisively diverted towards Pater. In Keats, it is balanced by the parallel insight that art wins its permanence only at the expense of organic life; the Grecian Urn, though a vision of fullness, is also 'cold pastoral', the nightingale's song is not only symbol but fancy, and fancy which 'cannot cheat so well/As she is famed to do, deceiving elf.' The ambivalence of the Odes is richly moving and is, indeed, inseparable from their greatness. Wilde, by concentrating on one side of the relationship between art and life and making the permanence of art straightforward proof of its superiority, distorted the balance which Keats kept and sacrificed truth as well as complexity in doing so. The distortion was dangerous as we now recognise, leading the aesthetes first to undervalue real experience, and then to lose all touch with it. One must admit, even so, that Wilde's insight was, and is, part of a complex truth. In expressing it through vigorous paradox he was not being deliberately foolish, as is often supposed, but was simply challenging stock notions in the cause of the realities he saw.

Wilde thought that literary modes, as well as individual styles, are more shapely and satisfying than anything in experience itself. The tragic, the heroic, the comic are triumphs of form which life, again, only hints at, and art alone can make real. 'Life,' says Gilbert in *The Critic As Artist*, 'is terribly deficient in form. Its catastrophes happen in the wrong way and to the wrong people. There is a grotesque horror about its comedies, and its tragedies seem to culminate in farce. One is always wounded when one approaches it. Things last either too long, or not long enough.' Our characteristic experience of real life, then, is of mixed motives, unforeseen outcomes, emotional *volte-faces* — in a word, of muddle. When the artist imposes on this flux his own order, his very success deludes us into thinking that the tragic, the heroic, the comic have more real-life validity than they do. He holds the mirror up to nature, we say, forgetting the degree to which he invents what seems to be reflected, and makes what is apparently seen. Wilde can go on to say, therefore, that the artist's pattern, though unnatural, and indeed *because* unnatural, is the 'true ethical import of experience', using the word 'ethical' easily enough despite the games which he chooses to play with the word 'moral'.

But the artist, who accepts the facts of life, and yet transforms them into shapes of beauty, and makes them vehicles of pity or of awe, and shows their colour-element, and their wonder, and their true ethical import also, and builds out of them a world more real than reality itself, and of loftier and more noble import — who shall set limits to him?

Why is the world of art 'more real than reality itself'? Because it has more form, and so more significance, than reality. And why has it true ethical import? Because its standards, even though they exist only in man's own achievements and nowhere else in any possible world, offer something concrete and valuable to live towards. A rose or an *objet d'art* is, for Wilde, the unique inspirer of conduct.

Wilde's emphasis leads, I have admitted, to distortion; but at least it guards against our taking any part of a work of art's 'truth', including its moral truth, for a direct transcript from life. E. M. Forster, a writer much greater than Wilde, bears this in mind when noting, in *Aspects of The Novel*, that the sensitivity of characters to one another in novels, and especially their moral sensitivity, is in some degree unlike anything in normal life whatsoever. 'The constant sensitiveness of characters for each other — even in writers called robust like Fielding — is remarkable, and has no parallel in life, except among people who have plenty of leisure.' In more recent treatments of the novel, especially those in the tradition of *Scrutiny*, there has been a tendency to overlook this aspect of the truth. The moral awareness of characters in novels is treated as though it related directly to life; in swinging away from Wilde's dissociation of morality and creative art, we have arrived at a stage when the two come close to being confused. Though I have, again, much sympathy with the modern view, and think that the errors of emphasis in *Scrutiny* on this matter are less dangerous than those of Wilde and the *fin de siècle*, I believe that Wilde saw part of the truth, and a part we can ill afford to lose. My main contention must again be made, that we should not allow ourselves to write off as deliberate perversity paradoxes which Wilde intended as a challenge to serious thought.

Attention must finally be called, before I leave this stage of argument, to the last and most important difference between art and life of which Wilde was acutely aware; the difference between our psychological responses to both. In real life, to put the distinction at its simplest, a man who slips on a banana skin and hurts himself is not funny, in art or in anecdote he is. Where, then, is the difference? The answer seems easy enough. If we are watching a play or hearing an anecdote, no one is really being hurt. We are freed from the obligation to feel appropriately, and exonerated from any duty to act; our response, to use Wilde's word, is aesthetic. The moral drift of the episode might please us (the man's fall will very likely be led up to in a manner emphasising its incongruity; the theme of pride going before a fall will be there, together with the arbitrariness of the world we live in). We may enjoy, too, a pattern: the action of falling might be multiplied and exaggerated, as in those delightful films of the silent days, when not one but dozens of men would be likely to be falling about at once. The differences between art and life turn out to be much what Wilde said they were. On the one hand art adds significant form to events; on the other it removes them from the flux of reality to an abstract world of its own devising.

In tragedy, similar considerations apply, though they are more complex. We feel for the tragic hero, it is true, yet we do not feel for him as we do for a man suffering in real life, where events are isolated and unpredictable, and where suffering happens in front of our eyes instead of being merely enacted. The tragedies of life have less shape than those of art, and more poignancy; outrage and impotence, grief and incredulity mingle with the classic responses of pity and fear. The participation of spectator and of actor is irrevocably different. Only in life itself are we actors, and then, Wilde would insist, very poor ones, in a bungled production and a feeble play.

From these considerations Wilde completed his aestheticism, noticing that our major pleasure in art comes from its form, which paradoxically consoles us almost in proportion to the intensity of the griefs being portrayed.

Form [says Gilbert in *The Critic As Artist*] is everything. It is the secret of life. Find expression for a sorrow, and it will become dear to you. Find expression for a joy, and you intensify its ecstasy. . . . Have you a grief that corrodes your heart? Steep yourself in the language of grief, learn its utterance from Prince Hamlet and Queen Constance, and you will find that mere expression is a mode of consolation, and that Form, which is the birth of passion, is also the death of pain. And so, to return to the sphere of Art, it is Form that creates not merely the critical temperament, but also the aesthetic instinct, that unerring instinct that reveals to one all things under their condition of beauty.

III

When Wilde's theories of art are in place, we can return to his wit and irony. His most characteristic habit is one of paradox. 'Work is the curse of the drinking classes,' he writes, and naturally we are delighted, but why? Partly, no doubt, because the mere intention to shock by way of reversing a respectable cliché always is amusing, not only to adolescents to whom it comes fairly naturally as a form of humour, but to the incurable iconoclast biding his time inside most of us. But the intention of shocking is only part of the story. The real joke is that the cliché Wilde reverses is itself hopelessly and perniciously stupid, so that there is irony at the expense of those who are actually shocked, as well as good-humoured laughter for those who are not. Do we really believe that drink is the curse of the working classes? Of course not. Do we say that we believe it? If we do, we deserve any fate a satirist might devise. Wilde's wit performs, therefore, the traditional task of irony, sorting its audience into sheep and goats by challenging to a response which is human and real instead of being conventional and dead. Though his pose is to shock for its own sake, the pose, in this instance, is his technique. Mistaking pose for real intention is precisely the trap Wilde sets for his readers, and the *raison d'être* of his irony.

If we examine more closely the clichés Wilde turns inside out, we shall see that almost always he has behind him either genuine insight (as in the theories of Art and Life I have already discussed), or genuine humanity (as in his great essay, *The Soul Of Man Under Socialism*), or genuine detestation of cant and humbug (as in his Comedies, and much of the recorded conversation). What looks like, and is intended to look like, a prolonged flirtation with cynicism is in fact a running battle against obtuseness, hypocrisy and cant. What seems at first sight an affront to responsibility is on second sight a jest at the expense of the pseudo-responsible. Stupidity and insincerity are confronted with formulae decked out to look more deplorable than themselves, yet actually pointing back towards the minimal respect for good sense and good nature which they violate.

A few quotations from Wilde's greatest, and most characteristic success, might bear out this claim. *The Importance Of Being Earnest* is undoubtedly one of the funniest plays in the language. In appearance it is immensely cynical, yet the audiences who laugh are not, by and large, a crowd of cynics. The force of the wit can best be translated into questions addressed to ourselves. Are we the sort of person who parrots 'money doesn't matter', or accounts it for righteousness to those who do? 'I do not approve of mercenary marriages,' says Lady Bracknell. 'When I married Lord Bracknell I had no fortune of any kind. But I never dreamed of allowing that to stand in my way.' Do we delight in telling people their faults for their own good? 'On an occasion of this kind,' says Gwendolen, 'it becomes more than a moral duty to speak one's mind. It becomes a pleasure.' Do we say (not in the 1960s admittedly), that the Upper Classes should set an example? 'If the lower classes don't set us a good example,' retorts Algernon, 'what on earth is the use of them?' Do we dismiss groups we cannot be admitted to as worthless? 'Never speak disrespectfully of Society, Algernon,' warns Lady Bracknell, 'only people who can't get into it do that.'

Wit of this order sets a delicate problem for the critic. It no more lends itself to analysis than champagne does. Attack is bound to seem heavy-handed, sober praise rather beside the point. But risking this, as one must: what *is* going on in passages like these? On the surface, there is aristocratic flippancy in the face of virtue, and flippancy, what is worse, reverberant with class-conscious overtones. If we did not know Wilde to be a socialist and a man of humane instinct, we might think he really meant it. Yet look again, and where is the cynicism? Any of Wilde's epigrams could be transmuted into serious insights, and transplanted into the most moral of dramas or novels. Once more, the substitution of cynicism for responsibility is only apparent; the real challenge is from honesty to pretence, from generosity to meanness. No doubt some of us do disapprove of mercenary marriages, despise the fleshpots, deflate our friends disinterestedly, look for a lead to our Betters. But for each of the genuinely virtuous (and is virtue quite the right word?) there must be dozens who make use of the formulae. These, as at all times, are Wilde's real target, for it is hypocrisy he hates, and the cruelty bred of hypocrisy, never true disinterestedness or warmth of heart. His humour, though sparkling, is merciless to the moral poseur, whether Insider or Outsider, fool or knave. And why, indeed, should it not be? To attack cant with flippancy is surely less vicious than to disguise selfishness with cant; and recognising the selfishness in humanity may be no bad preliminary to recognising the unselfishness that can co-exist with it as well. Wilde's cynicism, in any event, is born of a light-hearted generosity of spirit that can be better trusted than solemn professions, and certainly than the morality of the people he deflated. The unusualness of the irony is that his norms are to be found neither in what he says, nor in the reversal of what he says, but in the confrontation of moral humbug parading as righteousness with moral good-heartedness parading as flippancy. His tone is so gay that conventional moralists could neither see, nor afford to see, what was really happening. As we know, they had a fine revenge on him in the end; and their verdict, whether we like it or not, has influenced and obscured our view of his art, as well as of himself, ever since.

Wilde made no claim to being a saint, and the claim is un-likely to be made for him now. But a remark which Lady Windermere mistakenly makes about Lord Darlington really is true, I would say, of Wilde himself: 'Believe me, you are better than most other men, and I sometimes think you pretend to be worse.'

IV

When all this is said, a doubt remains. Is Wilde's shallowness only as apparent as I have urged? To suggest that he differs from most ironists simply in technique, and not in quality, may seem not enough, especially since the flamboyance which flavours his irony clearly belongs to his character as well. The temperament which poses as frivolous might be nearer to its pose than it assumes; the irony which works by concealing its moral credentials might start with precious few to conceal. Perhaps Wilde's wit does, as I have suggested, disturb only

L

corrupt habits, but if it wears a look of corruption itself, what has been gained? Long before his trial, the public took Wilde at his face value as a frivolous man; and we may wonder whether even malice and stupidity could so seriously have misunderstood, and maligned, a genuine moralist in this way.

The problem is to see why decency should be so reticent about itself; why it should again and again evade direct presentation, leaving irony to testify with more than usual obliqueness in its place. To acknowledge this problem, and to offer an answer, brings me to my last port of call, the fascinating and unjustly neglected essay, *The Soul of Man Under Socialism*. Wilde proceeds towards truth here, as he does in his aesthetic essays, by way of extravagant gestures in what he takes to be the right direction. 'The majority of people spoil their lives by an unhealthy and exaggerated altruism,' . . . 'The virtues of the poor may be readily admitted, and are much to be regretted,' . . . 'There is only one class in the community which thinks about money more than the rich, and that is the poor,' . . . 'Misery and poverty are so absolutely degrading, and exercise such a paralysing effect over the nature of man, that no class is ever really conscious of its own suffering. They have to be told of it by other people, and they often entirely disbelieve them.' Such dicta, though appearing to be at the expense of the poor, are no such thing; they spring from a sense of outrage which was the driving force of Wilde's socialism, and the force behind much that he wrote. I have discussed Wilde's aesthetic ideas in the hope of illustrating the seriousness underlying their paradoxes, so perhaps I can take his socialism for granted. The warmth and humanity of *The Soul Of Man Under Socialism* must be apparent to anyone who reads it with an unbiased mind, whether he agrees with the viewpoint, or is familiar with the background, or not. What I want to do here is to quote two or three passages in which Wilde comes as near to a direct statement of his positives as he ever did, except perhaps in the painful, and for our present purposes largely irrelevant, *De Profundis*.

It will be a marvellous thing — the true personality of man — when we see it. It will grow naturally and simply, flowerlike, or as a tree grows. It will not be at discord. It will never argue or dispute. It will not prove things. It will know everything. And yet it will not busy itself about knowledge. It will have wisdom. Its value will not be measured by material things. It will have nothing. And yet it will have everything, and whatever one takes from it, it will still have, so rich will it be. It will not be always meddling with others, or asking them to be like itself. It will love them because they will be different. And yet while it will not meddle with others, it will help all, as a beautiful thing helps us, by being what it is. . . .

. . . Now as the State is not to govern, it may be asked what the State is to do. The State is to be a voluntary association that will organise labour, and be the manufacturer and distributor of necessary commodities. The State is to make what is useful. The individual is to make what is beautiful.

. . . A red rose is not selfish because it wants to be a red rose. It would be horribly selfish if it wanted all the other flowers in the garden to be both red and roses. Under Individualism people will be quite natural and absolutely unselfish, and will know the meaning of the words, and realise them in their free, beautiful lives.

A comparison of *The Soul Of Man Under Socialism* with D. H. Lawrence's essay *Democracy* might be instructive; though the terminology and the tone of the essays differ, and the attitude to socialism itself differs, the underlying ideas are sometimes strikingly similar. Wilde, like Lawrence, believed in 'individualism' — in the fulfilment, that is, of the unique possibilities for beauty and fruitfulness which he took to be latent in Everyman. And he hated all attitudes, whether rooted in puritanism or jingoism, which stood opposed to such fulfilment. His socialism was grounded quite simply in the conviction that if private property were abolished, and poverty and public squalor eradicated, individuals would be free to develop naturally and grow into their own unique stature. The cant and humbug born of privilege would give way to a new acceptance of beauty and diversity; this in turn would bear fruit in gladness of mind and soul, love, generosity and delight.

That this hope was tinged with utopianism, and expressed with little sense of the practical, is apparent enough; Wilde himself would have been the last to deny it. Blake and Lawrence were also utopian and impractical, yet their dynamic decency survives this; their political ideas may be illiterate, but their grasp on human maturity is firm, and will be permanently admired. If one asks (as one must) why Wilde was unable to translate his own vision into positives as Blake and Lawrence did, the answer is probably twofold. On the one hand, he had less creative talent (Blake and Lawrence are, after all, among the great writers, and can we expect others, even the healthiest, to be as good?); on the other, he was a homosexual and therefore cut off from translating his vision of fruitfulness into anything like the normal terms that the greater, and more central, writers use. The realisation of doctrines of individualism must have been for him peculiarly difficult. His private life led, mainly no doubt through public hostility, to chaos. Even had he managed to accommodate a homosexual nature to a Blakeian philosophy, the results in 1890 would have been unpublishable. Perhaps it is not surprising that despite his generosity and vitality, the serious treatment of sexuality in the Comedies should centre on a dark foreboding concerning the cruelty of society to its sexual misfits; and that he should generate for the Mrs Erlynnes and the Mrs Arbuthnots who fall victim little more than a breathlessly sentimental, and very largely useless compassion. Society had traditionally forced on its oddities the role of jester, if not worse; the eunuch, the hermaphrodite and the dwarf might have their private sanities, but they are likely enough to end up amusing a Volpone, or the readers of the Sunday press as the case might be. The consciousness Wilde had of such dangers doubtless led him to write obliquely, and to sound stilted or evasive whenever he attempted to do otherwise. When one thinks in these terms, the co-existence of a warm and exuberant nature with a seemingly flippant and cynical style is no longer surprising. Nor is it odd that though our first instinct is to mistake his pose for the reality, a more detailed reading convinces us that the final truth is better than this, and to be found elsewhere.

CHAPTER 10

LYTTON STRACHEY:
THE TECHNIQUE OF DEBUNKING

I

THE publication of *Eminent Victorians* in 1918 was a portent. There had been iconoclastic onslaughts upon the Victorians before, but never of an especially effective kind. Butler had fallen largely on deaf ears, Oscar Wilde had been very satisfactorily dealt with in the end. 'De mortuis nihil nisi bonum' ... the Victorians had known how to protect themselves and their myth against almost any irreverence that could be devised. 1914, however, was the end of all that. When Lytton Strachey was ready to hurl his thunderbolt, the *Zeitgeist* was already on his side. A whole generation was ready to breathe freely in this new air; for air it was, though 'fresh air' might have seemed an excessive description even then.

But the whirligig of time brings its revenges; the recent past is taken for granted all too soon. Today, Lytton Strachey's reputation is at a low ebb; we find it hard to look on him as a serious biographer at all. Perhaps the best we can do for him at the present time is to think of him, as Noel Annan has suggested, as a polemical writer; a man with a mission, who made history serve his mission in any way that it could. In each of his biographies in turn he takes certain aspects from the lives of people who actually existed and constructs from these, wilfully but cleverly, very memorable if highly fictitious caricatures. It is not exactly that he cheats, though sometimes this has to be said as well. There is a certain integrity, in the way that even his most damaging assertions are supported with quotation. Froude really did say, 'The only good thing I know about Cranmer is that he burnt well'; Manning and Monsignor Talbot really did agree with the proposition that 'Dr Newman's spirit must be crushed'. But do we need to remind ourselves how

vulnerable any man is, if a damaging selection is to be made
from his life? Let a determined iconoclast loose, and who shall
'scape whipping? What we have to ask is whether Lytton
Strachey's picture is in any degree true, when the malicious
exaggerations have been allowed for. And we shall probably
agree that though some of the Victorians were fair game, others
get very much less than their due.

Literary criticism has to look at what is actually offered, and
Strachey is demonstrably less honest than any other ironist
concerning us in this book. His type of irony is, I would say,
an inherently bad one; it is also very pervasive, as a glance at
works like Ronald Knox's *Enthusiasm* or Rose Macaulay's
Letters To A Friend will show. In the account that follows I shall
be sounding a more adverse note than usual, so perhaps I
should make clear at the start that I enjoy reading *Eminent
Victorians*, and think there are still ways in which it can be of
interest and value. Strachey is very amusing, witty, civilised,
stylistically distinguished; his viewpoint is a liberal one, which
badly needed a hearing when he wrote. Much of what he said
is undoubtedly true; and if middle-class taste wins further
victories in the later twentieth century, much of it may soon
need saying all over again. In these and other ways I am
sympathetic; but the frequent dishonesty of his technique, and
of his usual tone of voice, cannot be ignored.

II

The most notable feature of his irony is its conscious elegance,
the antecedents of which are in the eighteenth century; he
chooses to write in the style of Hume and Gibbon. The strategy
in this kind of irony is very different from Swift's or Butler's.
The reader is not exposed to attack but admitted to an alliance,
upon which the whole force of the rhetoric depends. Strachey's
intention is not to criticise his own age but to flatter it. His
readers are invited to a place of implied equality, where they
can share an amused examination of manners, beliefs and
customs inferior to their own.

The atmosphere of this tactic I have already referred to;
writer and reader are incorporated by the writer's rhetoric in
an immense solidarity of opinion, in an atmosphere where

nothing needs to be proved since everything depends on the proof being taken for granted. The writer has no need to defend his own opinions, or to attack those of his adversaries with frontal tactics of logic or ethics, since what he chooses to draw attention to is implicitly discredited from the start. The reason why he has chosen this subject is in order to enjoy its absurdities in the company of other enlightened and right-minded men. This gratifyingly elevated atmosphere, exemplified supremely by Gibbon, was one of the fine fruits of eighteenth-century assurance, the apotheosis of the doctrine of ridicule as a test of truth.

But even in Gibbon, when we admitted his success, there were still certain radical weaknesses to observe. There was his failure to understand or to sympathise with idealism, for instance. With all his common sense, intellectual vigour and shrewd understanding of the ways of self-deception, his treatment of the Early Church is weakened by his failure to grasp its essential sincerity. We do not criticise him for treating its religious experience as illusory, since this is a possible, though not self-evident, view of it. But we do criticise him for failing to distinguish between noble and explicable illusions, and merely irrational folly. His ironic dismissiveness is hard-hitting, and often justified, but there are times when it reveals merely an imaginative poverty in himself. The eighteenth century, of course, had its own good reasons for mistrusting enthusiasm; we should not blame Gibbon for sharing the general opinion of his age. It may be true, however, when the necessary allowances have been made, that the temperament which most naturally finds its medium in dismissive irony is not one which is likely to be sensitive to outstanding ideals. There is a certain objectivity of viewpoint, a certain pose of having seen through people and things in place of a sympathetic effort to see into them, a certain readiness to ascribe men's deeds to fear and self-interest instead of to the more idealistic motives they are themselves conscious of, which seems to preclude the insight and humility required for true biography. These limitations, which we notice even in Gibbon, are far more strikingly to be found in Lytton Strachey, where there are less positive qualities to serve to disguise them. Strachey is a very small-scale Gibbon at best; a Gibbon with fewer gifts, and a less positive philosophy, but consistently following in the footsteps of his master. What we notice in him, when we look even slightly below the surface, is a curious and unexpected vulgarity; not open vulgarity, it is true, but the coarseness which inevitably sets in when a tone of mannered superiority is in any degree less justified than it pretends.

One of Strachey's tricks is to indulge in straightforward ridicule of a kind which would be unpleasant in a schoolboy. He describes Clough, the poet, as follows: 'This earnest adolescent, with the weak ankles and the solemn face, lived entirely with the highest ends in view.'

What Strachey has said about Clough is that he was an earnest young man with the highest aims in life. What he has done, by introducing the weak ankles and throwing in that damaging word 'adolescent', is to turn him into an object of pure ridicule. The trick is on the same level, despite Strachey's apparent sophistication, as a crowd of street urchins jeering at a hunchback — equally heartless, equally irrational, and certainly not less to be despised. He is, of course, encouraging our very natural suspicion that anyone who looks like a saint is more plausibly a prig, and relying on this suspicion in his readers for the effect. In the essay on Dr Arnold he again juxtaposes irrelevant trifles with matters of real importance, so that the absurdity of the first appears to discredit the second: 'His outward appearance was the index of his inward character; everything about him denoted energy, earnestness, and the best intentions. His legs, perhaps, were shorter than they should have been.' The legs in this context, where outward appearance is said to be the index of character, serve to make the whole man seem stunted. This would be a hopelessly irrelevant jibe even if Arnold's legs had been short. But in fact they were not; Strachey made the whole thing up — and surely Arnold's pomposity would have been sufficiently amusing in itself, without recourse to malicious invention?

Strachey is adept at ridiculing whole institutions and societies, as well as individuals, with remarkable economy. His account of Oxford at the time of the Movement is heavy with drugged and narcotic imagery which tells its own story, or so we are encouraged to deduce. His survey of the Church of England just before the Movement (Manning II, para ii) is a master-

piece of amusing — and in this case justified — denigration.
He has, in addition, a keen eye for anecdotes and incidents with
the maximum potential of destructiveness, both to individuals
and to the Churches to which they belong. His urbane and
incredible summary of the Gorham case; his memorable
description of a scene between Pasha Gordon and a Levantine
merchant during the last days of Khartoum — these and many
other episodes, with their blending of clarity and irony, spring
to mind. Here, for example, is a passage from the essay on
Manning:

> Manning had been removing the high pews from a church
> in Brighton, and putting in open benches in their place.
> Everyone knew what that meant; everyone knew that a high
> pew was one of the bulwarks of Protestantism, and that an
> open bench had upon it the taint of Rome. But Manning
> hastened to explain. 'My dear friend', he wrote, 'I did not
> exchange pews for open benches, but got the pews (the same
> in number) moved from the nave of the church to the walls
> of the side aisles, so that the whole church has a regular
> arrangement of open benches, which (irregularly) existed
> before. . . . I am not to-day quite well, so farewell, with much
> regard—Yours ever, H.E.M.'
> Archdeacon Hare was reassured. It was important that
> he should be, for the Archdeacon of Chichester was growing
> very old, and Hare's influence might be exceedingly useful
> when a vacancy occurred.

By using a dispute about pews and benches, Strachey manages
to suggest that ecclesiastical arguments are all on this level of
triviality. 'Archdeacon Hare was reassured' reduces the
Archdeacon to a buffoon, and the final comment exposes
Manning as a hypocrite and an opportunist. More than this, by
quoting 'I am not to-day quite well, so farewell' . . . immediately after Manning's 'explanation', he invests the letter
with a very elusive perfunctoriness indeed — though the row of
dots preceding the sentence indicate an omission which would
make the ending less amusingly abrupt.

As a last illustration, I must quote Strachey's picture of Newman in Rome, naïvely* trying to explain his religious opinions
to the Cardinals:

Cardinal Barnabò, Cardinal Reisach, Cardinal Antonelli, looked at him with their shrewd eyes and hard faces, while he poured into their ears — which, as he had already noticed with distress, were large and not too clean — his careful disquisitions; but it was all in vain; they had clearly never read De Lugo or Perrone, and as for M. Bautain, they had never heard of him. Newman in despair fell back upon St Thomas Aquinas; but, to his horror, he observed that St Thomas himself did not mean very much to the Cardinals. With a sinking heart he realised at last the painful truth: it was not the nature of his views, it was his having views at all, that was objectionable.

The foolishness of Newman and the worldliness of the Cardinals are both clearly established. The intellectual integrity of the Church of Rome is very completely demolished. But we can notice also, behind all this, a sense of lurking horror: the horror of Newman's predicament as his attempts to come to grips with Holy Church meet with a Kafka-like unresponsiveness and frustration. His sense of bewilderment and dismay as the 'shrewd eyes and hard faces' of the Cardinals reduce him to silence might have come straight from *The Trial*. Our sympathy is held in check, however, by the urbane amusement of the tone. It is no part of Strachey's purpose to make his characters too humanly real for us.

Strachey's main strategy as a biographer, we may agree, is to denigrate the characters of his eminent Victorians and to discredit their motives. He is blind to their idealism, and makes little serious effort to come to terms with their thought. Manning, Florence Nightingale, Dr Arnold and General Gordon are little more, in his reading of them, than variations on a single theme. Their characters display a core of hard ambition and a thirst for personal glory; reinforced in each by a sense of religious vocation which they take to justify any means or ends that will serve; and disguised in each by an elaborate process of self-deception, which is nowhere clearer than in their prayers and meditations before God. Not for one moment does he suggest that their high moral beliefs might have had equally high origins, still less that their intellectual beliefs might have been in any sense true. He quotes Newman's views on flying houses and Dr Arnold's doubts about the parentage of Abijah's mother, but nothing which would lead us to suppose that these men were among the most intelligent of the nineteenth century. He is careful, indeed, to avoid mention of any of their opinions which do not fall foul of that very reliable English superstition 'common-sense'. He quotes Florence Nightingale's religious beliefs only, I suspect, because he thinks of them as a personal eccentricity, and is not aware of the tradition of Optimism in European thought since Leibniz, to which they belong.

III

This confirms us in our adverse opinion of Strachey as an historian, but gives a clue to his methods and purposes as a polemical writer. If we regard him as a creative writer, we shall be struck by the skill with which he balances minor characters one against the other, and subordinates them all to his portrait of the main character. This main character is, in each essay in turn, first magnified into a public legend, and then diminished and undermined with ridicule. The eminent Victorians are first presented from an external vantage point, and shown at the height of their power; then we are taken into their innermost counsels, to observe what fears and absurdities lurk behind the façade. But even with this second view, they do not become entirely absurd. The legendary figure has some reality behind it — it has, in fact, the driving power of a ruthless and un-qualified egomania. Strachey actually admires his eminent Victorians — rather as one might admire some formidable devil who was somehow unaware of his depravity. His very admira-tion, in this event, is as damaging to the 'real' Victorians as his ridicule; for the monstrous beings who thrill us by their proud inhumanity are unlikely to command any degree of respect.

Manning is built up from the first into a Tamburlaine-like figure, conquering the destinies themselves and irresistible in his rise to fame. 'It was as if the Fates themselves had laid a wager that they would daunt him, and in the end they lost their bet.' This image establishes itself in our mind, and recurs when Manning is at last within sight of the Arch-bishopric of Westminster. 'This time the Fates gave up the un-equal struggle; they paid over their stakes in despair, and

retired from the game.' In the introduction to the essay, before
any nearer view of Manning is given, we have a preview of him
in his glory. He is a splendid and striking spectacle, as fantastic
as some prince in the *Arabian Nights*:

> In Manning, so it appeared, the Middle Ages lived again.
> The tall gaunt figure, with the face of smiling asceticism, the
> robes, and the biretta, as it passed in triumph from High
> Mass at the Oratory to philanthropic gatherings at Exeter
> Hall, from Strike Committees at the Docks to Mayfair
> drawing-rooms where fashionable ladies knelt to the Prince
> of the Church, certainly bore witness to a singular condition
> of affairs. What had happened? Had a dominating character
> imposed itself upon a hostile environment? . . .

This external view remains with us as we read, and we return
to it, with the underlying egomania of the man now known to
us, towards the end of the essay:

> The spare and stately form, the head, massive, emaciated,
> terrible, with the great nose, the glittering eyes, and the mouth
> drawn back and compressed into the grim rigidities of age,
> self-mortification and authority — such is the vision that still
> lingers in the public mind — the vision which, actual and
> palpable like some embodied memory of the Middle Ages,
> used to pass and repass, less than a generation since, through
> the streets of London.

Florence Nightingale is likewise magnified into a huge and
almost superhuman being; into the legend which, in common
with the other eminent Victorians, she successfully made of herself. 'We are ducks . . . who have hatched a swan,' sighs her
mother, as she reflects upon the manner of daughter she has
begotten. 'But the poor lady was wrong,' comments Lytton
Strachey, 'it was not a swan they had hatched; it was an eagle.'
Florence's work in Scutari is given an epic ring: 'The reign of
chaos and old night began to dwindle; order came upon the
scene.' The bringer of order is fierce and relentless, however.
Strachey stresses her 'indomitable will', her 'harsh and
dangerous temper', 'something peevish, something mocking,
and yet something precise — in the small and delicate mouth'.
Dr Arnold is also presented as a memorable figure at the

height of his success — though since he is seen through the eyes of awed and cowed schoolboys, Strachey can now permeate the legend itself with irony.

He himself, involved in awful grandeur, ruled remotely, through his chosen instruments, from an inaccessible heaven. Remotely — and yet with an omnipresent force. As the Israelite of old knew that his almighty Lawgiver might at any moment thunder to him from the whirlwind, or appear before his very eyes, the visible embodiment of power or wrath, so the Rugby schoolboy walked in a holy dread of some sudden manifestation of the sweeping gown, the majestic tone, the piercing glance, of Dr Arnold.

Dr Arnold's preoccupation with the Old Testament is made the pretext for presenting him as a latter-day prophet. 'He would treat the boys at Rugby as Jehovah had treated the Chosen People.' No doubt this very amusingly captures the Headmaster's time-honoured technique of authority; it allows no hint of Dr Arnold's theological liberalism, or of his part in gaining acceptance in this country for the new Higher Criticism from Germany.

General Gordon, as we might expect, is the most exotic figure of all. First we are offered the usual external view of the public hero, though this time the 'faintly smiling Englishman' is made to seem enigmatic, terrible and invulnerable all in one:

Walking at the head of his troops, with nothing but a light cane in his hand, he seemed to pass through every danger with the scatheless equanimity of a demi-god. The Taipings themselves were awed into a strange reverence. More than once their leaders, in a frenzy of fear and admiration, ordered the sharp-shooters not to take aim at the advancing figure of the faintly smiling Englishman.

When we are admitted to his thoughts, we find him intoxicated with images of ambition clothed about with religious sanctions. As he sets out on his ill-fated mission to Khartoum, regarding himself as an instrument marked out by Providence for this moment, and sublimely isolated within his own insights, 'A thousand schemes, a thousand possibilities' sprang to life 'in his polluting brain'. From then onwards, he is increasingly a source of terror to those whom he commands and rules.

The legendary quality of these characters arises from an instinctive cruelty and ruthlessness that separates them from their fellows. Their own minds, for example, are dominated by thoughts of hell fire and damnation, which form a morbid undercurrent to their experience of life. The possible quotations are so numerous that I shall confine myself to one from each essay. Of Manning, we read: 'The more active, the more fortunate, the more full of happy promise his existence became, the more persistently was his secret imagination haunted by a dreadful vision — the lake that burneth for ever with brimstone and fire.' Of Florence Nightingale: 'It was in vain that she prayed to be delivered from vanity and hypocrisy, and she could not bear to smile or be gay "because she hated God to hear her laugh, as if she had not repented of her sin".' Of Dr Arnold, '. . . then, more than ever, he seemed to be battling with the wicked one. For his sermons ran on the eternal themes of the darkness of evil, the craft of the tempter, the punishment of obliquity.' And of General Gordon: 'He began to reflect upon his sins, look up texts, and hope for salvation.' This sort of morbidity is matched by a moroseness of temper and a diabolical disregard for other people that is sufficiently marked to inspire fear. Florence Nightingale is spoken of as 'this bitter creature', and pictured as a variety of unpleasant animals. Arnold and Gordon are both represented as maintaining discipline through terror. And Manning is made to seem even more remarkably inhuman. The speed with which he forgets his wife after her death is intended to shock by its unnaturalness; it is matched later by the completeness with which he forgets his old ally Monsignor Talbot, when that gentleman has been translated from his position of influence to a padded cell.

Strachey's aim is to produce a memorable and skilful portrait of his main character; his treatment of minor characters is wholly assimilated to this intention. It is possible to see these somewhat less eminent Victorians standing in roughly four different kinds of relationship to the main subject of each of the essays. Firstly, there are those who are worthy to be his opponents; then, those who are worthy to be his allies (though only Monsignor Talbot fully qualifies for this honour, since the eminent Victorians prefer to walk alone); then, those who are so many obstacles in his path; and lastly, those who are entirely his victims. These minor characters are carefully woven into Strachey's pattern, and allowed to have the type of reality we feel in a first-rate caricature. It need scarcely be added that they bear little resemblance to the historical personages whose names Strachey has attached to them.

Of the type who are merely obstacles in the path of the hero, we might instance Archdeacon Hare, whom Manning re-assured about the pews — or even better, 'poor General Simpson', 'whom nobody has ever heard of, and who took Sebastopol'. General Simpson plays little part in the narrative except as an example of incompetence; he contrasts strikingly with the efficiency of Miss Nightingale, and forms part of the unpropitious background against which she has to work. The portrait is short and vivid and has clear affinities with the art of Horace Walpole, whose unforgettable accounts, in a dozen letters, of 'the burlesque Duke of Newcastle' is one of the fore-runners of the line of irony in which Strachey stands:

> . . . for, while Lord Raglan had been too independent, poor General Simpson erred in the opposite direction, perpetually asked advice, suffered from lumbago, doubted, his nose growing daily redder and redder, whether he was fit for his post, and, by alternate mails, sent in and withdrew his resignation.

The minor characters who are worthy opponents of the hero include those who are themselves magnified to legendary pro-portions, in order that a clash of great wills or conflicting fanaticisms can take place. This occurs mainly in the essay on Gordon. The first of such characters is the fantastic Hong-siu-tsuen, a religious fanatic built on the same scale as Gordon himself, whose defeat at Gordon's hands is described with a mingling of irony and magnificence: 'In the recesses of his sera-glio, the Celestial King, judging that the time had come for the conclusion of his mission, swallowed gold leaf until he ascended to heaven.'

The Mahdi, as Gordon's central opponent, is also worthy of him, and even wins his grudging admiration. Both men exemplify 'the drunkenness, the madness of religion'. Strachey does not distinguish between the religious systems of each, but is concerned to demonstrate their similarity in terms of inner fanaticism.

The last and more numerous class of minor characters consists of those who are victims of the hero, and a foil to set him off. In the essay on Manning, Newman is chosen for this role. Within the first few pages, Newman's intellectual status is fatally undermined with an impression of gross credulity, in order that his naïveté will heighten the pathos of his predicament, and thereby reflect added discredit upon his tormenter. 'When Newman was a child,' Strachey tells us, 'he "wished that he could believe the Arabian Nights were true". When he came to be a man, his wish seems to have been granted.' After this clipping of Newman's wings, Strachey uses him as a focus for his attacks on the Roman Catholic Church in general, and on Manning in particular. There is, of course, an historic truth in this; no one doubts that Newman was treated disgracefully — nor, for that matter, that Manning was essentially a power-hungry man. But Strachey subordinates history to fiction as always; his semi-witted Newman is magnified into a figure of pure pathos. On the evidence of a chance remark, a letter or so, and one picturesque incident at Littlemore, he does not hesitate to write: 'Since his conversion, Newman's life had been one long series of misfortunes and disappointments,' and to fabricate years of misery and bitterness for the man who wrote in his *Apologia*, with a sincerity that even Strachey admits to be 'transparent', 'From the time that I became a Catholic . . . I have been in perfect peace . . . it was like coming into port after a rough sea; and my happiness on that score remains to this day without interruption.' Strachey assumes, of course, that Newman must 'really' have been ambitious, and must 'really' therefore have been desperately unhappy, despite the slight consolation of his religious beliefs. This failure to understand a man of Newman's cast demonstrates particularly his own limitations as a biographer.

The chief victim of Florence Nightingale was Sidney Herbert, but Clough is the most consistent example of a 'foil'. He is depicted by Strachey with more than usually savage ridicule, since he bumps into two of the eminent Victorians, and into the Oxford Movement as well for good measure, each time with

results disastrous to himself. Strachey not only uses him to set
off the main characters, but makes him exist in his own right as
a ludicrous example of misplaced idealism. He has the same
religious preoccupations as the main characters, but lacks the
ruthlessness which makes them great; there is nothing to shelter
him from open absurdity and collapse. His first encounter is
with Dr Arnold at Rugby, where under the Doctor's influence
he develops that intense moral nature which is to bring him
only torment and futility for the rest of his life. 'Never did Dr
Arnold have an apter pupil . . . He thought of nothing but
moral good, moral evil, moral influence, and moral responsibility.' After leaving Rugby, Clough falls victim to the Oxford
Movement, which first appeals strongly to his moral nature
(thereby illustrating how prone to illusions a moral nature is),
and then causes him, by reason of its inherent improbabilities,
to lose his faith (thereby indicating that even an earnest
adolescent with weak ankles could hardly be bamboozled for
ever). Of his loss of faith, Strachey writes:

> Clough the poet (with others) went through an experience
> which was more distressing in those days than it has since
> become: they lost their faith . . . Clough was made so uneasy
> by the loss of his that he went on looking for it everywhere as
> long as he lived; but somehow he never could find it.

With this nasty jibe, Strachey leaves Clough in mid-air. The
poet makes his final appearance as one of the minions of Miss
Nightingale, where his moral ideals at last find outlet in his
own little niche 'downstairs'.

> There were a great number of miscellaneous little jobs
> which there was nobody handy to do. For instance, when
> Miss Nightingale was travelling, there were the railway
> tickets to be taken; and there were proof-sheets to be cor-
> rected; and then there were parcels to be done up in brown
> paper, and carried to the post.

Perhaps we see Strachey at his most characteristic when,
having shown his hero as a public legend from the outside, and
as a dangerous egomaniac within, he finally admits us behind
the scenes, to the 'real motives' and the ultimate truths of their
lives. Here, for example, are extracts which analyse the 'actual'

M

motives behind Manning's rise to power — the motives in the
light of which his spiritual agonies, recorded in intimate documents and prayers, can be discounted as illusions and treated
as broad comedy. Why, we are led to enquire, did Manning
decide to take Orders? 'He entered the Colonial Office as a
supernumerary clerk, and it was only when the offer of a Merton
fellowship seemed to depend upon his taking orders that his
heavenly ambitions began to assume a definite shape.' But why
did he wish to be an Archdeacon? 'His vast ambitions, his
dreams of public service, of honours, and of power, was all this
to end in a little country curacy "agreeable in many respects"?'
Why did he join the Oxford Movement? 'It was a relief to find,
when one had supposed that one was nothing but a clergyman,
that one might, after all, be something else — one might be a
priest.' Why did he wish to become a Bishop? 'Nobody could
wish to live and die a mere Archdeacon.' Why, finally, did he
go over to Rome? 'The Church of England,' Strachey explains,
'is a commodious institution; she is very anxious to please; but,
somehow or other, she has never managed to supply a happy
home for superstitious egotists.'

Here, then, are the 'real' answers to such questions, and there
is little wonder that Manning's struggles, as he attempted to
find answers of his own, can be depicted for our light entertainment. When he is offered a post as sub-almoner to the Queen,
Strachey records: 'The offer threw Manning into an agony of
self-examination. He drew up elaborate tables, after the manner
of Robinson Crusoe, with the reasons for and against his
acceptance of the post.' These tables, after all, hardly affect the
issue. They are merely evidences of Manning's self-deception,
as he conceals the underlying realities from himself. In many
other passages, the meditations of the eminent Victorians are
held up for our laughter. It is here, perhaps, that we can most
clearly see Strachey's unfitness to come to terms with real
people, even if they were Victorians of an admittedly unusual
kind. I have already suggested that the life of any man might
provide material for a sufficiently determined iconoclast.
Idealists, in particular, are vulnerable to this technique, since
their high standards lead naturally to a sense of unworthiness,
·hich is recorded often enough in documents that were never
˰nded for publication; and their aspiration can very easily

be made to appear as a disguised form of pride. We can reflect further that mental unrest in one form or another is the common lot of great men, since there can be no aspiration without conflict. But Strachey finds in the mental agonies of his heroes signs only of neurosis and self-deception. He provides a picture which even elementary psychology must admit to be very wide of the mark.

IV

In closing, I should like to reassert that I enjoy reading *Eminent Victorians*; my personal sympathies are more with Strachey's own liberal humanism than with the beliefs of most of the Victorians he debunks. But the ironic tricks he uses are irresponsible ones, all the more so in that any party can adopt them readily enough when the tone has been learned. And any party can be corrupted by them.

CHAPTER 11

ALDOUS HUXLEY: AND THE TWO NOTHINGS

I

'CLASSIFIED, like a museum specimen, and lectured about, I felt most dismally posthumous.' This was Aldous Huxley, reminding us that donnish acclaim is not necessarily the summit of a writer's ambition. And if we feel that in his lifetime academic criticism was less than fair to him, to think in terms of posthumous amendment might be, by his own criteria, over-solemn. He has had a wide success after all, among readers who delight in intelligence as an end as well as a means; and time brings the Ph.D. thesis along with the worm.

But it remains odd that the universities have paid so little attention to an outstandingly intelligent writer: odd, and perhaps symptomatic of the mistrust with which intelligence is often viewed in Britain, especially by those who possess it. Not that this is the whole story, by any means. 'Sincerity in Art,' Huxley said more than once, 'is mainly a matter of talent.' The writer who specialises in such truths can be assured of a good many enemies. He is, moreover, an example of the type of writer, more congenial to the French than to the English, who has understood and condemned his own puritanism without in any great measure escaping from it.

My main concern in what follows will be with his irony, which links him with Swift not only in certain specific ways, such as its capacity for disgust and its nearness to tragedy, but also in its continuing relevance as an interpreter of life. 'Add to one touch of nature one touch of irony,' he writes, 'and you have a comment on life more profound, in spite of its casualness, its seeming levity, than the most eloquent ramblings of the oracles.' When such a comment is offered on Gibbon or Voltaire, we are disposed to agree; as a comment on Huxley himself, it runs into hesitations and doubts. Is he not, perhaps, too detached to be a major ironist, or too cynical? When his irony is given full play, are we not reminded of a surgeon with outstanding gifts of diagnosis, whose patients nonetheless always die? The knife cuts sharp and true, but there is no property of healing in it; or possibly the malignancy goes too deep. I shall argue later that Huxley specialises in ironic traps from which there seems to be no way out; that he has a genius for locking us in Doubting Castle and demonstrating that all the keys have been lost. At times, one even feels that his offer to the reader is a simple choice between two Nothings — the Nothing of Mrs Viveash's boredom in *Antic Hay*, and the Nothing of Mr Propter's mysticism in *After Many A Summer*. I shall be returning to this suggestion several times, but it is as well to remember that Swift also can spring traps of a notoriously effective kind; *Brave New World* has more in common with Book IV of *Gulliver* than a few tricks of style. If we look at Huxley's irony not in one work but over a period of years, the notion that he is chiefly a negative writer becomes increasingly hard to sustain. What I want to do here is to look in turn at five of the novels, which between them span the twenty years between the two world wars.

II

Huxley's first novel, *Crome Yellow*, is in the satiric line of Peacock. It is full of fun, as we too easily forget after putting it down, but while some episodes are simply amusing, others already hint at a profoundly disturbing astringency. The hero's torment as an intellectual endlessly wounded by self-knowledge is a clear pointer towards much that is to come.

Antic Hay, written in 1923 and the first to concern us here, is an altogether more important work. As in *Crome Yellow*, we meet a group of characters in whom intelligence is an unfailing source of disquiet. But the range is now wider, and Huxley's irony too subtle for simple analysis. He plays on our own capacity for uneasy self-knowledge with horrifying sureness of touch. More than any ironist I can think of, he evokes fear in his readers as an integral part of his technique. And in *Antic Hay* he explores, as he was to do often, the degree to which honest intelligence can lead to cynicism, self-loathing, mental paralysis rather than to knowledge, self-control and committal. For some critics, this is enough in itself to damn him. They see in it a sort of diabolical gravitation, a foil at best for Lawrence's opposite pull of the intelligence towards moral maturity. To take this view, how-ever, may well be to risk confusing art with morality. It over-looks the manner in which Huxley himself places negative attitudes, in his depiction of Coleman for instance. And it over-looks the difficulties which even Lawrence sometimes had in preserving his vision unspotted from the world. I shall return to this matter later, but wish simply to assert at this stage that the insistence upon degradation and disgust in Huxley's work is not fundamentally due to masochism — though this enters into it — but to his utterly ruthless and uncompromising honesty. What needs to be said, perhaps, is that the puritan tradition, of which we hear a good deal these days, has always included men of Huxley's temperament as well as men of Lawrence's. If moral earnestness, fierce energy, strong com-mittal are one side of puritanism, then revulsion from the body, savage denunciation, bitter irony are no less certainly the other. Huxley's puritanism, I would say, was of Swift's type, which increases rather than diminishes in fierceness as it senses its own impotence to alter anything. It is the puritanism which is compelled to approach the best, if at all, by way of the worst; so that if the worst proves too strong for it, the very energy on which it lives can turn to destruction. To accuse Huxley of frivolousness for not seeing eye to eye with Lawrence is just about as sensible as accusing an agnostic of frivolousness for not professing to believe in God. The difference between the two men is to be thought of in terms of temperament rather than of integrity. Both disturb us in their different ways be-cause they have too much honesty, not because they have too little.

Antic Hay, moreover, is nearer to the centre of twentieth-century literature than any single novel of Lawrence's; its pessimism is nearer to T. S. Eliot, James Joyce, Scott Fitzgerald, Franz Kafka, than is often supposed. In this sense Huxley can be seen as another reporter of the Waste Land; one in whom contemplation of the twentieth century produced a curiously un-English blend of laughter and despair. *Antic Hay* is his first important creative response to the type of society and situation that was later to be satirised equally amusingly, with greater urbanity but far less concern, by Evelyn Waugh.

But Huxley does not write only as a judge, nor does he suggest that any easy solutions exist for the evils and weaknesses that he sees. If the tribulations of the smart set seem well-merited as they progress through self-indulgence to boredom, we are also shown that introspection and self-doubt can afflict any thinking man, irrespective of his degree of moral guilt. When Huxley shows how anything can be grist to this particular mill, from the remnants of a Christian conscience to the newest of Freudian insights, his irony is not only a defensive mis-anthropy, but a glimpse into the traditional hell of ultimate despair. In portraying the unsuccessful painter Old Lypiatt, he undermines creative energy itself by putting its aspirations and pretensions into the mouth of a failure. And in casting doubts on the holiness of the heart's affections, he attacks the very citadel of romanticism; if hopes of self-fulfilment are made to seem as idle as hopes of Heaven, where is the romantic to turn? 'Poor Old Lypiatt' . . . the very formula is a secret nightmare for scores of would-be creative young men, as Huxley very well knew. Nor does he stop here, since Lypiatt has to peel off layer after layer of self-deception as one might peel an onion, until the nothingness of the centre of his life can no longer be doubted or escaped.

Now what is the point of a ruthless honesty like this? A Christian writer might conduct similar operations, as C. S. Lewis does in *The Screwtape Letters*, but as a prelude to grace. In Huxley, there is no *deus ex machina* in the wings, only the erosion of dignity and purpose as one illusion after another is exposed. 'Everyone's a walking farce and a walking tragedy at the same time,' he comments, poor consolation indeed for what has been lost. But we should not overlook the discriminations of cynicism which are already part of the satiric texture: if Coleman's cynicism is a sickness of the soul, Huxley's own cynicism is often the reverse side of the soul's passionate longing for health. *Antic Hay* opens by drawing attention to a dislocation which is at the heart of Huxley's own ironic vision. There are two Gods, one emotional, the other logical, and these two are not One. His hero Gumbril, who is both acutely aware of this dislocation, and afflicted with the characteristic torments of the young,

withdraws into a fantasy world of his own devising. He com-
pounds from elements aesthetic, messianic and erotic a fanciful
self-idealisation, which later impinges on his real life through his
farcical charade as the Complete Man. All of this, we might
agree, is good adolescent psychology, without being startlingly
new. But it is something more as well; there is an intensity of
perception which makes the word 'adolescent' more of a hin-
drance to the critic than a help. Gumbril is surrounded by
other characters who in various ways correspond to his most
cynical apprehensions. In Coleman, who verbalises and luxuri-
ates in filth as a connoisseur might in beauty, Huxley shows us
the last degradation to which accepted cynicism can lead. This
purest variant of hell is a foreshadowing of Spandrell in *Point
Counter Point*, Staithes in *Eyeless In Gaza*, Dr Obispo in *After
Many a Summer* — a whole sequence of cynics who remind us
that though the data for pessimism are such that no honest man
can afford to deny them, the acceptance of pessimism can be
no less than the cancer of the soul. Confronted with such
characters we are able neither to reject them easily, since so
much of what they say is true, nor in any sense to accept them
on their own terms. What Huxley *is* concerned to show, I
imagine, is that 'honesty' is a criterion which must be applied
at least as much to the manner in which a man holds his views
as to the nature of the views themselves. His most evil characters
have among their literary ancestors Iago and Bosola, both very
honest men in their way.

When we turn from Coleman to Mrs Viveash, as she walks
'her private knife-edge between her personal abysses', it is to
encounter another classic type of damnation. '"But I don't
like anyone," cried Mrs Viveash with terrible vehemence.' In
her, cynicism has produced not violence, but the annihilating
prospect of immeasurable boredom. Her eyes, we are told, 'had
a formidable capacity for looking and expressing nothing . . .
as though she were worshipping almighty and omnipresent
Nil.' She too is a prototype for important characters in later
novels — for Lucy Tantamount in *Point Counter Point* who is a
more terrifying variant, and for Helen in *Eyeless in Gaza*, who
is an altogether more rounded and moving one.

On the other side of the picture we find Gumbril Senior, the
first of yet another well-defined and increasingly influential

sequence of Huxley characters — Rachel Quarles in *Point Counter Point*, Miller in *Eyeless in Gaza*, Mr Propter in *After Many A Summer*. Old Gumbril shares with the other people in the novel their sense of futility, but not their propensity to despair. The body might be unredeemable, but there remains a realm of serene disengagement for the soul. What we have to do, he thinks, is to reject 'the wretched human scale' which is 'the scale of the sickly body, not of the mind'. His offer, as I have already hinted, is the possibility of exchanging for Mrs Viveash's Nil, which is the nothingness of the body, that other great Nil, which is the nothingness of the soul.

And this, as we can see looking back, is the true pointer to Huxley's own development as a novelist; the choice which in almost every novel he will return to, with greater or lesser realism as the case might be. But in the years immediately following *Antic Hay*, he was diverted by the influence of D. H. Lawrence into another type of exploration, which reaches its culmination five years later in *Point Counter Point*. 'Man is one,' wrote Lawrence, 'body and soul; and his parts are not at war with one another.' Huxley's sympathetic attempt to come to terms with this view, and his eventual failure to do so, are among the most interesting features of his development. By the early '30s he had reverted to the view of *Antic Hay*, which could be fairly summarised by turning the sentence I have just quoted from Lawrence inside out. In moving as close to Lawrence as he does in *Point Counter Point* however, he proves beyond doubt his own seriousness as a man and a novelist. He provides, too, an important critique of Lawrence himself, and one which it is time that we started to take note of again.

III

'If you only knew how dreadful love seems to somebody who doesn't love, what a violation, what an outrage.' This now familiar torment is Walter's, at the beginning of *Point Counter Point*, and he goes on to reflect as follows.

Perhaps we're brought up too wholesomely and asceptic-ally, he thought. An education that results in one's feeling sick in the company of one's fellow men, one's brothers — can it be good? He would have liked to love them. But love does not flourish in an atmosphere that nauseates the lover with an uncontrolled disgust.

The carry-over from *Antic Hay* is clear enough, but Huxley is ready now to extend his canvas. As the title implies, there is to be a greater variety of characters than before, indeed something of a representative survey. They are likened to the instruments of an orchestra, all of which play their own tunes 'equally right and equally wrong; and none of them will listen to the others.'

Among the characters who can be considered in any way happy John Bidlake is of immediate interest to a reader coming from *Antic Hay*. He is a painter who unlike Old Lypiatt really does have great talent, so that his *obiter dicta* on art are preserved from irony. He is also a lighthearted sensualist, practising sex while Rampion preaches about it, with rather less damage to his partners than readers of the early Huxley might expect. At the other end of the scale, Rachel Quarles finds happiness in renunciation of the flesh, and in the mystic way of negation. Somewhere between the two Lord Edward also achieves the happiness that comes of disengagement, in his case through the abstractions of science. Yet another character who finds happiness, of a kind, is the Fascist leader Webley. Though his pride is the sort which proverbially goes before a fall ('He wants to be treated as though he were his own colossal statue, erected by an admiring and grateful nation'), it is the authentic pride of the prophet — fiercely dynamic for all its arrogance, undeterred by self-doubt up to the actual moment of death.

All of these characters have some measure of contentment with their lot, but the limits within which this happiness exists are sharply defined. Rachel Quarles and Lord Edward win serenity at the expense of human concern. Though the one is a mystic, the other a scientist, both cultivate a degree of detachment which cannot easily be distinguished from indifference. Webley's limited success as a leader rests on the dubious foundation of fascist theory bolstered up by violence; when he is murdered, it seems little more than poetic justice. Even Bidlake's zest and good humour fail to survive the tumour in his stomach, or to see him through with dignity to the grave.

And what then are we to make of Mark Rampion — whose

happiness seems better based than that of the others, and his energy a remarkable triumph, for once, of body and spirit working together? Rampion, one need hardly add, is closely modelled on Lawrence, and his wife Mary on Frieda. The chapter where his first meeting with Mary is described brings to mind Mellors's meeting with Lady Chatterley, as well as Lawrence's personal history. But almost at once, we are struck by something very odd about his place in this novel. Alone among the characters, with the possible and decidedly ironic exception of Webley, he seems not just one instrument singing his own tune, but the very theme the whole orchestra might exist to develop. The pivotal question in this novel, and indeed in Huxley's career as a novelist, turns out to be simply this: is Rampion big enough to contain the whole novel, or is he not? As it turns out, he is not; mainly, one senses, because Huxley's emotional prejudice in his favour cannot finally overcome the weight of creative intuition that works against him. We are not convinced in the end that Rampion is talking about realities; and this is because Huxley himself is not convinced, despite the very best will in the world.

Nor is this any great reason for surprise. Lawrence's attraction to him is at least in part the attraction of opposites. As we hear Rampion expounding Lawrence's ideas in Huxley's prose, there is an unmistakable falsity of tone: everything is familiar, but it is like a lecture on Lawrence rather than the man himself. And alone among Huxley's characters, except for the mystically inclined, Rampion is insulated against the prevailing atmosphere of irony. In a book written by an author to whom irony is something of an instinct, and never more so than when the body is being extolled, this insulation seems doubly artificial. Not that we doubt the sincerity of Huxley's admiration for Rampion. 'He can smell people's souls,' says Mary Rampion, making just the claim for her husband that Lawrence would most have wished. And just for a chapter or so it looks as though Rampion might really swing the whole novel, with its galaxy of bored and wicked people and its disastrous events, into the ambience of his personal vision. The magic is strong enough, at any rate, to hold Huxley's normal vision in balance against something very like its opposite; we can understand how he came, under the spell of it, to write on Lawrence one of the brilliantly seminal critical essays of our time. But in the end, Rampion's dynamic decency doesn't win the day. He vanishes from the novel before its climax, and when the irony of point-counterpoint reasserts itself, it is grimmer and nearer to tragedy than before. Rampion hasn't explained, for all his good sense, the complexities of sexual depravity which Lucy Tantamount, Walter and Burlap in their different ways exemplify. He has analysed but not saved Spandrell, whose nihilism plays a terrifying part in the novel's climax. Above all, he has been unable to exorcise certain *facts*, which haunt Huxley's imagination in all that he writes. There is the cancer which kills Bidlake, for instance ('Deplorable,' writes Philip, 'to see an Olympian reduced by a little tumour in his stomach to the state of sub-humanness'). There is the murder of Webley — the joint outcome of Illidge's social grudges and Spandrell's unmotivated, unassuageable hatred of life. There is the meningitis which kills Philip's young son, with its mindless cruelty, its terrible cat-and-mouse game with its prey.

The novel returns, then, through its vision of the worst that can happen, to Huxley's usual sense of life; that matter is evil, the body a torment and a trap. Philip Quarles, writing about Rampion in his diary, says: 'The chief difference between us, alas, is that his opinions are lived and mine, in the main, merely thought.' This glib and partial antithesis between 'thinking' and 'living' has been taken up by some critics, as though it were also the major difference between Huxley himself as a writer and Lawrence. I have already tried to establish how superficial any such notion would be. Huxley rejected Lawrence in the long run for the same reason that he rejected incarnational religion; attractive though the redemption of the flesh is as a belief, plausible as it can on occasion be made to sound, it didn't *feel* convincing to him in the end. This may have been his tragedy perhaps, or it may have been a simple difference in temperament, deeper than any theorising can plumb. But we cannot doubt that Huxley was as honest in his own way as Lawrence was, equally sensitive and intelligent in his search for truth, though the report that he came back with was darker. His true affinity, as I have already hinted, is with Swift; with the vision of Lilliputian man, incurably small, and Yahoo man, incurably dirty. One of the most perceptive remarks ever made about Swift is Huxley's, and it applies with equal, if not greater force to himself. Swift, he wrote, 'could never forgive man for being a vertebrate mammal as well as an immortal soul'.

What we come back to is the need to distinguish in *Point Counter Point* between cynicism of Spandrell's type, which is the cancer of the soul, and pessimism which might look very cynical, but is the simple refusal of Huxley's personal honesty to abdicate. It is Elinor Quarles who makes, towards the end of the novel, the fullest statement of its main theme: 'But the very possession of a body is a cynical comment on the soul and all its ways. It is a piece of cynicism, however, which the soul must accept, whether it likes it or not.'

'To be with Lawrence,' Huxley wrote elsewhere, 'was a kind of adventure, a voyage of discovery into newness and otherness. For, being himself of a different order, he inhabited a different universe from that of common men — a brighter and intenser world, of which, while he spoke, he would make you free.' Rampion is Huxley's generous salute, as a novelist, to this spell, but the clause 'while he spoke' cannot be overlooked. After *Point Counter Point* Huxley moves off again in his own direction, no longer expecting that the war between flesh and spirit will ever be ended. He intensifies instead his search for man the Houyhnhnm — for the mental abstraction, disguised maybe as an animal, who will offer the spirit an escape from the evils it can no longer hope to cure.

IV

Brave New World, written in 1932, is the best-known of Huxley's novels, and inside its conventions very possibly his best. The theme is an old one; where is happiness to be found? Like many previous explorers, including Dr Johnson in *Rasselas*, the answer Huxley appears to offer is 'nowhere'. 'At the time the book was written,' he commented in 1946, 'this idea, that human beings are given free will in order to choose between insanity on the one hand and lunacy on the other, was one that I found amusing and regarded as quite possibly true.' The novel is similar in structure to Book IV of *Gulliver*, particularly in that the direction the irony seems to be taking is devastatingly reversed halfway through, and everything thrown in the melting-pot again. We are presented at first with a world set in the future; a seeming utopia of a non-moral kind, which turns out to be the creation of applied science harnessed to a totalitarian state. Babies are made and conditioned in test-tubes, luxuries abound; sex has been dissociated at long last from procreation, and freed to compete on equal terms with the other amusements. Dirt and squalor have been done away with, since in a promiscuous society hygiene and cleanliness are everywhere a *sine qua non*. Most sources of tension have dis-appeared with the taboos that engendered them, but if life still threatens to become disquieting, a 'holiday in eternity' can always be obtained with the drug *suma*: 'Christianity without tears,' as Huxley calls it.

The presentation of this Brave New World is shot through with irony, as we should expect. In doing away with pain the scientists have also made an end of greatness. 'Civilisation has absolutely no need of nobility and heroism,' says the Controller, 'these things are symptoms of political inefficiency.' They have also abolished freedom, since the conditioning of babies for happiness has necessarily curtailed their power of choice, and as the Controller also says, what *is* happiness but 'liking what one *has* to do'? Other casualties of the utopian society include liberalism, democracy, Shakespeare and God. There used to be such things, but they were all found conducive to pain, guilt and an unstable society. The individual has absolutely ceased to matter, since if some accident overtakes him, he can readily be replaced from a test-tube. Only the State is unique, and therefore uniquely entitled to preserve itself.

The main ironic points here are clear enough. Reversing his grandfather's belief that science is the generous friend of man, Huxley sees it as his last and deadliest enemy. And anticipating such nightmares as Orwell's *1984* and David Karp's *One*, he foresees the process of conditioning by which a totalitarian regime might abolish the human race as we have hitherto come to know it. He makes the further ironic point that sexual pro-miscuity, though superficially making for happiness, is to any sensitive soul the very negation of it. As we know from his essays, he agreed with Lawrence in thinking that free love is as dangerous, or very nearly so, as 'that melancholy sexual per-version known as continence'. 'Too much liberty is as life-destroying as too much restraint,' he says, and again, 'Nothing is more dreadful than a cold, unimpassioned indulgence.' In the Brave New World of the future any sexual relationship that lasts long enough to suggest emotional attachment is opposed, and 'mother' has become a supremely dirty word.

The trap in the novel is sprung when Huxley turns to the other side of the picture: to Bernard, whose conditioning in the test-tube went wrong, so that his spirit yearns for things other than he has; to the Savage, who continues the old way of life in an artificially preserved New Mexican settlement, until he is disastrously brought face to face with the new. Bernard, who strives towards just the standards by which the new society is tried and found wanting, turns out to be a typical early Huxley hero. His sexual self-consciousness leads to disgust rather than to liberation; and sexuality, when it ceases to be trivial, reverts to being a torment. As to the New Mexican settlement (its location chosen, one wonders, out of fading deference to Lawrence?), it turns out to be every bit as dirty, degraded and neurotic as the London of *Antic Hay*. When the Savage is brought face to face with the new utopia his response to it is so morbid that we feel it to be almost justified after all. The Savage's obsession with Shakespeare proves to be fully as dangerous as the creators of the Brave New World would have anticipated; when he can no longer dramatise himself as Ferdinand he casts himself instead as Othello, the whole force of outraged idealism turning into hatred and violence. His obsession with Jesus shows itself to be if anything worse. In his hatred of amoral pleasures he cries out to be hurt; pain will both prove his manhood, and expiate his guilt. But his disillusionment with Lenina/Miranda is at least as much a satire on himself as on her. When his search for pain turns into action, it can be seen as the cruelty of the puritan temperament having its fling.

In the powerful scene between the Savage and the Controller, both talk the same language, but from opposite camps. The Savage can think of the stable society of 'nice tame animals' only as an outrage; the Controller claims that it is the best of all possible worlds, without pretending that the best is especially good. In his 1946 Introduction, Huxley said that were he rewriting the book he would include a further alternative for the human species. Between lunacy and insanity, there would now be something more positive than a vacuum. The passage is of such key interest that I should like to quote it in full.

If I were now to rewrite the book, I would offer the Savage a third alternative. Between the utopian and the primitive horns of his dilemma would lie the possibility of sanity — a possibility already actualised, to some extent, in a community of exiles and refugees from the Brave New World, living within the borders of the Reservation. In this community economics would be decentralist and Henry-Georgian, politics Kropotkinesque and co-operative. Science and technology would be used as though, like the Sabbath, they had been made for man, not (as at present and still more so in the Brave New World) as though man were to be adapted and enslaved to them. Religion would be the conscious and intelligent pursuit of man's Final End, and unitive knowledge of the immanent Tao or Logos, the transcendent Godhead of Brahman. And the prevailing philosophy of life would be a kind of Higher Utilitarianism, in which the Greatest Happiness principle would be secondary to the Final End principle — the first question to be asked and answered in every contingency of life being: 'How will this thought or action contribute to, or interfere with, the achievement, by me and the greatest possible number of other individuals, of man's Final End?'

The relevance of this to Huxley's later work is beyond question; but in 1932 he chose to leave humanity poised between two types of madness. In later years would his intentions in re-writing have changed again? More than most of our writers, with the supremely honourable exception of Bertrand Russell, he remained flexible amid the rapid vicissitudes of twentieth-century history. The rewriting of philosophies and with them such novels as may be indebted to philosophies has become a major pressure on honest writers today as never before. One wonders what changes Lawrence might have been disposed to make in his world had he lived on into the atomic age.

V

Eyeless In Gaza, published in 1936, might have been Huxley's greatest novel, but unhappily it is badly flawed. The characters all talk too much, holding up the narrative for chapters on end. The hero sprawls through the novel, in essays and jottings more shapeless than one would have thought possible.

The obviously controversial thing about *Eyeless in Gaza* is its bold experiment with time. Like *Tristram Shandy*, it abandons a chronological sequence in favour of a flash-back technique of great complexity. The main events span a period of more than thirty years. Each chapter is headed with the date on which its events take place, and the chapters are interspersed in what appears to be a random fashion.

Now what does Huxley hope to gain by this method? Mainly, I would say, psychological suspense. For much of the time we are wondering *why* the characters are as they are, and the author deliberately holds back key events until we have been able, from their behaviour, almost to deduce what has happened in the past. The extremely important episode surrounding Anthony's relationship with Brian at the time of his death is kept until near the end, when it comes almost with the shock of recognition. Several times Huxley is enabled by his freedom with time to supply vital clues to his characters at moments when these are most useful to our total understanding of them. And we are less disposed to commit ourselves to hasty judgement when certain vital clues from the past are still likely to be revealed. There is, too, something curiously and usefully disturbing about the rapid transitions between (say) Mary Amberley's youthful brilliance, and her squalid degradation in middle age.

The technical experiment is strikingly successful, then, in some ways, but there are losses to balance the gains. Perhaps a novelist can justify the strains put upon us when he tampers with the time sequence only if he has other excellencies of an unusually gripping kind. Sterne can capture our attention with his characters, who are so marvellously vivid and idiosyncratic that the order in which things happen to them hardly matters. James Joyce can hold us, in *Ulysses* if not in *Finnegans Wake*, with his splendid manipulation of theme and symbol. And Virginia Woolf unfailingly captivates us with her style: in which other writer is the tension between an aristocratic tone and a deeply troubled consciousness so poignant, or the gift for writing prose with the intensity of poetry so finely achieved?

N

Huxley, who has none of these virtues to the same degree, is left too nakedly depending on ideas to sustain our interest. Even his visual sense is not good. In *The Doors of Perception* he has harsh things to say of writers who too readily assimilate what is felt to what is thought, perhaps recognising this as a major weakness in himself.

A further disadvantage in the technique is that it distorts certain moments in the past by making them more statically important to the characters than they normally would be. Mr C. B. Cox has made a similar point about Virginia Woolf, and it seems to apply with equal if not greater force to *Eyeless In Gaza*. The importance to Hugh, for instance, of the moment in school when he is caught masturbating by some of his schoolfellows, suggests nothing so much as arrested development. The criticism one has to make on this score is twofold. On the one hand, we are shown Hugh's schoolfellows actually recalling this episode, much later in their lives, behind his back. In other words, Hugh's fears that it will make him permanently ridiculous are not, Huxley would seem to suggest, groundless. But surely in fact they would be — for who cares whether a man has been found masturbating in his schooldays or not? This may seem a minor point, but its implications are rather larger than they appear to be. The great American novelist, Scott Fitzgerald, makes one of the characters in *Tender Is The Night* say this: 'Most people imagine that the attitude of other people towards them swings through great arcs of approval and disapproval.' Fitzgerald, with his unerring sense of social realities, places this fear for what it is. In Huxley, such fears are regarded as normal; indeed, the reader himself is frequently played upon through potential neurosis of the same kind in himself.

The second point that must be made is that moments from the past have this static importance not only for Hugh, who is of a recognisably neurotic temperament, but for Anthony and Helen as well. And when the normal time sequence is departed from, perhaps to some degree this is unavoidable. The different episodes become almost like a series of framed photographs; we compare them with one another with heightened feelings of nostalgia or irony, but the sense of cause and effect is curiously weakened.

Even more than *Point Counter Point*, this novel is punctuated by scenes of violence and disgust, which shape as well as symbolise its central crises. There is Helen's revulsion as a child from the feel of butcher's kidneys, and her disgust and self-disgust when a pet cat dies. There is Brian's violent and terrible death by falling; the amputation of Staithes's leg (after an intolerable delay while Miller discourses on Buddhism); the murder of Ekki by the Nazis. Above all, there is the notorious scene early in the book when Anthony's lovemaking on the roof is cut short by the arrival of a very dead and very messy dog (a misfortune that Mellors himself mightn't have survived, as Huxley could even have reflected when conceiving it). The scene demonstrates the hypersensitivity to suffering of both Helen and Anthony; it also marks a turning point in their relationship, since Anthony comes to realise that he loves Helen as well as he desires her at the very time that Helen is deterred from any further physical intimacy with him. As a symbol of human brutality it is as fierce as anything in Hardy; and I think we feel it is a valid symbol and not merely contrived, since Huxley's revulsion from the natural world is so clearly adequate to it.

Certain of the characters from the early novels reappear, but to be treated with greater realism, so that one is able to feel for them more. Staithes is in the line of Coleman and Spandrell, a Thersites-like commentator bent on 'forcing humans to be fully *verbally* conscious of their own disgustingness'. His description of the making of scent from the excrements of a pole-cat is Swiftian in intensity, yet he is by no means a puppet, since we are permitted to see more clearly than in earlier novels the vulnerability behind his restless arrogance. When he allows his wounded leg to rot away, the desire for pain reminds us of the Savage in *Brave New World*. When he is eventually anaesthetised and the ghastly amputation is taking place, his face in repose has the untroubled innocence of a child.

Helen, too, reminds us of earlier characters — of Mrs Viveash and Lucy Tantamount, though she is more real than the one, and altogether more human than the other. Caught in her 'ordinary hell of emptiness, and drought, and discontent', she has nothing but her own torments to offer to those who are closest to her. Yet the intimacy with which Huxley draws her is remarkable; for once he seems to be exposing himself more than his readers in doing so. And the fact that her affair with Ekki brings her temporarily to life and hope, as though Fate had prepared a crowning savagery for her rebellious and over-sensitive nature, brings her nearer to tragic status than Huxley's characters usually come.

Anthony, who is an extended portrait of the familiar self-wounding, self-consuming intellectual, is also curiously sym-pathetic — if only because he has more to be tormented about, more real cause for guilt, than his earlier prototypes. In spite of his long, shapeless essays, and his endless spiritual exhibition-ism, we are able to feel concern as well as interest for his predica-ment. The tragedy of Brian's death, for which he is morally responsible, has aggravated (as we later learn) his search for safety at all costs. His cynicism, his sexual promiscuity, his intellectual evasiveness are all part of his quest for peace and quiet. When he is forced back into the vulnerable world of emotional relationships again — first by his love for Helen, later by his long-deferred committal to a cause — it is with feelings of the deepest disquiet. Even so, the Cause which eventually attracts him has more to do with mysticism — with the ultimate escape from committal — than with any clear-cut social dynamic. And this, we cannot help remembering, is in 1935.

The picture of Mrs Foxe as a woman in whom genuine charm and religious principle turn, unperceived by herself and under the pressure of almost incestuous possessiveness, into cruelty, is remarkably good of its kind. She is perhaps the one character of Huxley's who might have been created by George Eliot. In the ill-fated relationship between Brian and Joan, Huxley explores with compassion as well as irony yet another classic trap in the no-man's-land between love and sex. Brian is the victim equally of Mrs Foxe, who uses prudery in the service of possessiveness; and of Mary Amberley and Anthony, who allow free love to become an excuse for betrayal. The puritanism of Brian's mother, the licentiousness and treachery of his best friend, alike conspire to bring about his death. The passages leading up to this are among the finest things Huxley achieved as a novelist. But in carrying his art to this new level of psycho-logical realism, he demonstrated how far he was from any belief in earthly happiness, at least for the great majority of human beings as they actually are. The plight of Helen is such that neither dancing (in which she for a moment 'lost her identity, and became something larger than herself'), nor art, nor sexual ecstasy can offer more than momentary respite from the unbearable loathing of self-knowledge. 'Tortured by pleasure, tortured by pain,' she reflects, 'at the mercy of one's skin and mucus, at the mercy of those thin threads of nerves' . . . this is the reality about life, if one is honest. Miller alone among the characters has a genuine hope, which is to escape from this cycle altogether into the untroubled serenity of Nirvana. Again the two Nothings hang in delicate balance, for all the added psychological realism that has been achieved.

VI

The last novel I want to mention, very briefly, is *After Many A Summer*, which brings the wheel full circle. The theme, as the title discloses to those who know their Tennyson, is cruel immortality; the horror of prolonging the life of the body without at the same time arresting its decay. (Here, Book III of *Gulliver*, as well as the inevitable Book IV, springs to mind.) Though in parts very amusing, the novel is wrecked by Mr Propter, whose exposition of man as a 'nothingness capable of free power' sprawls monstrously over half of it. Its theme is nowhere more amusingly stated than in the comments of its ill-starred heroine when she sees two baboons copulating ('Virginia clapped her hands with pleasure. "Aren't they cute!" she cried. "Aren't they human!"'). Dr Obispo's disgust as he examines Mr Stoyte, the would-be immortal, and reflects on 'the whisperings and crepitations inside the warm smelly barrel before him', brings us on to equally familiar ground. The last scene of the novel, a supremely cynical apotheosis of the human beast, is for once comparable, in its sheer audacity, with the denouements of Evelyn Waugh. But an amusing last chapter does not make a major success; *After Many A Summer* has neither the psychological interest of *Eyeless In Gaza*, nor the consistent interest as fable of *Brave New World*. What it does provide for us is the purest expression in the novels of Huxley's constant dichotomy between flesh and spirit. The human animal becomes simply Yahoo, the human soul simply Houyhnhnm; the one loathesome, the other a devitalised abstraction at best. The mysticism which Mr Propter discourses upon as a 'liberation from personality' may strike us as an even greater threat to the individual than the machinations of the scientists in *Brave New World*. Even the small degree of committal suggested to Anthony by Miller's mysticism in *Eyeless In Gaza* has disappeared again, since the idealism of the reformer is just as vain, in Mr Propter's view, as the fornication of the rake. Huxley returned, then, to the total disbelief in worthwhile committal which characterised his early work. And even if the spirit's Nothing had become a shade more emphasised than the body's, a liberal critic would no doubt feel that *here* is the tendency in Huxley that has to be resisted.

VII

From here I can perhaps summarise the case against Huxley, as it is sometimes presented. In moving on to the phase represented by *After Many A Summer* and his later work, does he not offer an impossible dilemma? Instead of *suma*, which came in for ironic treatment in 1933, we are presented with mescalin, of which we are expected to approve. Instead of the Nothing of Mrs Viveash's boredom, we have the Nothing of Mr Propter's religion: a very dubious exchange we might think, in that Mrs Viveash is at least conscious that her Nothing is an emptiness, whereas Mr Propter thinks that his Nothing is everything there is. After the traps have all closed, and the circle of humiliation and suffering is complete, are we not left more or less where we started, having gained from intelligence only a very full insight into its own futility?

The force of this criticism is inescapable, and any answer to it must be of a personal kind. I began by asserting that Huxley had understood and condemned his own puritanism, even though he had never managed to escape from it. Though the events in his novels seem sometimes almost to justify the Colemans and Spandrells, Huxley never fails to discern in them the very sickness of the soul. His own irony, I have argued, is born in the ruthlessness of honesty; if he sets out to shock us, it is as a challenge to new thought, new directions, not to apathy and despair. 'Those who are shocked by truth,' he said himself, 'are not only stupid, but morally reprehensible as well.' How then did he differ from his own most despairing characters? Not, perhaps, by offering a cause we can be devoted to, or by proposing answers to the various problems with which he deals; but by continuing to trust to honesty and intelligence as goods-in-themselves, however dark their data and their situation; by remaining lively, alert, even exuberant whatever the story that he had to tell. I had occasion when writing on Swift to draw attention to an important ambivalence which inheres in the irony of this kind: though its content may sometimes deny the possibility of civilised values, its style actually embodies such values as it goes along. Huxley's exuberance, moreover, was inseparable from his restless curiosity, his constant readiness to change his opinions, or develop them, or reaffirm them as the century unrolled its own surprises and ironies to his gaze. Whereas the Colemans and the Spandrells luxuriate in negation, Huxley himself never ceased to fight against it. In his essays, he frequently made as strong a stand for the liberal decencies as Lawrence himself. The two collections published shortly before his death reminded us that he was not only one of the most intelligent of writers — an endless source of delight to everyone who enjoys ideas — but also one of the most ruthless opponents of cant, prudery, hypocrisy. On art and music he wrote with special authority, since he was not only a connoisseur, but one whose range extended equally to all the arts, and co-existed with creative talents of the most flexible kind. About art he was never cynical, though it had always been something of a mystery to him: how can a race so squalid as ours perceive or create so much beauty? He was, too, always fascinated by the various ways in which art hints at immortality — through the static endurance of its form, so much longer lived than the men who create it; through its suggestion that beauty is, after all, an absolute, upon which windows can sometimes be opened. In *The Doors Of Perception* and *Heaven And Hell*, the part which art played in forming his religious mysticism became clearer than ever before. These two long essays are, I need hardly add, among the most exciting of his writings. They are far more plausible than most of the reviewers suggested, and by no means a further instalment of Mr Propter, as readers of *After Many A Summer* would naturally fear.

In closing, there is one further point which I think should certainly be made. Huxley is often spoken of these days as negative, and resented for a number of reasons, some of which I have discussed. But I think myself that we are faced with a much more terrifying type of cynicism, which is perhaps in the very bones and marrow of the atomic age. Too often these days even liberal writers adopt a tone of portmanteau knowingness — a tone in which protest is automatically made to sound naïve, and moral earnestness the prerogative of the crank. Huxley himself, for all his ironic intelligence, was a writer who still believed that intelligence and irony matter. Whatever the abysses opened up in his novels, he continued to seek for the truth, in a direction which has a respectable history, whether we subscribe to it ourselves or not. And confronted with the brutal or the stupid, he was willing to offer a face-to-face challenge, as were Shaw, Russell and Orwell. Today we need voices that are angered by injustice, but urbane and civilised as well as uncompromising in their anger. I think that Huxley is pre-eminently a writer that university students should be reading, however their teachers may hold aloof.

CHAPTER 12

EVELYN WAUGH:
AND THE MYSTERIOUSLY DISAPPEARING
HERO

I

SHORTLY before the 1959 General Election Mr Waugh was asked by *The Spectator* how he intended to vote. He replied that he would not presume to advise his Sovereign in her choice of ministers: an abdication of civil rights faultlessly urbane, as one would expect, and prompted by the absence of any issues worthy of their retention. More recently, he is reported as saying that he sees nothing objectionable in the total destruction of the world provided that it comes about, as seems likely, inadvertently.

In quoting Waugh from memory (and these dicta were no doubt meant to be ephemeral) I do him an injustice. Much of his success depends on the fineness of his style; 'fine style' thought of in the old-fashioned way, as felicity of utterance, wit, charm, rather than as a vital union of form and moral content. His *bons mots* deserve to be repeated exactly. Take away the verbal precision, and you crash down too violently on the meaning. This very risk, however, might remind us of the twin dangers lying in wait for any discussion of a humorist: you can take him too seriously, or you can take him not seriously enough. To accept Waugh's urbane savagery at its face value might seem monstrous; yet his novels are nearer to Aldous Huxley than to P. G. Wodehouse, when all is said. Thinking back over the sequence, one remembers how often he has taken the equivalent of a Hola or a Nyasaland in his stride, without finding any pressing need to cast a vote; how often his leading characters have suffered a total destruction, inadvertently, in which he appears to find nothing objectionable. His very style poses a problem. It is a civilised style, modifying in the act of saying what is said; guaranteeing, one would imagine, an achieved urbanity beyond the cynicism. Yet Waugh frequently suggests, through his own characters, that such a style can be appearance rather than reality; the *tone* of a polite age, surviving the values that gave birth to it, and remaining as a dangerously misleading façade.

The world which Waugh wrote about best in his early days was the Mayfair world, where such a possibility is most clearly to be discerned. Satiric ruthlessness is tempered, especially in *Vile Bodies*, his funniest book, with bitter-sweet nostalgia for the scenes and people satirised, 'Youth is brief, and Love has wings; Time will tarnish, 'ere we know, the brightness of the bright young things. . . .' In *Decline and Fall*, the first novel, the hero who falls among Mayfair wolves is an average English gentleman of his time. Good-natured, well-educated as theories of education go, an ordinand with an Anglican training and background, placid rather than fiery in his dealings with the world, not very bright but by no means a half-wit, he is the born victim of a corrupt society which he is ill-equipped either to understand or to resist. The Prelude to the novel finds him being sent down from Oxford for indecent behaviour. In no real sense is he guilty, but neither in himself, nor in his associates, nor in the powers-that-be is there a will to establish this. Misfortune throws him back on teaching, and on the engaging cynicism of Dr Fagan of Llanabba Castle.

'I have been in the scholastic profession long enough to know that nobody enters it unless he has some very good reason which he is anxious to conceal. But, again to be practical, Mr Pennyfeather, I can hardly pay one hundred and twenty pounds to anyone who has been sent down for indecent behaviour. Suppose that we fix your salary at ninety pounds a year to begin with?'

The carelessness of the Waugh universe which Paul meets at this stage is a prelude to his more serious disgrace later, and to his gradual disappearance as a real human being. His association with Margot Beste-Chetwynde leads him unwittingly into the white slave trade. When arrested, the remnants of a liberal upbringing fit him only to take the blame in silence. Again, he is in no real sense guilty, but the power, or will, to establish justice does not exist.

Waugh's irony is directed partly, of course, at the fashionable

world in which Paul is lost, but it is in no way motivated by
liberal idealism. On the contrary, the liberal tradition is
satirised at least as strongly as the curruptions. In equipping
Paul with his futile blend of decency and naïveté, it has prepared him as a sheep for the slaughter. When he meets Margot
Beste-Chetwynde he is simply impressed by her. The gaiety,
the charm, the appearance of fragility convince him, and he
sees nothing else of what is there. An education conducted
along impeccably Arnoldian lines has turned him into a waste-
land character, without convictions, without insight into evil,
without any felt or understood values. Given the loneliness of
modern man as well, he seems fated to mistake appearance for
reality; to become an incarnation of the liberally nurtured
innocent abroad.

Just over halfway through the novel, in 'Interlude In Bel-
gravia', Waugh comments on his intentions directly.

> For an evening, at least, the shadow that has flitted about
> this narrative under the name of Paul Pennyfeather materia-
> lised into the solid figure of an intelligent, well-educated,
> well-conducted young man . . . This was the Paul Penny-
> feather who had been developing in the placid years which
> preceded this story. In fact, the whole of this book is really an
> account of the mysterious disappearance of Paul . . .

From this point onwards, concern for Paul as a person is
avowedly withdrawn; 'Paul Pennyfeather would never have
made a hero, and the only interest about him arises from the
unusual series of events of which his shadow was witness.'
At the end, his supposed death, narrated with mock-heroic
echoes of Tennyson's *Morte D'Arthur*, is at the level of satire a
comment on the final stage of his mysterious disappearance. His
'resurrection' is an ironic bow to the resilience of such shades
in the waste land, and in no sense a re-establishment of concern.

II

The interesting feature about the irony is its lack of a centre.
Waugh is dealing here, as he frequently does later, with material
for a bitter indictment of humanity against its own highest
ideals. Few writers have been better acquainted with the shams,
the meanness, the bleakness of the human heart; with what he

calls elsewhere the 'seven-league boots of failure'. In the event, however, it is the ideals themselves, rather than their infringement, which attract his bitterest scorn. No ambition wonderfully to mend the world can be discerned. The liberal parson, Prendergast, is treated with greater irony, for his doubts and his good intentions, than Margot Beste-Chetwynde; at least she survives, while he dies as a martyr without honour. Waugh's insight appears to be of the self-protective kind; his cynicism an armour against idealism, not an offensive weapon in its battles. It is a love–hate relationship that he conducts with human follies; repelled by them, yet savouring them as a connoisseur; reporting them shrewdly, but expecting too little of men to be deeply indignant.

The world of *Decline and Fall* is tough in more ways than one; man is not the only source of inhumanities to man. Little Lord Tangent is the first, but not the last, young victim of a universe which matches human carelessness with a sinisterly ludicrous unconcern of its own. The lack of compassion for his plight, as an accident at the school sports turns by degrees into a death wound, is more than a satiric indictment of his parents. It is an embodiment of the moving spirit of the novel as a whole. Absence of compassion — indeed, a deliberate withholding of compassion — seems at the heart of Waugh's irony. As the leading character, and minor characters, disappear, one feels not only that society doesn't care, and that nature doesn't care, but that the author doesn't care himself. The causes of Paul Pennyfeather's mysterious disappearance are neither explored nor regretted. At the very point where one would expect a writer to be most engaged, Waugh's interest explicitly and aggressively ends. The nearest approach to serious comment is in the form of an assertion of dogma, of unquestioned certainty, which at the very end impresses (and *is* this ironic?) Paul's disillusioned shade.

> Then the lecturer came in, arranged his papers and began a lucid exposition of the heresies of the second century. There was a bishop in Bithynia, Paul learned, who had denied the Divinity of Christ, the immortality of the soul, the existence of good, the legality of marriage, and the validity of the Sacrament of Extreme Unction. How right they had been to condemn him!

Two years after *Decline and Fall* Waugh became a Catholic;
but the tone of his novels remained unchanged. From this time
on, the toll of major characters is formidable. One after another,
they strut and fret their hour upon the stage and then are heard
no more. There is Angela Runcible, whose good-natured
irresponsibility epitomises the bright young things ('too
bogus'), and whose fate it is to be finally faded out by them.
There is the blameless William Boot, who through a series of
misunderstandings is transformed into a foreign correspondent;
who serves, in his innocence, as a superb instrument for Waugh's
ironic survey of Fleet Street, and of politics among the outposts;
and who after further misunderstandings reverts to his old
identity, vanishing without the pangs of actual death at the
moment when some credit might be due. There is Tony Last
in *A Handful of Dust*, whose dull good nature is complexly im-
posed upon, and whose final disappearance into the clutches of
Mr Todd, and an endless round of Dickens in the swamps, is
the most exuberantly audacious annihilation that even Waugh
has conceived. There is Prudence in *Black Mischief*, whose desire
to be eaten by her fiancé (such wishes in a Waugh novel are not
safe) is magnanimously granted. There is Aimee, the loved one,
who vanishes to that Heaven where once a year she will wag
her tail and remember.

In all these novels, the disappearing heroes are similar to
Paul Pennyfeather: a mechanism for social satire, but in themselves scarcely important. Yet the fact that Waugh uses them in
this way robs his satire of much human sting; an irony used to
evade humanity is very far from the tradition of Swift, of
Gibbon, of Voltaire, of Orwell. This becomes clearer when one
notices the two more positive emotions which break fitfully
through the prevailing carelessness; tenderness, and nostalgia.
There is tenderness in Waugh's picture of John Andrew in *A
Handful of Dust* (one of the most human characters he has
created), and in the final reflections of Prudence as she sets out
for home in *Black Mischief*. There is nostalgia, of a richly memorable kind, in the opening chapters of *Brideshead Revisited* as well
as frequently elsewhere. Clearly, Waugh is not lacking in
human feeling. What he lacks, it seems, is any confidence in it,
at least as a reality to trust. When tenderness is turned into
social action, he recoils in scorn from the stupidity. When it

arouses personal expectation, as in *Brideshead Revisited*, betrayal
is always in the offing.

III

I have mentioned *Brideshead Revisited*, and this is the novel on
which discussion of Waugh is bound to centre. It is his greatest
success, and his most regrettable failure; a central example of
his strengths, and his weaknesses, as a writer. From the opening
pages, one feels that Waugh is writing altogether more seriously
than usual. Sebastian and Charles develop more realistically,
more sympathetically, than any previous characters. At last, the
characters really matter, it seems — to the author himself, if
not perceptibly to the universe they inhabit.

The first half, 'Et In Arcadia Ego', fully bears out the promise;
it is, indeed, Waugh's one claim to belong to the main tradition
of the English novel. This makes the shock of the second section
even greater, when the expectations aroused are most rudely
shattered: almost, one is tempted to feel, as though Waugh goes
out of his way to be revenged on writing which has taken him
on to more dangerously human ground than he wishes. Instead
of Sebastian's *malaise* being further explored, it is distanced and
abandoned. The inner realities of his unsuccessful rebellion
against his mother, and against his religion, are nowhere
touched on; the reasons why his great natural gifts of gaiety,
good nature, happiness, and with them the idyllic promise of
springtime Oxford, should fail, are simply evaded. Instead, he
turns out to be yet another mysteriously disappearing hero. A
shadowy existence remains, which we hear of occasionally from
the outside, and are told might be religiously acceptable in
some way that the novel fails to make clear; but as a character
Sebastian is no longer there. Nor is this all. The other erring
Catholics are brought back to their fold, by as sorry a piece of
supernatural manipulation as I can recall, and the intervention
of 'grace' is a virtual rejection of the distinctively human
development promised — or so one had assumed — earlier.

The position of the agnostic narrator, Charles, is of especial
interest. As Sebastian vanishes, Charles moves into the centre
of the picture in his own right. Waugh doesn't, it is important
to acknowledge, weight the scales against him. He is allowed to
exist with a viewpoint which to the Catholic mind appears as

invincible ignorance, but which is represented, nonetheless, as intelligent, morally sincere and at least plausible as an interpretation of events. He is forced to consider Catholicism closely because his relationships with the Marchmain family deeply affect his own happiness. He remains, throughout the main action of the novel, intellectually and morally unconvinced. Because of this, his personal closeness first to Sebastian, and later to Julia, is thwarted; his attempts, in Forster's terms, to 'connect', break against the barriers of creed. Not only is he obliged to let Sebastian vanish beyond the reach of any hope, or wisdom, he might himself offer, but later he loses Julia as well. The affair between them founders on the Catholic objection to remarriage after divorce. Julia, whose love for Charles is represented as the greatest human experience of her life, renounces him; the faith which leads Sebastian to become the drunken hanger-on at a monastery drives Julia also into her willed loneliness.

If Waugh had succeeded in representing Julia's faith in human terms demanding respect equal to Charles's agnosticism, the novel might, despite everything, have been great. Instead, the pull of Catholicism is talked of as a mysterious compulsion; partly explained, no doubt, by the antiquity of the family, and the considerations of class and privilege which also enter in, but also supposed by the Marchmains themselves to be an inevitable, rather than a pathological, part of the Catholic consciousness. Charles's position can be explained in terms of the integrity of human relationships, and the claims of love and loyalty to make their own laws, and to work out their own salvation. Against this, what Julia has to offer (and I can think of no more telling passage in Waugh's writings) is this: (She is replying to Charles's question 'What will you do?' which follows her decision to leave him).

'Just go on — alone. How can I tell what I shall do? You know the whole of me. You know I'm not one for a life of mourning. I've always been bad. Probably I shall be bad again, punished again. But the worse I am, the more I need God. I can't shut myself out from His mercy. That is what it would mean; starting a life with you, without Him. One can only hope to see one step ahead. But I saw to-day there was

one thing unforgivable — like things in the schoolroom, so
bad they were unpunishable, that only mummy could deal
with — the bad thing I was on the point of doing, that I'm
not quite bad enough to do; to set up a rival good to God's.
Why should I be allowed to understand that, and not you,
Charles? It may be because of mummy, nanny, Cordelia,
Sebastian — perhaps Bridey and Mrs Muspratt — keeping
my name in their prayers; or it may be a private bargain
between me and God, that if I give up this one thing I want
so much, however bad I am, He won't quite despair of me
in the end.

'Now we shall both be alone, and I shall have no way of
making you understand.'

Julia is seeing her relationship with Charles, it appears, not
as he does in terms of human loyalties and responsibilities, but
as part of a spiritual game of chess. She is bad, and if she gives
up the one thing she wants most — it happens to be Charles —
possibly God will forgive her for other sins. In this calculation,
Charles features purely as an object; as though he were a
Chinese vase of a rather precious kind, or at the best a habit of
promiscuity. As a real person, he counts not at all; and the
notion of a God who sets an absolute wedge between the best in
human love, and love of Himself, is in no way challenged by
Julia. It is particularly interesting that Julia should revert, in
the course of explaining herself, to the terrors, comforts and
authorities of the nursery: one is left wondering whether Waugh
includes this imagery in a spirit of defiant paradox, or whether
it is an unconscious give-away of the selfishness and immaturity
of her choice.

In this speech, Julia herself vanishes — as a 'real human
being', to quote Waugh's earlier words on Paul Pennyfeather.
This time, however, the disappearance is with the connivance
of the author (or so one imagines): indeed, with his approval.
Brideshead Revisited, which begins like a masterpiece, ends with
the most explicit of Waugh's evasions. We are not *shown* who is
twitching upon the thread, but my guess, for what it is worth,
would be Sebastian's also vanished Aloysius. Little wonder that
Waugh normally prefers his shrewdly journalistic irony to the
sending down of plummets into the human heart.

In *The Ordeal of Gilbert Pinfold* Waugh places the scolding and mocking voices, inside or outside, which demand engagement, firmly in the realm of hallucination. Mr Pinfold, having exorcised them, claims the right to continue his secluded, inoffensive life; kindly rather than cruel; good-natured to his friends; irascible when intruded upon; free from either the obligations or the discomforts of a 'social conscience'. In itself, this is normal and pleasant enough: a choice of the sabine farm, far from the madding crowd's ignoble strife. There are, however, two reservations which such an attitude — and in a large part Waugh might be proposing this ideal for himself — entails. The first is that it does not make for great art, which presupposes, indeed, the rejection of such an attitude, in favour of exactly the costly identification with suffering humanity here refused. The other is that it does not confer the right to satirise the liberals, the idealistic — the 'do-gooders', if one likes — as Waugh habitually does. It is no accident that so many of his main characters disappear mysteriously at the point when to an engaged artist they would become most challenging; and that the quality of his detachment might have to be defined, in the end, as an irony of moral withdrawal.

IV

I have said enough to indicate my own view that Waugh is not a major writer. It is equally necessary to discover the reasons why one continues to read him with pleasure, and to sense that he has a distinctive place, with certain others not unlike him, in the literary tradition. To regard him merely as a 'symptom', or as one more journalist of the waste land, is less than adequate. As a stylist he excels; as a writer who can make one laugh aloud he has few equals (Wodehouse, Amis, not many others) among living British writers. As a reporter of certain types of setting — the Mayfair smart set, the British colonial, the officers' mess in wartime — he is scarcely surpassed. It would be nearer the mark, possibly, to say that though he lacks the moral seriousness which major writers in one way or another share, he does, to a high degree, have the gift of creating his own world: a world which convinces us, if we submit to it, by its internal coherence — its 'flavour', which pervades everything, cannot be confused with any other literary experience, and can never be wholly

o

forgotten. This gift is seldom talked about in literary criticism these days; it is shared by certain other early twentieth-century writers, in themselves totally dissimilar, (Chesterton, Kipling, Beerbohm, T. F. Powys, for example) who are praised, if at all, with caution. It is, I suspect, in itself a rare form of literary distinction; one which contributes greatly to the success of any writer who pleases many and pleases long; and one which is shared with most of the great writers by certain others, less great, yet oddly haunting in their appeal.

The problem raised by a writer's 'flavour' — especially when he is otherwise less than great — is admittedly difficult. How far can disbelief, and especially moral disbelief, be suspended? — how far should it be? Even writers of the stature of Swift can pose the problem. In Book IV of *Gulliver*, for example, we are almost persuaded while reading that man *must* be either a Houyhnhnm or a Yahoo. The analysis, preposterous though on a moment's reflection it is, receives such force from Swift's style that we submit at the time, and can never afterwards wholly forget the particular impact of the work. An O'Neill play can really convince us, for an hour or two, that a claustrophobic, self-pitying group of failures embodies the ultimate truths about the nature of man. Later, one knows it is not true; yet it is a partial truth, and so strongly conveyed that it remains, unexorcised, with its power to extend human sympathy and understanding.

Swift and O'Neill are great writers in a way Waugh is not. The experience they offer, though incomplete (and who, except Shakespeare, *is* complete?) includes important partial truths shot through with deep human concern. This concern is exactly, I have argued, what Waugh lacks. His novels do not extend our awareness of *why* people are as they are, and they inhibit rather than create compassion. Yet he, too, offers important partial truths. In the realm of sophisticated and well-educated worthlessness there *are* people like Margot Beste-Chetwynde and Brenda Last; no theory of man which overlooks them is really safe. The realism at this level is much enhanced by the flavour of Waugh's novels: unique, unforgettable, waiting with something of the quality of an old friend, despite everything, wherever one chooses to enter. I think it unlikely that this body of work, any more than Chesterton's or Wilde's, or Kipling's, will ever be wholly neglected.

CHAPTER 13

ORWELL: IRONY AS PROPHECY

I

'THE durability of *Gulliver's Travels* goes to show that, if the force of belief is behind it, a world-view which only just passes the test of sanity is sufficient to produce a great work of art.' These are the concluding words of 'Politics vs. Literature', Orwell's famous essay on Swift. They were written in 1946, a year or so before the publication of *1984*, but they strikingly anticipate the problem he was soon to be offering himself.

Since I have started here, Orwell's debt to Swift must be briefly touched on. It is more a similarity of temperament, perhaps, than a direct debt of style — and a partial similarity at that, since Orwell seems to me perhaps saner, if not greater, than Swift. Both men were prone to a tragic pessimism, which colours their irony in a distinctive way. There are not a great many resemblances of ironic technique, but some of the situations in *1984* remind us of Orwell's recent interest in *Gulliver*. In the Black Book of the supposed rebellion, for instance, Winston Smith reads of fantastic experiments conducted by scientists in violation of all common sense:

> In the vast laboratories of the Ministry of Peace, and in the experimental stations hidden in the Brazilian forests, or in the Australian desert, or on lost islands of the Antarctic, the teams of experts are indefatigably at work. Some are concerned simply with planning the logistics of future wars; others devise larger and larger rocket bombs, more and more powerful explosives, and more and more impenetrable armour-plating; others search for new and deadlier gases, or for soluble poisons capable of being produced in such quantities as to destroy the vegetation of whole continents, or for breeds of disease germs immunised against all possible

antibodies; others strive to produce a vehicle that shall bore its way under the soil like a submarine under the water, or an aeroplane as independent of its base as a sailing ship; others explore even remoter possibilities such as focusing the sun's rays through lenses suspended thousands of kilometres away in space, or producing artificial earthquakes and tidal waves by tapping the heat at the earth's centre.

The scientists at Balnibarbi also carried out extremely foolish experiments, which Swift writes about in somewhat similar terms. An even more interesting resemblance exists between the austerities of the world of *1984* and the Utopian aims and achievements of the Houyhnhnms. The very programme of the Party, as O'Brien on one occasion describes it, might pass for an account of the Houyhnhnms: 'The sex instinct will be eradicated. . . . There will be no curiosity, no enjoyment of the processes of art.' The Houyhnhnms, like the rulers of *1984* in fact, are concerned to diminish individual consciousness by every means open to them, in pursuit of a systematic social purpose.

These similarities do not, however, go very deep: or perhaps one should say that the differences are what chiefly matter. Swift's scientists are at least well-meaning in their folly, but Orwell's are the puppets of an infinitely sinister State. Swift's Houyhnhnms aspire to brotherhood and serenity, to the un-ambiguous betterment of their race, but Orwell's Party wants only fear and annihilation: the unfettered reign of rage, fear, cruelty, madness and despair.

My main concern is not, however, to compare the two works, but to pursue Orwell's own judgement of Swift, as it might be turned upon himself. Does *1984* proceed from 'a world-view which only just passes the test of sanity'? Let me say at once that the view of *1984* as a simple excursion into mania seems to me wholly untenable. Even though Orwell admitted that the shadow of illness fell over his last work ('It wouldn't have been so gloomy if I hadn't been so ill'), there is no escape by this route from *all* the gloom that is cast. If the author of *Burmese Days* and *Homage To Catalonia* is not sane, then who is? What might have to be conceded, however, is that though pre-eminently a guardian of our radical sanities, he was prone from

his earliest days to moods of sullen bitterness with life. This
bitterness is a curiously complex affair, part personal, part
philosophical, part political. It ranges from tragic pessimism at
its most noble, to sullen indifference at its most depressed. There
seems to have been scarcely a moment when he was not haunted
by the spectre of the worst that might happen, both to himself
as an individual, and to the human race. An inversion of
romantic optimism can often be detected in him: yet an inversion which is so far from being purely personal, that we feel it,
at times, as the imagination of the twentieth century itself. In
the Black Book of *1984* the following passage is to be found:

> . . . in the general hardening of outlook that set in round
> about 1930, practices which had been long abandoned, in
> some cases for hundreds of years — imprisonment without
> trial, the use of war prisoners as slaves, public executions,
> torture to extract confessions, the use of hostages, and the
> deportation of whole populations — not only became com-
> mon again, but were tolerated and even defended by people
> who considered themselves enlightened and progressive.

Whatever we may decide about *1984* as a whole, the truth
of this passage can scarcely be challenged. If it is nightmare,
then it is the nightmare of us all. Beside it, one might set words
written more recently by another of our great radical prophets
of doom. In an article sponsored by *The Observer* on the occasion
of his ninetieth birthday, Bertrand Russell had this to say:

> Ever since 1914, at almost every crucial moment, the wrong
> thing has been done. We are told that the West is engaged in
> defending the 'Free World', but freedom such as existed
> before 1914 is now as dim a memory as crinolines. Supposedly
> wise men assured us in 1914 that we were fighting a war to
> end war, but it turned out to be a war to end peace. We were
> told that Prussian militarism was all that had to be put
> down; and, ever since, militarism has continually increased.
> Murderous humbug, such as would have shocked almost
> everyone when I was young, is now solemnly mouthed by
> eminent statesmen. My own country, led by men without
> imagination and without capacity for adaptation to the
> modern world, pursues a policy which, if not changed, will

lead almost inevitably to the complete extermination of all
the inhabitants of Britain. Like Cassandra, I am doomed to
prophesy evil and not be believed. Her prophesies came true.
I desperately hope that mine will not.

The oddity of Russell's life is instructive, as he suggests himself. A liberal Victorian, born thirty years before motor cars or
aeroplanes were thought of, and forty-two years before the
First World War, he lives on in judgement upon us from that
near yet almost unthinkable past. To have retained an exceptional degree of talent and urbanity to so great an age, yet to
be regarded by large sections of the popular mind for this very
reason as both senile and delinquent, is surely an ironic
denouement. The role Russell has inherited, in his own view of
it, is that of Cassandra, one of the classically ironic *personae* of
antiquity. Any century which can treat an eminent Victorian
in so unlikely a way has a remarkable capacity to surprise.

George Orwell was born later than Russell and died earlier,
but his radical consciousness of the modern world is in some
measure akin: hence the violence of his despair. Most satirists
sense some kind of abyss between actual human behaviour and
the ideal, and use exaggeration in pursuit of reform. But the
satirist who senses that the ideal is actually unobtainable may
find his very exaggeration taking on prophetic force. Eventually
he may move away from satire altogether, towards a deeply
tragic view of life. The darkness of *1984* would surely have
amazed and horrified even Swift. *A fortiori*, it would have
amazed and horrified almost any eminent European one could
name who happened to be born during the three or four
centuries immediately preceding our own. This is one of the
reasons why Russell's perspective can be especially useful to a
critic of *1984*. It is becoming fatally easy just now, I shall
suggest, for familiarity with apocalyptic forebodings to breed
for them a dangerous contempt.

II

1984 is best approached by way of the early Orwell, rather
than as a phenomenon on its own. Sir Richard Rees has discerned in Orwell, in his recent excellent biography, four
apparently contrasting strains: the rebel, the paternalist, the

rationalist and the romantic. He has reminded us that Orwell was a man in whom a passionate desire for justice and a passionately bitter pessimism were always apt to meet. Possibly in some sense this could be said of all major satirists, but in Orwell the conjunction seems especially close. His anger is curiously poised between the constructive and the negative. There is genuine hope for moral improvement in men as a realisable ideal, and genuine fear that such improvement may be incompatible with human nature as it is. The hero of *Keep The Aspidistra Flying* is a fairly obvious example of a man in whom anger begins in hope, but ends in blackness and despair. He rages against hypocrisy and cant, and the ideal he fights for — a more egalitarian, more vital humanity — would be acknowledged by many great rebels of the modern world. But this idealistic anger readily merges into something very different from itself, an 'evil mutinous mood', to use Orwell's own term. Self-pity and laziness, cruelty and despair tinge and colour the anger, until it becomes an insupportable burden to the hero himself, and to everyone he is concerned with. Notoriously, anger is a chameleon emotion, changing colour and mood unnoticed, and very subtly allowing the best in a man to offer sanctions to the worst. The uniqueness of Orwell's anger is that he was entirely conscious of these dangers, as he shows in this fairly early work, yet entirely unable to escape from their implications. His consciousness of the worst that can happen, both for one individual man and for humanity, was almost obsessive. The worst enforced itself upon him as more powerful, because more plausible than the best: indeed, as more powerful because more plausible than the second-best, in so far as this can be equated with a world of mixed good and evil, guilt and expiation in which most men conceive their lot. His anger becomes, at such times, his awareness of life itself. One can no longer distinguish it from a grim sense of some hostile inevitability, against which moral idealism is fated to wrestle in vain.

In the early Orwell as well as in the later, one sees side by side with pure ideals of justice and humanity this pure doubt about whether men are capable of achieving such ideals. It is not only his attitude to the working class that is notoriously ambivalent, but almost equally his attitude to that smaller class to which he himself reluctantly belonged: the well-educated, middle-class

intellectuals, aspiring to intelligent committal and goodwill in
an increasingly chaotic world. The working-class characters in
his early novels may not be as grotesquely inadequate as the
sheep in *Animal Farm* or the proles in *1984*, but they offer little
social hope for a rational mind. In the same way, the real-life
intellectuals of the '30s may have been less systematically
corrupt than Napoleon or O'Brien, but in Orwell's eyes they
were no trustworthy architects of a better world.

He had, in fact, a very English dislike of intellectuals,
suspecting that anyone willing to wear such a label would be
diminished and depraved by it. He mistrusted the utopian
aspirations of many left-wingers, feeling that behind their true
radical decency there was a fatal failure to *see*. What did they
fail to see? Partly, that pacifism was parasitic on exactly the
forces and people it scorned (he quotes with approval Kipling's
famous jibe, against those who mock 'the uniforms that guard
you while you sleep'); partly, that an élite mentality can be
both arrogant and unrealistic in assessing its own importance
to the world. Most of all, however, he thought the left-wing
idealists failed to see those evil forces of which he was almost as
conscious in his early life as when he came to write *1984*: the
harsh realities of power, underlying parties of the left as well as
of the right, and making any simple formula of good versus
evil dangerously trivial and naïve.

Orwell's scepticism centres on his feelings about power, but
he had doubts about the human body as well. Salvation by
Freud convinced him as little as salvation by Marx. It is not
that he is hostile to the body, as Aldous Huxley so often is.
On the contrary, he accepts sex with almost Lawrentian completeness. He was on the side of the body against its moralistic
detractors, whoever they were. In *1984* the fact of sex becomes
a possible hope for humanity, when nearly every other hope
has failed. Nevertheless, he differs from Lawrence in the length
to which this hope can be made to go. Winston Smith's affair
with Julia in *1984* is strikingly unlike Mellors's affair with Lady
Chatterley, and the difference is at least partly accounted for by
Orwell's superior realism. Whereas Lawrence's vision of sex is
an idyllic fantasy, Orwell's is infused with the ruthless clear-
sightedness which he brought to politics, and to every depart-
ment of life. Like Huxley, he doubts the body's ability to stand

up to the wear and tear of salvation by sex. Even his early heroes are ordinary rather than outstanding men. They are tormented with anxieties about false teeth, bald spots, growing paunches, disabilities which Lawrence's men either did not have, or which they somehow took in their stride. Sexually, they are competent performers rather than athletes. The last hero, Winston Smith, is recognisably within their line. Long before the cruel onslaught against his body in the Ministry of Love, he is conscious of his poor appearance, his tiredness, his false teeth. Sex has always been as much a burden to him as a delight. After the bitter poetry of the furtive and the unhappy, he has found himself soiled and still alone.

Even his affair with Julia, when almost impossibly it comes about, is touched with ambiguity. Julia has more will than he has, but less imagination. The frankness with which sensuality is given and taken redeems it from shame; there seems to be a real hope for freedom and honesty in the unconquered compulsions of physical need. Nevertheless, the love between Winston and Julia is broken in the end and turned to hate: by the agency of a hostile society, it is true, yet by a society which uses the intrinsic, and even inevitable weaknesses of the body to achieve its aims. In the Ministry of Love Winston is submitted to physical indignities more extreme than any envisaged by Swift, or even Huxley, in their grimmest moods. O'Brien is able to present Winston to himself, after weeks of torture, as a being hideously and irreparably broken in body and mind. The passage is one of the most terrifying in the book, but it is also one in which Orwell makes explicit certain fears, or perceptions, which haunted his imagination from the start. O'Brien is speaking:

'Look at the condition you are in,' he said. 'Look at this filthy grime all over your body. Look at the dirt between your toes. Look at that disgusting running sore on your leg. Do you know that you stink like a goat? Probably you had ceased to notice it. Look at your emaciation. Do you see? I can make my thumb and forefinger meet round your bicep. I could snap your neck like a carrot. Do you know that you have lost twenty-five kilograms since you have been in our hands? Even your hair is coming out in handfuls. Look!'

He plucked at Winston's head and brought away a tuft of hair. 'Open your mouth. Nine, ten, eleven teeth left. How many had you when you came to us? And the few you have left are dropping out of your head. Look here!'

He seized one of Winston's remaining front teeth between his powerful thumb and forefinger. A twinge of pain shot through Winston's jaw. O'Brien had wrenched the loose tooth out by the roots. He tossed it across the cell. 'You are rotting away,' he said; 'you are falling to pieces. What are you? A bag of filth. Now turn round and look into that mirror again. Do you see that thing facing you? That is the last man. If you are human, that is humanity. . . .'

We are faced here, admittedly, with the gloating of a sadist who, as Inquisitor, has truth as well as power on his side: it is the madness of one man, and of the system for which he stands. But mortality and corruption are not exclusive to madness and sadism, as we too well know. Is our terror in responding to this not to some degree for humanity itself, inevitably broken on the wheel of time? Any purely humanistic programme for human fulness must take account of these betrayals of the flesh. It was Orwell's fate to be particularly obsessed by them, even before the last illness during which he wrote *1984*. He was compelled it seems to confront the worst that can happen before allowing himself to place very much reliance on the best. And confronted with the worst, he doubted whether the luck needed to ward it off could be trusted to hold: Room 101 overshadows his creative imagination from the first. In the passage I have just quoted, O'Brien deliberately sees Winston not as one man, but as a microcosm — as Everyman, or what is left of Everyman after the worst has come about. But as early as *A Clergyman's Daughter* (a very fine novel, though Orwell turned against it himself) a foreshadowing of this situation can be found. There is an unforgettable night scene in which the heroine, reduced to utter destitution, finds herself among the homeless and outcast in Trafalgar Square. In literary terms, the scene owes much to the Circe episode in Joyce's *Ulysses*, but the nightmare quality is all Orwell's own. There is an indictment of society as in *1984*, but the degradation seems to embody, beyond this, some ultimate fear. In *Keep The Aspidistra Flying* the hero sinks gradually and wilfully through the very worst degradation he can find. Though his rejection of society starts in idealism, it degenerates into bitter hostility to all moral effort. His one aim, after a time, is to sink to a place where rage, love, hope, shame are all dead.

Obviously Orwell is not identified with his hero at this point, but we can hardly doubt that the temptation was his own. To call it a death-wish would be true, but too simple; just as the diagnosis *nostalgie de la boue* would be too simple, though some close relationship can be acknowledged between the moods. There is no glamour in Orwell's depiction of degradation, any more than there is in Joyce's in *Ulysses*. What there is, rather, is fear: the fear that Orwell himself, and perhaps humanity with him, belongs with the worst, as a final and fitting home.

In his own life, Orwell renounced his upper-class education and career, and identified himself with the down-and-outs of London and Paris. He found his home with humanity at what Eugene O'Neill in *The Iceman Cometh* called 'the last port of call'. He did this without glamourising the down-and-outs, in fact with an almost nauseous sense of their sheer, physical smell. The proles in *1984* are a last, and especially unpleasant, embodiment of Orwell's constant intuition about last-ditch humanity. 'If there is any hope,' Winston Smith always reflects, 'it lies with the proles.' The irony of this is near to the centre of Orwell's life.

I have stressed this side of Orwell's sensibility partly because the gulf between his last novel and everything that he wrote before has often been exaggerated. It remains true, of course, that his sense of human dignity and resilience is equally strong in very nearly everything he wrote. Against the dark vision of man, and the forebodings, he posed a passionate and unrelenting radicalism: he was determined that humanity should triumph and be great. It is these latter qualities which help to make him a major writer in a way that Aldous Huxley, for all his honest intelligence, is not. The sourness of life cannot by itself produce art as important as we feel Orwell's to be. In Orwell, the sourness is held in tension with creative vitality of unusual generosity and warmth. Like the other great moderns (as Stephen Spender has recently reminded us), he often seems a true Atlas-figure, bearing the whole weight of our twentieth-century consciousness alone.

In *Keep The Aspidistra Flying* Orwell presented a picture of the worst that might happen inside one man. The horror was alleviated, but hardly cancelled out, by the hero's half-ironic capitulation to the aspidistra in the end. In *1984*, he presents a picture of the worst that might happen to the human race. This time, no escape route is offered on the concluding page. Exclusion of hope (the massacre of hope, one might call it) is a central purpose of the work. As readers and critics we are confronted with questions of most urgent relevance to our own world and destiny. Is this vision of evil a disease, which Orwell merely projects upon the world in which he lives? Or are his evil apprehensions prophetic, and unfamiliar to us only in so far as we desperately wish to evade the truth? The antithesis can be put in a more literary form. Is *1984* a genuine satire, in the sense that it exaggerates an evil possibility in order to warn and deter? Or is it saying that the evil possibility is now the only one? That of the many possibilities for good and ill that have faced the human race, only the very worst can now come true?

III

But first, a few words about *Animal Farm*. Though based on the Russian Revolution and its aftermath, this grim little parable is by no means about Russia alone. Orwell is concerned to show how revolutionary ideals of justice, equality and fraternity always shatter in the event. The ironic reversals in *Animal Farm* could be fairly closely related to real events since the work was written (this is not the least of their effectiveness) as well as to the events on which they were based.

The charting of disillusionment is not new to our political scene. Shakespeare in *Julius Caesar*, Hobbes in *Leviathan*, Milton and the Romantic Poets, have all had their say. What *is* new about our modern disillusionment is its scale. More insistently than ever before, revolutionaries have proclaimed the liberation of the common man; more ironically than ever before, the common man has had to pay for revolution with his liberty, his happiness and sometimes his life.

But Orwell was never himself committed to revolutionary hopes, as the left-wing poets of the '30s were, and his charting of disenchantment was to this degree less extreme. He fought in Spain, but with grave doubts about his own side, which events did everything to confirm. His critique of revolution is basically simple, and embodies the same doubts about human nature which made benevolent paternalism more realistic for him, perhaps, than the ideal of a People's Republic. *Animal Farm* offers insights which were later spelt out, more abstractly, in the Black Book of *1984*. There always have been three classes of society, and there always will be. These are the high, the middle and the low. The war between the classes is necessary, and in normal circumstances could never have an end. The basic political reality is a struggle for power, and the basic reality of power is the ambition and self-aggrandisement of the few at the expense of the many. In this battle, ideals of justice, liberty and brotherhood are so many counters, which the various parties at different times find useful. The middle class is especially adroit in its use of them when it needs to enlist the superior numbers of the lower class in what is essentially its private cause. These ideals are emotionally explosive for two main reasons. The first is that they receive lip-service from most of us, so that politicians are enabled to manipulate the worst in us by way of what we are accustomed to regard as the best. The second is that a handful of idealists really do believe them, and those who do (such as Boxer in *Animal Farm*, or Shakespeare's Brutus) become enormously helpful by reason of their prestige. The politicians who use such slogans are, however, motivated by conscious cynicism of the deepest kind. It is a cynicism more realistic, if less amiable, than the hopes of the men whom they dupe.

In this broad approach to his theme, Orwell agrees with Bertrand Russell in taking the lowest possible view of politicians. He sees them not as ordinary men caught up in events too big for them, and forced against their will into evil moulds, but as depraved men, who have been drawn to politics in the first place by the corrupting search for power. 'Sensible men do not have power,' he once wrote, and the obverse of this is that the men who do have power are evil, since 'sensible' in this context is a moral term. It is interesting to notice that Orwell agrees with most revolutionaries in his estimate of the men who are actually ruling us, but differs sharply in his assessment of what will happen when they are swept away. The new masters will not be saviours, restoring to us a primitive freedom. On the contrary, they will be oppressors in their turn, resembling their predecessors in ambition and cruelty, and differing only in the extremes to which these motives will lead them when stability and tradition have been removed.

Orwell's heart is with the political idealists, but his head gives its verdict the other way. In *Animal Farm* the rise of the pigs to power is presented as inevitable. Our sense of inevitability is mediated through the pervasive irony, which uses a tone of almost bedtime cosiness to unfold the horrors of the tale. We observe the pigs coming into the ascendancy almost at once, as they persuade their fellow animals through a characteristic interplay of idealism and fear. When the machinery of naked power passes into their hands, idealism is totally replaced by fear. We are shown the ensuing power struggle among the pigs at the top, with the emergence of the more evil of the two to supreme power. Events continue to unfold with something of the unassailable logic of a dream. The defeated pig is transformed into an enemy, who can both canalise hatred and justify oppression. The ruling pig is apotheosised into human semblance, and ends in alliance with the hated humans who were originally deposed. These events are intensified by our sense that human nature itself is on trial. If we detect some inevitability in the progress of events, Orwell relies on no dialectic of history to sustain this, but only on his profoundly depressing assessment of political power. The whole range of contributory causes unfolds as we watch — the cruel intelligence of the pigs, the brutality (so easily harnessed) of the dogs, the casual selfishness of the cat, the vanity of the donkey, the heroic stupidity of Boxer, the moronic stupidity of the numerically preponderating sheep. Even when writing *The Road to Wigan Pier*, Orwell had been sufficiently sickened by his experience of imperialism to record: 'At that time failure seemed to me the only virtue.' In *Animal Farm*, the only virtue is Boxer's failure: yet can a man at once so decent and dynamic as Orwell rest in perceptions such as these?

IV

'It was a bright cold day in April, and the clocks were striking thirteen.'

1984 begins with foreboding. The clocks keep Continental time, but the hour chosen to indicate this is ominous. The first paragraph initiates us into the London of the future in images of staleness, claustrophobia and break-down: the 'vile wind', the 'swirl of gritty dust', the varicose ulcer, the broken lifts, the hallway smell of 'boiled cabbage and old mats'. Anyone who can remember eating in a British Restaurant during the last war will know that particular smell. The whole passage is rather like a bad day from the Blitz petrified into eternity.

The main theme of *1984* is similar to Aldous Huxley's in *Brave New World*. It is about the ways in which a powerful state might so diminish and reduce consciousness that humanity as we have known it might cease to exist. Winston Smith is haunted through much of the action by three dreams, one associated with hope (the Golden Country), one with guilt (his childhood greed, mentally linked with his mother's death) and one with fear (the threat lurking in darkness, which turns out to be waiting for him in Room 101). These three dreams suggest, even if they do not formally symbolise, three possibilities for the human race. The first is utopian and primitivist, a dream of natural freedom outside the fetters of social taboo. At its centre is the image of a young girl, throwing aside her clothes with a gesture of pure spontaneity:

What overwhelmed him in that instant was admiration for the gesture with which she had thrown her clothes aside. With its grace and carelessness it seemed to annihilate a whole culture, a whole system of thought, as though Big Brother and the Party and the Thought Police could all be swept into nothingness by a single splendid movement of the arm.

The second dream is nearer to the traditional religious consciousness, of a world in which sin and guilt dominate men, but the possibility of expiation also exists to give meaning and dignity to life. The third dream is pure nightmare: a foreboding, with no clear image, of enigma, anxiety and pain.

In *1984* the nightmare predominates, but there are moments when the utopian dream seems on the verge of breaking through. The novel falls into three sections, which underline the movement of its thought. Part I envisages the world of the future petrified, like the picture of London from which it starts, into eternity. Perhaps 'fixity' would be a better word than 'eternity' to describe this unending present, cut off from any possibility of change. The obliteration of the past has been virtually the obliteration of the future as well, since 'future', in any culturally meaningful sense, requires the past. In this first part of the novel the human march towards disaster is very nearly complete, but certain sources of hope remain. The second part is an ironic idyll, in which it seems that such hopes might still come into their own. When Julia throws off her clothes Winston is reminded of the girl in his Golden Country, and the rhythm of freedom is seen still to exist. The third part of the novel, however, returns to and intensifies the horror of the first. The masters of *1984* are shown to have anticipated, and provided for, every conceivable weakness in their structure. The hopes of Part II are savagely dashed, and the horror becomes embodied in physical images of torture, as appalling as anything in serious fiction I can recall.

The sources of hope which are hinted at in Part I, developed in Part II and destroyed in Part III are of varying kinds. Orwell uses them to chart the distinctive weapons of true human culture in its long historical struggle to survive. There is hope, he suggests, in the simple sanity of *fact*: as long as two and two make four, tyrants will face some limit to their power. There is hope, perhaps as an extension of this, in the past: while historical records remain, choices from the past for the future will always exist. When Winston Smith joins (as he thinks) the Brotherhood, accepting O'Brien as a friend, the two agree to drink a toast. Winston proposes as the subject of this 'the past' — and O'Brien gravely agrees, knowing that the past is indeed an enemy the Party must fear. By yet another extension, there is hope in the language we speak: words are the growing point of our awareness, our guarantee of superiority to the brutes. And this, in turn, indicates the hope of political rebellion, either by subversion originating inside the Party (an upsurge of literacy and intelligence from very near to the top), or by direct action from outside ('If there is any hope, it lies in the proles'). Yet another source of hope, different from these others but interpenetrating them, is found in the fact of sex. Life, honesty and humanity might make their last-ditch stand in the very compulsions of the flesh.

1984 demonstrates first the nature of these hopes, and then their systematic overthrow by the Party. In the past, Orwell suggests, all political tyrannies have been defeated sooner or later, by one or other of these forces, or by two or more of them acting together. The peculiarity of *1984* is that its masters are intelligent enough to have analysed and understood all the possibilities, and powerful enough to have circumvented them. The past itself has been attacked through the rewriting of history, and the reconditioning of individual minds. It is suggested, indeed, that the past exists only in documents and in memories, and that when these have been effectively controlled there is no 'real' past at all. The attack on language has proceeded side by side with this, and as part of a radical offensive against books. Like Huxley in *Brave New World*, Orwell suggests that great literature is a permanent threat to the totalitarian mind. If creative art is the attempt to explore and extend meaning, Newspeak and Doublethink could be described as exactly the reverse. The aim of the Party is to limit consciousness, until men are no more capable of real communication, or change, than are the brutes. Newspeak is the systematic method of diminishing words: in the first place by pushing them in the direction of orthodoxy, and in the second by pushing them towards unconsciousness itself. The suggestion that orthodoxy is a halfway house to unconsciousness is developed in the description of Newspeak. Orwell associates orthodoxy, through the sinister philosophy of Syme, with murder, and assimilates Newspeak to the gloating brutality of the Party itself.

The attacks on the past, and on language, are aspects of an ultimate onslaught upon *fact*: that two and two make five, if the Party says so, is a principle O'Brien wants passionately to display. If we can be made to doubt whether the past did or did not happen, we are already being moved into a realm where neither communication nor sanity have much meaning.

If we can further be made to doubt whether the present is happening as we think it is, the abolition of man as *animal rationnel* is near to being complete.

Solipsism is to be translated therefore from the study, where Hume was content to leave it, on to the stage of world affairs. It fits in, together with all the allied perceptions of *1984*, with Orwell's temperamental preoccupation with 'the worst'. The possibility of rescue from this nightmare through political action leads to new levels of ironic reversal: the Black Book actually exists, with its apparently saving perspective from the past, but its author is O'Brien, and what it amounts to is a final triumph of Doublethink itself. At the very moment when Winston is reading the book, he learns that the subversive movement is run by the State, and that his one friend is the enemy always lurking behind the most terrible of his dreams.

The irony of *1984* is fittingly translated at this point into the pattern of Winston Smith's relationship with O'Brien. From the earliest pages of the novel, Winston has been aware of an affinity between himself and O'Brien. In his third dream (as I have called it) a phrase occurred which he comes to regard as a prophecy. The passage is so important, that I should like to quote it in full:

> Years ago — how long was it? Seven years it must be — he had dreamed that he was walking through a pitch-dark room. And someone sitting to one side of him had said as he passed: 'We shall meet in the place where there is no darkness.' It was said very quietly, almost casually — a statement, not a command. He had walked on without pausing. What was curious was that at the time, in the dream, the words had not made much impression on him. It was only later and by degrees that they had seemed to take on significance. He could not now remember whether it was before or after having the dream that he had seen O'Brien for the first time; nor could he remember when he had first identified the voice as O'Brien's. But at any rate the identification existed. It was O'Brien who had spoken to him out of the dark.
>
> Winston had never been able to feel sure — even after this morning's flash of the eyes it was still impossible to be sure — whether O'Brien was a friend or an enemy. Nor did it even

seem to matter greatly. There was a link of understanding between them, more important than affection or partisanship. 'We shall meet in the place where there is no darkness,' he had said. Winston did not know what it meant, only that in some way or another it would come true.

We are reminded of some of the great handlings of this theme in nineteenth-century and modern literature. Dostoevsky is still unrivalled in his depictions of the deeply perverse relationship between Inquisitor and victim, but Kafka added his own insights in *The Castle* and *The Trial*, by depersonalising the agents of inquisition and stressing their enigma. In a lesser but still impressive way, we have had two handlings of the theme in more recent times. The clash between Martin Eliot and Sawbridge in C. P. Snow's *The New Men* uses the affinity between Inquisitor and victim to underline the irony of a liberal's dilemma in the modern world; Thom Gunn's poems 'The Beaters' and 'Innocence' spell out the sexual implications of such encounters with disturbing but useful directness.

In *1984* the link between Winston and O'Brien turns out to be a nightmare, where all normal presuppositions dissolve; it becomes the central insanity of the work. The very distinction between friend and foe — blurred in Winston's mind from the first, as the above quotation makes clear — dissolves in the giving and taking of pain. At the climax of his torture, Winston loses even his sense of *belonging* with O'Brien; he can feel only the pain itself, and gratitude when the pain is made to stop. His sense of O'Brien's wisdom grows with his suffering and bewilderment. O'Brien becomes a kind of god, worshipped in proportion to his superior attributes of intelligence, cruelty and power.

The relationship between Winston and O'Brien is an apotheosis of the novel's claustrophobia and despair. In the light of it, all the incidental ironies take on a new edge. There is our discovery, for instance, that the apparently solid figures on the political scene do not even exist. Goldstein and Big Brother are as much figments of the imagination as that Comrade Ogilvy whom Winston, in his official capacity, invents. The nearest we come to seeing the actual architects of *1984* is O'Brien himself. Madness and cruelty seem incarnate in him, yet he is almost as weighed down with tiredness as his victim, and too shadowy to be fully recognised as a man. Up to the time of interrogation, and even during the early stages of it, Winston has clung to the hope that behind the horror of *1984* there might be some remnants of paternalism, however misplaced. But O'Brien dispels this illusion, in words that come very close to some of the classic definitions of Hell:

> Power is not a means, it is an end. . . . The object of persecution is persecution. . . . The object of torture is torture. The object of power is power. . . . If you want a picture of the future, imagine a boot stamping on a human face — for ever.

In most irony, the sting is that a topsy-turvey picture is *nearer* to being true than we normally admit. Here, Orwell suggests that a topsy-turvey world *is* true, and that our attempts to evade this knowledge are so many exercises in self-deceit. Things which ought to be exaggerations for satiric purposes are represented as fact; statements which ought to be nonsensical or unthinkable are presented as simply true. 'War is peace' ought to be an exuberant exaggeration, but politicians have turned the nonsense into sense. 'Love is hate' ought to be a Freudian paradox at best, but the relationship between Winston and O'Brien transforms it into a political fact. The absurdity of events outstrips any humorous possibilities, and we have no temptation to laugh. Even worse, it outstrips any tragic possibilities, since tragedy depends on our sense that man is glorious as well as doomed, but this is exactly what the masters of *1984* have been most determined to destroy.

V

1984, like Book IV of *Gulliver*, is a hypnotic work. Orwell presents life as pure nightmare, yet we feel that life really is — or could be — like this as we read. Perhaps all great literature offers the illusion of completeness, but it is surely unusual for a work so totally given over to fear and horror to convince as this one does.

The critic's task is first to testify to the power of the work, and

then to stand back and ask questions. Are the various hopes for
humanity which the novel rejects fully realised in terms of the
story itself? Are its fears recognisably to do with waking life, or
is their spell nearer to those that come in sleep?

One aspect of our difficulty with *1984* arises from its undeniable imaginative success. Intellectually we want to fault
it, but emotionally we are all too likely to be convinced. The
issues at stake are certainly momentous, and the decisions we
make about them directly reflect our apprehension of the
modern world. Are we faced with a failure of nerve in one very
sick man? Or is this a true prophecy, of the failure of the human
race?

The moment one does stand back, it becomes clear that the
modern world is not entirely as Orwell makes out. In London
or Washington, as in most of the capitals of Europe, the smell
of freedom is still in the air. One doubts whether manipulation
by Secret Police and Tele-screen ever could be as complete as
Orwell represents them in his fable. (Yet the power of tyrannies
to perpetuate themselves has enormously increased since 1930,
and would one take this complacent view if one were a pre-
1956 Pole, or a South African today?) The metaphysical
problem of external reality is posed by Orwell in a somewhat crude form, and most philosophers would want to
quarrel (though not, perhaps, in the Ministry of Love)
with the assumptions on which O'Brien's logic rests. Orwell's
depiction of the proles is also open to objections of a serious
kind. The old man whom Winston tries to cross-question
in a pub rings depressingly true in that we have all met old
men like that (and a grave rebuff to optimistic humanism
they can seem): but such an old man is by no stretch of
the imagination *typical*. This is what Orwell makes him, and in
doing so he reveals the degree of oversimplification that is at
work.

The whole philosophy of power, as Orwell offers it in his last
two books, is controversial to at least an equal degree. When
Wordsworth wrote *The Prelude* in the very early years of the
nineteenth century, his account of the French Revolution was
coloured by pessimism, not dissimilar to Orwell's, if of a lesser
kind. The shock of Napoleon's treachery struck at the roots of
his idealism, and he came very close to 'yielding up moral

questions in despair'. But time alters the aftermath of revolution, as well as the revolution itself: which historians today
would be tempted to take this view? Given the perspective of a
century or more, we no longer associate the Revolution with one
man, no matter how outstanding his part may have been.
Most of us would probably judge the French Revolution a good
thing, on balance, rather than a bad — though we tend to
think of it as a fact, or an inevitability, rather than as something
offering itself to be judged. In a similar way, the Russian
Revolution is already passing into history, and Stalin becomes
one figure in a story that continues to unfold. Will future
historians, if there is a future, go on judging? If they do, it will
not be in Orwellian terms, we may be fairly sure.

In his recent biography of Orwell, Sir Richard Rees made a
telling point against the logic of *1984* which ought also to be
mentioned at this point. The implications of Winston's break-
down, he suggests, might reflect a curiously disguised and even
arrogant puritanism. The love between Winston and Julia is
proved to be worthless because under the stress of the most
extreme fear that can be devised for them, each will sacrifice
the other to escape. Room 101 becomes not only the ultimate
fear but the ultimate testing, by which all they say or do must
be tried. But is this not an impossibly puritanical yardstick to
apply? Can we accept as a standard for ordinary decency trials
which the greatest of heroes might scarcely survive?

Orwell might reply that the breaking of Winston is psychologically valid, and this, I think, would have to be allowed.
What one doubts is whether it is also symbolically valid, as an
assertion of the final crushing of the spirit of man.

Further objections might be made to the notion that unseen
manipulators could gain, and keep, such power. The Secret
Police appear to get little material benefit, and would their
loyalty be as absolute as it is made to seem? The very existence
of the Black Book is surely a danger, in that intelligence capable
of conceiving it is almost by definition intelligence capable of
changing its mind. What we feel, I think, is that Orwell under-
estimates the flexibility and resilience of the human intellect:
or maybe that he overestimates the degree to which human
cruelty is bound to triumph if society provides for it a suitable
soil.

There is one hope in *1984* I have not yet touched on, but it might strike many readers as the greatest hope of all. Winston and Julia are impressed, at the moment of their first love-making, by the spontaneous singing of a nearby thrush. Later they remember it when they hear an old woman singing, a few moments (as it turns out) before they are caught:

'Do you remember,' he said 'the thrush that sang to us, that first day, at the edge of the wood?'
'He wasn't singing to us,' said Julia. 'He was singing to please himself. Not even that. He was just singing.'

Almost immediately, the passage dissolves in terror. The ghastly repetitions of words and phrases with which the Secret Police announce their presence is the very antithesis of spontaneous song. In the noise and scuffle, the old woman's washtub is thrown across the yard, and her song ends in a sudden cry of pain. All of this seems especially ironic, yet the fact that the woman has sung and that the lovers have loved remains true (or doesn't it?), despite all that O'Brien can say.

All of these reservations about *1984* one is anxious to express, yet a very uneasy suspicion remains. Why do we so urgently want to make them? Is it not a tribute to Orwell's imaginative achievement that we do? There has been a tendency among recent critics, I fancy, to undervalue *1984*: to suggest that political events have not developed in this manner, and that there was never any real likelihood that they would. Against this, I would like to propose a midway position, as probably coming nearer to the truth. In detail Orwell's prophecies seem mercifully wrong, at least for England, but may we not be nearer to the spirit of *1984* than we normally think? The centrality of *1984* to modern literature is surely this; that the infection of the creative imagination which it acutely embodies is present, in a chronic form, almost everywhere we look. We live at a time when it is much easier to take our fears seriously than our hopes; when our most courageous men have forebodings, and our sanest men often turn into prophets of doom. There is hardly a serious novel of the past thirty years in which cruelty and fear have not played some considerable role; novels about the future predict disaster almost as a matter of course. There is scarcely a poet under thirty (as Edward Lucie-Smith has recently reminded us) who does not constantly revert to themes of suffering and pain.

Our very familiarity with the facts of the modern world can sometimes blind us to them, so that we think Orwell further from the perspective of normal sanity than he is. In the pages of the Black Book there is a remarkable analysis of the technique of Cold War, which is very much closer to the realities of the world today than even its original readers fifteen years ago could have foreseen. We have lived through Korea, Suez, Hungary, the Summit fiasco, Cuba since Orwell wrote — and we take it for granted that we shall be at the brink again, for this reason or that, in a matter of time. Every crisis has seemed sharper and more ominous than the last, for developing behind them have been plans for eliminating all human life from the earth.

Look back again at the list of scientific projects from *1984* which I quoted at the start: are the actual scientific projects we have heard about since Orwell's time less grim, or more grim, than these? Consider the assumptions of power-mania in all politicians, including our own, which underlie nearly all political comment today: are these less extreme than Orwell's assumptions, or merely better disguised? Undeniably we accept violence and injustice as inescapable evils, in a way that civilised men of the past would not have done. We pay lip-service still to the idea of human brotherhood, but to practise brotherhood would seem to most of us dangerously naïve. We accept the State's superiority to the individual, even in the 'Free World', in a manner that would have profoundly shocked us even thirty years ago. The very air is polluted by bomb-tests, and we know it is useless to complain about it.

If an eminent Victorian could be resurrected to see the modern world, what would he be most likely to think? Would his first feelings be of simple incredulity, or of dawning horror and dismay? Would Orwell's *1984* seem to him the fevered obsession of a sick man, or might he think it almost unbelievably close to the truth?

Any objective view of the present is hard to come by, and I throw these questions out only for what they are worth. It seems clear to me, however, that there is an infection in the creative imagination of modern writers, which cannot be wholly dissociated from the world in which they live. 'Imagination,' said Keats, 'may be compared to Adam's dream: he awoke, and found it truth.' If Orwell's imagination is in any sense truly representative of his century, we must hope that the awakening will be long deferred.

EPILOGUE

In these studies, my emphasis has repeatedly fallen on tone. No two ironists are wholly alike, whether in their temperament, their background, or their creative manipulation of words. For the critic only very close attention will suffice, to local nuances of tone, as well as to the structure of the whole.

Our main attention in these pages has been given to works where irony is a primary aim, but the tone of irony pervades many writings of which this could not be said. In eighteenth-century prose, irony is seldom absent as a possibility, even when no specific deflation is implied. The very slightest inflection could infuse this, for instance, with mockery, yet Bishop Butler's mood is serious, and he appears to mean exactly what he says:

> It is come, I know not how, to be taken for granted, by many persons, that Christianity is not so much a subject for enquiry; but that it is, now at length, discovered to be fictitious. And accordingly they treat it, as if, in the present age, this were an agreed point among all people of discernment; and nothing remained, but to set it up as a principal subject of mirth and ridicule, as it were by way of reprisals, for its having so long interrupted the pleasures of the world.

To ask whether this *is* ironic is to probe deeply into eighteenth-century culture itself. Elegance and urbanity lend themselves to ironic modulation, and ridicule was widely regarded as a test of 'truth'. There is, moreover, in ironic writing, that concession from reason to unreason which most truly rational men are prepared to make; a flickering at the edge of reason's candle, where light reaches towards the darkness round about. Butler's exposition, in the passage just quoted, is tinged with ironic overtones; it is as though he turns irony back on itself, capturing the scorn of unbelievers as a tone to be relished against themselves.

In my Preface, I emphasised the dangers of trying to harden ironic usages towards general formulae, yet for anyone engaged on this theme the lure of generalisation persists. One would not wish to deny, for instance, that at one end of an imagined scale a purely moralistic irony can exist: an irony, that is to say, where anger springs with savage directness from moral outrage, and no complications of malice, petulance, fear, or iconoclasm for the sake of iconoclasm, intervene. Dr Johnson well illustrates what I have in mind, in his classic reply to Soame Jenyns's *Free Enquiry into the Nature and Origin of Evil*:

> Many a merry bout have these frolick beings at the vicissitudes of an ague, and good sport it is to see a man tumble with an epilepsy, and revive and tumble again, and all this he knows not why. As they are wiser and more power-ful than we, they have more exquisite diversions, for we have no way of procuring any sport so brisk and so lasting, as the paroxysms of the gout and stone, which undoubtedly must make high mirth, especially if the play be a little diversified with the blunders and puzzles of the blind and deaf.

Soame Jenyns, it will be recalled, had defended the philo-sophic view known as Optimism, which holds that the world we live in, though imperfect, is the best of all possible worlds. The suffering of living creatures is justified in terms of the happiness of their natural superiors in the chain of life. Our well-being as men depends upon the sufferings of the animals who die to feed us, and may not our sufferings, in turn, be necessary to the well-being of higher, though invisible, creatures in the scheme of things? In France, this apologia for suffering met its ironic nemesis in *Candide*, where Voltaire infused it with the gayest and deadliest exuberance he could command. Dr Johnson, dealing with his English Pangloss, is sterner and more exalted than Voltaire. He pushes the implications of Jenyns's beliefs to their logical end, translating the complacent abstrac-tions of Optimism into concrete realities of flesh and blood. In doing so, he demonstrates that savage anger at such proposi-tions is the only fittingly human response we can make. The damage to Optimism seems to me even more extensive than Voltaire's; and indeed, purely moralistic irony, though rare, is more potentially destructive than any other kind.

Against purely moralistic irony we might be tempted to set purely exuberant irony, as a balancing concept, but this would almost certainly be a mistake. Exuberance is a quality which can co-exist with extreme maliciousness, as it sometimes does in Lytton Strachey, or with extreme pessimism, as it sometimes does in Swift; or, indeed, with purely moralistic irony, as it does in the piece by Dr Johnson quoted above. In ironic contexts, perhaps exuberance cannot exist 'on its own'; since if it did, it would be *simply* delightful, and this irony never sets out to be. Even Peacock is not simply exuberant, as I have already tried to show; and Dickens, who might also spring to mind if one thinks of his earlier work, could always combine zest and savagery with cutting effect:

> Mr Gamfield growled a fierce imprecation on the donkey generally, but more particularly on his eyes; and running after him, bestowed a blow on his head, which would inevitably have beaten in any skull but a donkey's. Then, catching hold of the bridle, he gave his jaw a sharp wrench, by way of gentle reminder that he was not his own master; and by these means turned him round. He then gave him another blow on the head, just to stun him till he came back. Having completed these arrangements, he walked up to the gate, and read the bill.

Our instinct here, I take it, is to laugh out loud ('Having completed these arrangements' and so on), but the actual content of the passage, particularly in its implications for Oliver, can only appal. The clash between meaning and tone is almost demonic: pure exuberance, we are reminded again, is very far from the ironist's intent.

The diversity of tone, and the diversity of subject; to these we fittingly return. My theme has been irony as a rhetorical technique, and it is upon this that attention has therefore centred: on the traps and surprises, the intellectual gymnastics, the virtuoso exuberance, the intrinsic delights. The reader who is sufficiently interested in such techniques to have followed these studies will be interested also, of course, in the other kind of irony, seldom absent from the minds of ironists in our primary sense: irony as a vision of the universe itself. Whether in Swift or Fielding, Mark Twain or Orwell, we constantly return to this larger theme: to the perception of cross-purposes, of absurdity, of tragic suffering, in the enigma of events that happen to us, and in 'the crazy fabric of human nature' itself.

A famous and possibly apocryphal story has been told about Gertrude Stein. Lying on her death-bed, she exclaimed over and over again: 'What is the answer?' But shortly before she died she sat up and said: 'What is the question?' Our ironists, one is reminded, keep us wondering upon both scores. If we discover the question even, when dealing with some of them, we shall have done rather well.

SELECT BIBLIOGRAPHY

THIS list is not intended to be comprehensive. It simply acknowledges works which have interested me, and to which I am conscious of being in debt.

When critical anthologies are given I have not listed the contents as well. Thus, Dr Leavis's famous essay on Swift is reprinted in two of the Swift collections, and parts of it are available in a third. I have not, however, given it a separate entry, since users of the bibliography will quickly discover the contents of anthologies for themselves.

General

James Sutherland, *English Satire* (C.U.P.).
L. J. Potts, *Comedy* (Hutchinson's University Library).
Wayne C. Booth, *The Rhetoric of Fiction* (Chicago).

Swift

John Middleton Murry, *Jonathan Swift* (Jonathan Cape).
Ricardo Quintana, *Swift: An Introduction* (O.U.P.).
  The Mind and Art of Jonathan Swift (O.U.P.).
Irvin Ehrenpreis, *Swift, the Man, his Works and the Age, Vol. I* (Methuen).
Bonamy Dobrée, *English Literature in the Early Eighteenth Century, 1700–1740* (O.U.P.).
Milton Voigt, *Swift and the Twentieth Century* (Wayne).
John Traugott (Ed.), *Discussions of Jonathan Swift* (Heath & Co., Boston).
Robert A. Greenberg (Ed.), *Jonathan Swift's 'Gulliver's Travels'* (Norton Critical Edition, N.Y.).
Ernest Tuveson (Ed.), *Swift* ('Twentieth Century Views', Prentice-Hall Inc., New Jersey).
Basil Willey, *The Eighteenth Century Background* (Chatto and Windus).
Aldous Huxley, *On Art and Artists* (Chatto and Windus).

Fielding

F. Homes Duddon, *Henry Fielding, His Life, Works and Times* (2 Vols.) (O.U.P.).

225

John Butt, *Fielding* ('Writers and their Works', No. 57, Longmans).
Ian Watt, *The Rise of the Novel* (Chatto and Windus).
John Middleton Murry, *Unprofessional Essays* (Jonathan Cape).
Ronald Paulson (Ed.), *Fielding* ('Twentieth Century Views', Prentice-Hall Inc., New Jersey).

Sterne

Walter Bagehot, *Literary Studies* (Everyman).
Arnold Kettle, *An Introduction to the English Novel, I* (Hutchinson's University Library).
Dorothy van Ghent, *The English Novel: Form and Function* (Harper and Row).
Virginia Woolf, *The Second Common Reader* (Penguin).
James L. Clifford (Ed.), *Eighteenth Century English Literature* (Galaxy Book, O.U.P.; Article by Rufus D. S. Putney).

Gibbon

E. M. W. Tillyard, *The English Epic and its Background* (Chatto and Windus).

Peacock

Ian Jack, *English Literature 1815–1832* (O.U.P.).

Thackeray

Gordon Ray, *Thackeray: The Uses of Adversity, 1811–1846* (O.U.P.). *The Buried Life* (O.U.P.).
Geoffrey Tillotson, *Thackeray the Novelist* (Methuen).
Kathleen Tillotson, *Novels of the 1840s* (O.U.P.).
David Cecil, *Early Victorian Novelists* (Penguin).
Arnold Kettle, *An Introduction to the English Novel, I* (Hutchinson's University Library).
Dorothy van Ghent, *The English Novel: Form and Function* (Harper and Row).

Mark Twain

Lionel Trilling, *The Liberal Imagination* (Secker and Warburg).
Charles Feidelson Jr. and Paul Brodtkorb Jr. (Eds.), *Interpretations of American Literature* (Galaxy Book, O.U.P.; Articles by Leo Marx and James M. Cox).
H. N. Smith (Ed.), *Mark Twain* ('Twentieth Century Views', Prentice-Hall Inc., New Jersey).

Samuel Butler

G. D. H. Cole, *Samuel Butler* (Home and Van Thal Ltd.).
Malcolm Muggeridge, *The Earnest Atheist* (Eyre and Spottiswoode).
Basil Willey, *Darwin and Butler: Two Versions of Evolution* (Chatto and Windus).

Lytton Strachey

F. A. Simpson, 'Max Beerbohm on Lytton Strachey', (*Cambridge Review*, Vol. LXV, 1943).
Noel Annan, *Introduction to Lytton Strachey's 'Eminent Victorians'* (Collins).

Aldous Huxley

D. S. Savage, *The Withered Branch* (Eyre and Spottiswoode).

Evelyn Waugh

Frank Kermode, *Puzzles and Epiphanies* (Routledge and Kegan Paul).
Bernard Bergonzi, 'Evelyn Waugh's Gentleman', (*The Critical Quarterly*, Vol. V. No. I).

George Orwell

Richard Rees, *George Orwell: Fugitive from the Camp of Victory* (Secker and Warburg).
Raymond Williams, *Culture and Society 1750–1950* (Chatto and Windus).
John Wain, *Essays on Literature and Ideas* (Macmillan).

INDEX

Jl